and comprehensive read. Thanks to this easy-to-understand guide, you can stop feeling overwhelmed about crypto and start feeling educated and empowered."

Eric Clarke
CEO, Orion

"Perhaps the single most exciting thing about the blockchain is that, in this case, if it sounds too good to be true, it can be true. Blockchain technology promises to solve trillions of dollars of wasted cost, whisk away eons of hours spent waiting, and eliminate the need for entire, redundant professions. The potential transformation inside the financial services industry is astounding. *The Truth About Crypto* introduces you to this exciting innovation and helps you make sense of it all. *The Truth About Crypto* is definitely the best read about digital assets yet. Ric makes the topic so fun and accessible, you almost forget you're learning something. Read it and your life will never be the same."

Dani Fava
Head of Strategic Development, Envestnet

"Innovation is a driving force in financial services, and digital assets will certainly be a significant contributor in our industry going forward. It's no surprise that Ric Edelman, who is always an innovator, is at the forefront of the conversation."

Bernie Clark
Managing Director, Head of
Schwab Advisor Services

"*The Truth About Crypto* is an approachable and thoughtful summary of digital assets and blockchain technology—which represent one of the biggest economic innovations in history. Ric demystifies the concepts and offers insights for readers at all levels of experience and expertise. For financial advisors in particular, I think it's a must-read!"

David Canter
Head of the RIA and Family Office Segment,
Fidelity Investments

Advance Praise for *The Truth About Crypto*

"Blockchain technology is driving one of the most revolutionary periods in finance since the Renaissance. As we stand upon the threshold of this moment, investors of every type should be paying close attention and reading voraciously. *The Truth About Crypto* is an excellent place to start."

> Downtown Josh Brown
> CEO of Ritholtz Wealth Management,
> star of CNBC's *Halftime Report*

"While many financial advisors remain skeptical about investing clients into digital assets, their broad adoption by consumers means that advisors at least have an obligation to get educated on the topic. Ric Edelman's *The Truth About Crypto* provides an excellent foundational understanding of what it's all about, from digital assets to the underlying blockchain technology, so advisors can make more informed decisions about whether or how to implement within their own practices."

> Michael Kitces, MSFS, MTAX, CFP, CLU, ChFC
> Chief Financial Planning Nerd, kitces.com

"Investing in crypto is complicated. As Ric tackles it, though, it becomes accessible, actionable, achievable. If you've felt like a blockhead about blockchain, this is the place to begin."

> Jean Chatzky
> CEO, HerMoney Media, and Bestselling Author

"Ric Edelman has long been known within financial services as a visionary and purveyor of financial education. Fortunately for us, his seemingly unquenchable thirst for learning and innovating, combined with a willingness to question and test his own beliefs and understandings has led him to expand, explore, gain, and now share expertise in such areas as exponential technologies, blockchain technology, and digital assets. *The Truth About Crypto* is a must-read for anyone who wants to gain knowledge—or challenge what they think they already know about their financial future."

> David Smith
> Co-Founder & Director of Third-Party Content
> *Financial Advisor* magazine

"Ric has done it again! He's taken a wide-ranging and constantly evolving subject and made it relevant and accessible to the widest possible audience. *The Truth About Crypto* is incredibly clear and very difficult to put down. Ric provides convincing evidence that ignoring crypto is the least rational response to it, and he offers a wealth of advice on how best to embrace this explosive innovation. This book should be required reading—not just for individual investors, but for legislators, regulators, financial advisors, and tax professionals as well."

Gary L. Perlin
Retired CFO, The World Bank and Capital One
Financial Corporation

"For decades, Ric has had one eye on the moment and the other looking to the future—for all us. Most of us missed the Agricultural and Industrial Revolutions, but the new "cyber revolution" will be the biggest and fastest. *The Truth About Crypto* gives us Ric's keen insight into the Blockchain and Digital Asset Revolution, and his commitment to elevating everyone's knowledge sets the stage for all of us to participate with confidence."

Craig Pfeiffer
President & CEO, Money Management Institute

"Brilliance is a phrase many use but few deserve. Edelman has proven himself to be an exceptional talent in the financial world by consistently breaking down complex ideas and concepts so that they're understandable and actionable. His newest book, *The Truth About Crypto*, is no different and won't disappoint. It's a worthy read for ANY investor or financial advisor considering, contemplating, or discussing digital assets."

Michael Jay Markey Jr., MRFC, BFA
Vice-Chairman, International Association of
Registered Financial Consultants

"Trying to decode the new world of digital assets? You don't need to be an investing genius; all you need is a trusted voice to guide you. Generations of investors have benefited from Ric Edelman's wisdom and his ability to cut through the noise with no-nonsense advice. In his new book, *The Truth About Crypto*, Ric deciphers and brings clarity to the subject, with a fun

"Ric Edelman has written the introductory book to crypto that needed to be written. I won't buy a copy when it comes out, I'll buy ten—to give to people who need a readable introduction to the exciting technology of the blockchain. I didn't know that Ric was an OG (original gangster) by buying his first bitcoin in 2014. That was early days. Of all the advice in the book, the best is his emphasis of using dollar cost averaging when it comes to bitcoin—buying over time. I can't endorse that approach enough."

Jan van Eck
CEO, VanEck Funds

"Bitcoin offers investors an unprecedented opportunity, and in *The Truth About Crypto*, Ric Edelman makes clear the compelling reasons why this is so—and arms the reader with the key information they need so they can quickly, easily, and successfully incorporate this new asset into their investment strategy."

Michael Saylor
Chairman & CEO, MicroStrategy

"Ric Edelman is one of the best-known voices in the wealth advisory field. Remarkably successful, having built one of the nation's top financial planning firms, Ric has spoken with tens of thousands of advisors and clients over the years, and he knows best how to communicate in a way that helps both advisors and individual investors get educated so they can live healthier financial lives. In *The Truth About Crypto*, Ric once again educates us, making accessible an exciting new asset class that we all need to learn more about. With his wit, storytelling, examples, and illustrations—armed with his four decades of experience—Ric makes us better prepared for the digital investment future that is upon us."

Shirl Penney
Founder & CEO, Dynasty Financial Partners

"Want to understand crypto? Here's everything you need, all in one place. Ric has done an incredible job of demystifying blockchain and digital assets with this book, and he makes the subject easily accessible for readers. Everyone who is interested in understanding digital assets should read this."

Marty Bicknell
CEO & President, Mariner Wealth Advisors

"Ric's practical idea for investing in digital assets can be easily understood and applied by anyone who wants to add digital assets to their portfolio. *The Truth About Crypto* is the perfect resource if you want to learn about this revolutionary new asset class."

> Stefan Cohen
> Partner, Bain Capital

"Ric Edelman once again uses his visionary insight, practicality, and deep knowledge to give readers an easy-to-understand, comprehensive, and practical guide on blockchain and digital assets for financial advisors and investors who are trying to understand the massive investment opportunities available. *The Truth About Crypto* is a must-read if you want to understand this massively important new investment marketplace."

> Anthony Scaramucci
> Founder & CEO, SkyBridge Capital

"Written from the perspective of one of the top financial advisors in the country, *The Truth About Crypto* translates the complex world of blockchain and digital assets into an easy-to-follow guide for anyone who wants to understand more about this new topic. The book has convinced me that this is not just a fad—and although values may fluctuate and certain ones may fail, blockchain technology is not going away. If you are an accountant, attorney, tax advisor, estate planner, trustee, executor, or anyone who deals with financial assets, you're going to need this information, sooner or later. Imagine being the executor of an estate that contains digital assets . . . ! Read this book and keep it as your reference guide! The book is fantastic and I'm glad I took the time to read it."

> Ruth Flynn Raftery, JD, CPA, AEP®
> President & Co-Founder,
> Advanced Planning Educational Group

"Anyone planning to profit in the future needs to read this definitive guide to digital assets. Ric's humor and helpful analogies make *The Truth About Crypto* an easy read. This comprehensive primer will convince even the greatest skeptic to take digital asset investing seriously."

> Russell M. Parker, CIMA®
> CEO & Founder, rpmAUM

"The impact of digital assets on global commerce and investment management will be profound. If you want to understand this transformational new asset class, *The Truth About Crypto* is a must-read."

Ray Sclafani
CEO, ClientWise

"Congratulations to Ric Edelman on another fantastic book. An influential thought leader who always looks ahead, Ric offers a fascinating and timely guide on an important but poorly understood topic: digital assets and blockchain technology. This book is a must-read for all of us, from an author who is a genius at making complex topics easy to understand. Those of us who worry about our retirement better get ready for the future—and there's no better way than reading *The Truth About Crypto*."

Ali Houshmand
President, Rowan University

"Ric Edelman's *The Truth About Crypto* gives readers a thorough overview of the entire digital asset space, covering the whats, hows, and whys of crypto in a comprehensive and well-researched guide. Edelman succinctly explains the state of the market, where it is going, and why and how it will get there. *The Truth About Crypto* also gives investors the tools to make informed decisions about the risks, opportunities, capital allocations, and portfolio management choices in this still-growing multi-trillion-dollar asset class. He closes the book addressing common investor concerns in a simple-to-understand Q&A format. With a deft hand and effortless command of his topic, Edelman delivers on the book's promise to lay out the truth about crypto."

Prof. Del Wright Jr. (@cryptolawprof)
UMKC School of Law
Author of *A Short & Happy Guide to Bitcoin,
Blockchain, and Crypto* and *Bitcoin and Crypto:
In a Nutshell*

"When I first delved into crypto back in 2013, Ric was the only person in the financial services industry who had an open ear. He recognized and understood how this new technology [could] provide opportunities for investors. Now, with this book, Ric has done a great benefit to both investors and advisors by providing a comprehensive and insightful view of how this bold new world can help all investors reach their financial goals."

Jack Tatar
Co-author, *Cryptoassets: The Innovative Investor's Guide to Bitcoin and Beyond*

"The digital asset ecosystem is growing at such a rapid pace that it can be difficult to truly understand it all. In *The Truth About Crypto*, Ric does a phenomenal job laying out the complete picture of the digital asset space and separating fact from fiction. *The Truth About Crypto* is now my go-to reference for anyone seeking to learn more about digital assets!"

Michelle Bond
CEO, Association for Digital Asset Markets

"With so many different sides to crypto, it can be very complicated to understand and, as a result, for many, something to be avoided. Thankfully, Ric demystifies this dynamic new asset class in a digestible, comprehensive manner. I highly recommend anyone interested in learning more to read *The Truth About Crypto*."

Bill Capuzzi
CEO, Apex Fintech Solutions

"Ric has the uncanny ability to distill a universe of complex information into a form that is accessible, insightful, and intriguing. Ric and his organizations sit at the nexus of information, education, and thought leadership within the digital asset and financial advisory communities, and we're all lucky to benefit from his focus on this new, emerging paradigm. If you're not engaging with this wealth of quality content, then you're not paying attention."

Daniel Eyre
CEO, BITRIA

"Crypto is the most important technological breakthrough of this generation, and *The Truth About Crypto* is the best introduction to it I've read. Ric manages to explain everything crypto—what it is, what it isn't, and how it will reshape our future—without resorting to jargon, technobabble, or hype. An incredible introduction to a very important topic, if you're looking to understand crypto as an investor, start here!"

Matt Hougan
Chief Investment Officer, Bitwise Asset
Management

"With enlightening research and engaging analysis and anecdotes, Ric Edelman clearly illustrates why digital assets are changing the way the world invests. He shows why blockchain is so transformative, illuminates the differences between the multitude of coins and tokens, and reveals the reasons for investing in digital assets. He even dives into regulation and compliance for financial advisors—and the tax section is a big bonus for every reader, complete with references. The comprehensive lists of companies providing investments, products, and services in the digital asset space is alone worth many times the price of the book. Buy this now so you can understand how this transformative technology will change your life!"

Zac Prince
CEO, BlockFi

"The first decade of bitcoin and crypto have been full of both market signals and noise. Ric's book, *The Truth About Crypto*, illustrates for the reader the important market signals needed to navigate this fast-paced industry, and most importantly, how bitcoin and crypto interface with our personal financial lives via retirement savings, money, and more. Ric's deep knowledge of financial markets and blockchain technology enables his book to be relevant for the average reader, while in-depth and accurate enough for the advanced crypto enthusiast to enjoy as well."

Ryan Radloff
CEO, Choice

"Ric does an excellent job breaking down the complexities of blockchains and crypto assets into easy-to-understand concepts. The timing of his book couldn't be better to help investors and advisors formulate their plans on how to participate in the next generation of the world's financial markets. This is the go-to guide to build crypto into your strategy!"

Tim Rice
Co-Founder & CEO, Coin Metrics

"Ric Edelman has written an important primer for anyone interested in investing in crypto. His expert knowledge and insight take readers through an important journey of discovery and understanding of how blockchain technology and digital assets are revolutionizing the way we invest. This book is an excellent guide."

Brett Tejpaul
Head of Coinbase Institutional

"This approachable introduction to digital assets and Distributed Ledger Technology arrives just as crypto has found its way to mainstream finance. An essential guide to this pioneering new sector for those looking for an efficient way to better understand the future of money."

Dmitry Tokarev
CEO, copper.co

"The digital asset market is expanding at an exponential rate, creating tremendous investment opportunities for those who know where to look. Ric's ability to break down complex topics into actionable insights makes *The Truth About Crypto* the ideal guide for investors who want to take advantage of this once-in-a-generation opportunity."

Kevin Kelly, CFA
Co-Founder, Delphi Digital

"Few people can explain bitcoin and blockchain as clearly and concisely as Ric can. Investors at every level will find incredible value in this extremely well written book. Finally, a book written for investors and financial advisors who can now understand the complex topics of bitcoin and blockchain."

Christopher King
Founder & CEO, Eaglebrook Advisors

"For years, Ric Edelman has been at the forefront of investing in digital assets. He walks the reader through the topic, using his vast knowledge and straightforward, practical approach. I recommend this book as a must-read for every investor, advisor, and allocator who wants to take advantage of the most exciting investment opportunity of the next decade."

Mike Kelly
President & Chief Investment Officer,
FS Investments

"At FTX, we believe that blockchain technology presents the opportunity to fundamentally improve our financial system. However, as we've seen with other transformative technologies, there is an education gap which can prevent one from participating with confidence. Ric's book helps to bridge that gap and make crypto more accessible to the average investor. With all of his success as a financial advisor and his reputation as an objective expert, I can't think of a better person to help educate and empower people about crypto."

Nate Clancy
VP of Business Development, FTX US

"*The Truth About Crypto* is a timely guide to the basics of blockchain, crypto, and everything in between. Ric Edelman's ability to simplify key concepts around this revolutionary technology is unmatched among today's thought leaders in the digital asset ecosystem."

Kristen Mirabella
Director, Business Development, Gemini

"Ric is an aficionado of all things crypto. In webinars he is an articulate blockchain champion and go-to guy for how or how not to invest in digital assets. Given his vast network, command of the subject, and common-sense approach, this book is a must-read for all financial planners and investors."

Mitchell Dong
CEO, Pythagoras Investment Management

"Ric presents an easy-to-understand primer on what bitcoin is, why it is important, and the transformative impact it is having on an emerging digital world. Readers will benefit from the history that led to bitcoin's introduction, and a breakdown of the concepts that explain the innovation."

Jason Les
CEO, Riot Blockchain

"Ric is a master communicator. His storytelling approach creates an easy-to-read book, despite the complex topic. If you're an investor or an investment advisor and want to learn about blockchain and digital assets, I highly recommend *The Truth About Crypto*."

Jake Ryan
Founder & Chief Investment Officer,
Tradecraft Capital

"In *The Truth About Crypto*, I found myself highlighting almost every page as Ric did a phenomenal job simplifying the complex topic, without watering down his great findings!"

Andres Garcia-Amaya
CEO & Founder, Zoe Financial

ALSO BY RIC EDELMAN

The Truth About Your Future

The Truth About Money

The Truth About Retirement Plans and IRAs

The Lies About Money

The Squirrel Manifesto

Rescue Your Money

Ordinary People, Extraordinary Wealth

Discover the Wealth Within You

The New Rules of Money

What You Need to Do Now

THE TRUTH ABOUT CRYPTO

YOUR INVESTING GUIDE TO UNDERSTANDING BLOCKCHAIN, BITCOIN, AND OTHER DIGITAL ASSETS

RIC EDELMAN

Simon & Schuster

NEW YORK   LONDON   TORONTO
SYDNEY   NEW DELHI

Simon & Schuster
1230 Avenue of the Americas
New York, NY 10020

First Simon & Schuster hardcover edition May 2022

SIMON & SCHUSTER and colophon are registered trademarks of Simon & Schuster, Inc.

For information about special discounts for bulk purchases, please contact Simon & Schuster Special Sales at 1-866-506-1949 or business@simonandschuster.com.

The Simon & Schuster Speakers Bureau can bring authors to your live event. For more information or to book an event, contact the Simon & Schuster Speakers Bureau at 1-866-248-3049 or visit our website at www.simonspeakers.com.

Interior design by Paul Dippolito

Manufactured in the United States of America

10 9 8 7 6 5 4 3 2 1

Library of Congress Cataloging-in-Publication Data has been applied for.

ISBN 978-1-6680-0232-2
ISBN 978-1-6680-0234-6 (ebook)

In Memory of Anne-Marie Bottazzi
"Friendship is a rainbow between two people"

Helpful Lists You'll Find Inside

The Investments, Products, Services, and Companies in the Blockchain and Digital Assets World

Contents

Part Two: Understanding Bitcoin and Other Digital Assets

Part Three: Investing in Digital Assets

Part Four: Regulation, Taxation, and Compliance

Chapter 21: Operations and Compliance

Part Five: Getting Started

THE TRUTH ABOUT CRYPTO

Foreword

My ah-ha moment on digital assets came during a discussion with Ric Edelman. But the revelation didn't come from Ric.

I was interviewing him at a conference I was hosting for *Barron's* "Hall of Fame" financial advisors. To even get into the room, they had to clear a very high bar: 10 years or more as a top-ranked Barron's advisor. This was not merely an elite group; it was the elite of the elite. (And three times, Ric was #1 in our rankings.)

I wanted to get a sense of the crowd—how rudimentary would we need to get in order to give them the information they needed on bitcoin and other digital asset investment opportunities? After all, this wasn't exactly a Silicon Valley tech-bro confab. Ric and I were onstage in the elegant ballroom of a 125-year-old hotel on the ocean in Palm Beach. The advisors we were addressing were mostly well past their 50th birthdays and had spent decades constructing smart, resilient portfolios of stocks, bonds, and alternative assets. They warn their clients against chasing fads, and while they take calculated risks, they manage money for people who are already rich, and who don't want to have to get rich twice.

I speak with financial advisors regularly in my role at *Barron's*, and most of them are crypto-skeptics. They're used to measuring intrinsic value based on cash flow and other metrics; all digital assets—even bitcoin and Ethereum—fail these tests. Many of the advisors work for companies that won't let them buy digital assets for client accounts even if they want to. About half are "fiduciaries," meaning they are legally bound to put their clients' interests ahead of their own.

So, there Ric and I were, talking to nearly a hundred of his peers, the nation's most successful financial advisors. I asked them, "How many of you own digital assets in your personal accounts?" Well over half of

1

them raised their hands. Shocked, I asked, "How many include digital assets in client portfolios?" Again, far more than half the hands in the room went up. To get around their firms' restrictions, some of the advisors quietly point clients in the right direction. That could not only get them in trouble with their compliance officers, it also could cost the advisor—if clients remove funds from their accounts to buy crypto elsewhere, that leaves a smaller asset base on which to charge fees. But these advisors had decided, to my surprise, that it was in their clients' best interest to own digital assets. So, they were fulfilling their fiduciary duty by helping them do so.

We've come a long way since 2018, when John Oliver described cryptocurrencies as "everything you don't understand about money combined with everything you don't understand about computers." Now, a group of fairly conservative, highly sophisticated money managers, working with some of the nation's wealthiest individuals, have converted. These men and women did not chase the dot.com bubble, they didn't hop on the SPAC bandwagon, they hadn't poured money into Bernie Madoff's scam. But they've decided digital assets belong in a well-balanced portfolio. They join a long list of establishment types—pension funds, endowments, and even a small 401(k) provider—who have embraced digital assets as well.

Ric, of course, has been urging all of them to do so for a long time. They are probably kicking themselves for not listening to him sooner. I certainly was a skeptic. As an editor at *Barron's*, I first became aware of bitcoin in 2013 when it was priced at $31. I watched as it climbed, and thought of it as the greater fool theory at work—you bought bitcoin simply in the hope that someone else would pay a higher price. And did they ever; 2,210 times higher by November of 2021. Had I invested a mere $200 back in 2013 and cashed out near the recent high, I would have covered one of my children's college education for the cost of a high-end toaster.

While I haven't ruled out the possibility that we are witnessing the greater-fool theory on steroids, I now think of digital assets as analogous to the internet in the '90s. Sure, there were excesses, but like the internet, I see this new technology as a transformational force, changing the future more than most of us can imagine. Yes, some of today's highflyers will become the Pets.com of our era (Dogecoin, anyone?), but as Ric lays out in the pages that follow, the utility of blockchain technology is undeniable.

The ability to tokenize illiquid assets can allow investors to own a share of almost anything, or an aging couple to tap the equity of their home without a pricey reverse mortgage. Photographers and songwriters and even makeup artists will be able to profit from their intellectual property in ways they never could have imagined. Ric predicts that the US government will create a stablecoin by the end of this decade. Why would the government do that? For one thing, digital money will allow governments to track transactions, meaning they can tax them.

So, I am doing my part to educate people, particularly financial advisors. As I say to skeptics, it's not my place to tell advisors how to construct portfolios, but I assure them that basic knowledge of digital assets will be a prerequisite for a thriving practice. Your clients may not expect bitcoin in their portfolios, but their children will.

A time machine can be a helpful decision-making tool. Imagine, 10 years from now, uttering this sentence: "Damn, I wish I had not learned about that emerging technology that was minting billionaires and transforming the world of finance."

Enjoy the journey!

Jack Otter
Global Head of Wealth & Asset Management
at *Barron's* and host of *Barron's Roundtable*

Welcome

I'm really excited you're here! You're about to embark on a fascinating journey, one that I began in 2012. I was interviewing famed futurist Ray Kurzweil for my PBS television show at his faculty office at Harvard. While chatting afterward, Ray encouraged me to attend the Executive Program at Singularity University. He cofounded the institution with Peter Diamandis to help world leaders learn how to apply technology to solve global challenges and build a better future for the planet. With Ray's help, I was accepted into the nine-day, deep-dive program on exponential technologies. The course covers Artificial Intelligence, Robotics, Machine Learning, 3D Printing, Big Data, Nanotech, Biotech, Fintech, EdTech, AgriTech, and more.*

It was there that I first heard the word *bitcoin* and the notion of a "cryptocurrency." It made no sense to me (despite—or because of—my knowledge and experience in the financial field). Nevertheless, I was intrigued. So, I explored bitcoin throughout 2013 and began investing in 2014. As my knowledge grew, and as I got to know many of the folks involved, I became acutely aware of two facts:

First, blockchain technology and the digital assets it makes possible are revolutionary. This is the most profound innovation in commerce since the invention of the internet.

Second, few people realize this—including the vast majority of financial professionals.

Although the crypto community has created an astonishing array of products and services, it hasn't learned how to reach investors like you. And the bulk of the financial services industry, which in the United

---

* Upon completing the program, I was invited to become a guest lecturer and invest in the organization. I did both.

States manages two-thirds of all investors' money, doesn't fully realize the incredible investment opportunities available in this new asset class. Nor does the financial field yet know how to give its clients access to these opportunities.

That's why, in 2018, I created the Digital Assets Council of Financial Professionals. Today, DACFP is widely regarded as the premier resource on this topic for Wall Street and corporate America. We are the bridge connecting the crypto community with the financial services field. Our role is to provide financial professionals with the education they need so they can explain these new technologies to their clients, helping everyone gain access to these investment opportunities. (Already, thousands of financial professionals have enrolled in DACFP's program to attain their Certificate in Blockchain and Digital Assets.)

Over the past decade, I've trained thousands of financial advisors and corporate executives on blockchain and digital assets. Ironically, the more investment knowledge and experience these folks have, the harder it is for them to comprehend this new asset class. Indeed, I've found that the more college degrees, professional designations, and years of investment and financial experience an individual has, the more they struggle with this topic. That's simply because blockchain and digital assets technologies have nothing in common with anything financial professionals have learned about or experienced anywhere in their careers.

So, if you know nothing about economics, finance, asset management, or portfolio analysis—well . . . *congratulations!* You have a distinct advantage over all those Wall Streeters!

And if you are (sorry) one of those financial folks with years of investment and financial experience, then I urge you, as you read these pages, to set aside your well-earned knowledge and experience for a little while. I know that's a big ask—I've got 37 years in the financial field and six professional designations myself, and if someone were to tell me to ignore what I know, well, yeah, I'd call that a big red flag. All I can say is that I understand how you feel. I felt the same way when I started exploring this new asset class, too. But I quickly learned that, instead of *helping*, my knowledge and experience were actually a hindrance. I had a lot of presumptions, expectations, and judgments to overcome. I now see that my initial resistance *interfered* with my journey toward comprehending this new technology and all it offers. So, you can either benefit from my experience and proceed as I suggest—which will save you a lot of time and aggravation—or you can trudge along as I did at first. Up to you.

Let's Use the Right Words

Automobiles were once known as *horseless carriages*—but imagine the look you'll get today if you tell someone you want to buy one. Likewise, bitcoin was introduced as *cryptocurrency*—and if that's what you call it, you'll be as outdated as folks who wear galoshes on a rainy day.

So, let's use the correct terminology. It's the best way to demonstrate you're knowledgeable.* The tech is new, and so are many of the words. They are often derived from or similar to familiar words and terms, but some are just bad jokes.

I'll explain them as we go, but a few key terms are worthy of mention here.

First, there's *Bitcoin* (capitalized). Then, there's *bitcoin* (lowercase). *Bitcoin* refers to the computer network; *bitcoin* refers to the

---

* It's also how you can immediately tell if someone you're talking to truly knows about this topic. People who use outdated terms don't know as much as they think they do—and you'll come upon them pretty much every time you have a conversation about this topic.

asset that's used on the network. So, you buy and sell bitcoin on the Bitcoin network.

Yes, you can use *bitcoin* in the plural, but only in certain circumstances. You'll notice how I handle it throughout this book. You'll get the hang of it. But if in doubt, go with the singular; it's more of *deer* and *deer* than *cat* and *cats*. As in "I own lots of bitcoin," not "I own lots of bitcoins."

Also, it's okay to say *crypto* when talking shop with fellow insiders, as I did 10 paragraphs ago. But generally, it's better to use *digital*. It's a lot friendlier than scary *crypto*, and, besides, everyone's familiar with *digital*, since we now live in a digital world—Twitter and other social media; PayPal, Venmo, Zelle, and other online payment apps; Amazon and other online stores; and so on.

Zelle

As for the second half of *cryptocurrency*, well, we now need to split it into two parts: *currency*, yes, but also *assets*. Don't mention one when you mean the other. We'll talk more about this in chapter 8. For now, just realize that there is a difference.

One more item: *fiat currency*. You'll encounter this phrase a lot. Fiat currency is issued by a government but isn't backed by anything (such as gold); instead, citizens put their faith in the government's willingness and ability to support the currency. When a currency is backed by, say, gold (as the US dollar was prior to 1973), the amount of currency that can be printed is limited by the amount of gold held by the government. By replacing gold-backed currency with fiat currency, the central bank can more freely control how much money

> If I don't like the term *crypto*, why did I use it in the title of the book!?
>
> Because the term is, sadly, still the common nomenclature. My publisher felt this would be the best way to attract readers,* and I found it difficult to disagree. But hopefully, you now know why it's best to stop using the term.

---

* It worked, huh!

is printed. Today, just about every currency in the world, including the US dollar, is a fiat currency.

Disclosure

This book describes many digital coins and tokens by name, and my wife, Jean, and I own many of them. The book also contains the names and descriptions of many companies, and I have relationships with many of them, too. In some cases, Jean and I have invested money in those companies' coins or tokens. In other cases, we have invested in the company sponsoring those investments. Finally, some companies are sponsors or advertisers of DACFP, or my media company, The Truth About Your Future (thetayf.com), which is devoted to teaching consumers and investors about blockchain and digital assets and related topics. Finally, I'm a customer or user of some of the products or services mentioned in the book.

Therefore, on each page containing the first mention of each of these coins, tokens, or companies, you'll see icons (and footnotes if additional disclosure is needed). The icons and their meaning are:

 As of this writing, Jean and I own the asset under discussion. We therefore have an economic interest in its success.

 As of this writing, Jean and I have equity, stock options, warrants, advisory shares, convertible debt, bonds, or other debt of the issuer being discussed (or whose product, service, or investment is being discussed). We therefore have an economic interest in the issuer's success. If you buy, hire, subscribe to or otherwise use these products, services or investments, the issuer gets revenue, which could in turn benefit Jean and me.

As of this writing, the company under discussion, or the company behind the product or service under discussion, is a sponsor or advertiser of DACFP and/or TAYF. I have an economic incentive for you to buy, hire, subscribe to, or otherwise use its products or services (especially if you tell 'em I sent ya!), so I can increase my chances of persuading them to maintain or increase their sponsorship and advertising campaigns with my companies.

 As of this writing, I am a customer or user of the product or service mentioned.

There are only two ways for me to avoid these conflicts of interest: Jean and I could divest ourselves of all ownership of digital assets or cease our business activities, but, hey, that ain't happening. Or, I could omit any reference in the book to any such asset or company. That would be a huge disservice to you. It would also render the book rather pointless, as I wouldn't even be able to use the word *bitcoin* (which appears in these pages 718 times).

So, since these conflicts can't be avoided, we are doing the next best thing by disclosing them to you. This way, with your own good judgment, you can reach your own conclusions.

As you evaluate the performance data presented in these pages, keep in mind that past performance does not guarantee future results. Also, I've compiled dozens of lists to help you find the investments, companies, and vendors providing products and services you'll find helpful as you engage in the world of digital assets. Although I have strived to compile lists that are accurate and complete, I take no responsibility for any errors or omissions. You should use these lists as a starting point in your own research efforts, and not rely on them to make any decision to purchase any product or service referenced.

Now, You're Ready to Begin!

In the first part of the book, I'll introduce you to block-chain technology—how it works and why it's so transformative for our global economy. In the second part, you'll learn about bitcoin and other digital assets. In the third part, you'll discover the investment opportunities: how to select the ones that are right for you, and how to incorporate them into your overall investment portfolio. In the fourth part, we'll cover regulation, taxes, and compliance. **Singularity University** And in the fifth part, I'll help you get started by answering your most common concerns.

Let's get started!

PART ONE

Understanding the Technology

Chapter 1

The Four Most Transformative Innovations in the History of Commerce

All human advances are due to innovation—from new ways of thinking to the invention of new tools. In the world of commerce, it's been suggested that the four most impactful innovations are:

Fire

The wheel

The internet

The blockchain

It's easy to agree that the first three changed history. But blockchain?

"You shouldn't have asked me to show you how it works."

Yeah, blockchain. Think of it as Internet 3.0. The first internet connected people on a mass scale—think Facebook and social media. You know how impactful that was (and still is). That led to Internet 2.0 (more commonly called IoT, the Internet of Things). This internet connects things to each other—my dog wears a collar that tells my phone if she leaves the yard. And at the grocer, a QR code tells the automated checkout kiosk that I'm buying a banana.

Internet 3.0 is the Internet of Money, aka blockchain. Connecting money via the internet is as transformative to commerce and society as the Internet of People and the Internet of Things have been, and because "money makes the world go 'round," Internet 3.0 will prove to be even more impactful than its predecessors. The wealth-creation opportunities on a global scale are truly unprecedented.

Indeed, Nasdaq says blockchain technology "holds great promise in allowing capital markets to operate more efficiently with greater transparency and security." The Bank of England (Great Britain's central bank, comparable to our Federal Reserve) goes even further, saying blockchain technology could transform the world's financial system. More than 90% of the world's banks are developing blockchain technology; in 2021, Bank of America alone filed more than 160 patent applications involving digital payment technologies. JPMorgan Chase says banks will save $120 billion a year. Banks and other companies spent $6.6 billion on blockchain R&D in 2021 and will spend $19 billion annually by 2024, according to market intelligence firm IDC. Already, almost all the nation's top colleges and universities offer courses in blockchain and digital assets, and blockchain engineers are now the highest-paid programmers in the country, earning $175,000+ a year. (According to LinkedIn, US job postings for "crypto" and "blockchain" positions skyrocketed 1,000% in 2021. Major financial services firms, including JPMorgan Chase, BNY Mellon, Deutsche Bank, Wells Fargo, Citigroup, Goldman Sachs, Morgan Stanley, Capital One, UBS, Bank of America, Credit Suisse, and Barclays, hired 40% more crypto employees in 2021 than in the prior year. Jobs include sales professionals, workers designing crypto offerings for consumers, and engineers building blockchain platforms for banks.)

Excitement isn't limited to the financial sector. MarketsandMarkets reports that the blockchain market will grow 53% per year, reaching $3.2 billion by 2026. For example, *Billboard* magazine says blockchain "offers solutions to intractable problems, such as song rights monitoring and reliable distribution of royalties and event tickets."

All this helps explain why PricewaterhouseCoopers says blockchain technology will add nearly $2 trillion to the $80 trillion global economy by 2030. Transformative, indeed.

Chapter 2

Why Blockchain Is
So Transformative

Blockchain technology will be so impactful because it revolutionizes business. And it all starts with the humble ledger.

What's a *ledger*? It's a place where you record deposits and withdrawals. Your checkbook is a ledger. So is an Excel spreadsheet. Both are private; you alone have access to them, and you alone decide who gets to see the information. If you want to cheat, you can create a second ledger with false information—and you can show the fake one to others instead of showing your real ledger. (This is known as a "second set of books" and was Al Capone's downfall.)

Ledgers are used throughout the world's financial system. Because every ledger is private, they're expensive to manage and maintain, and they allow for fraud and abuse. Thus, the global accounting industry is a $120 billion business, according to IBISWorld. No wonder banking costs are so high!

Now, consider a ledger that exists on a blockchain. It is broadly distributed to everyone who has an internet connection, which is why blockchain is also known as DLT, *distributed ledger technology*. Instead of being private, DLT is public; anyone can see it anytime, for free (simply visit https://www.blockchain.com/explorer). But although everyone can see the data, no one can alter it. Indeed, data on a blockchain can never be erased, changed, or copied by anyone.

What I've just described is revolutionary.

You see, when I look at data on your private ledger, I am forced to trust you when you say the data is legitimate. This is why our global financial system is known as the trust economy. We do business with each other because we trust each other.

But trust has limits. So, I hire auditors to confirm that what you're telling me is true.

Trust (or lack thereof) is the reason buying a house is so cumbersome. After you sign the sales contract, you hire a settlement attorney to conduct a title search—to verify that the seller really does own the deed and has the legal right to sell it to you. Then, you buy title insurance in case the title search was flawed. Meanwhile, you apply for a mortgage and the lender verifies that you really do have the income and assets you claim to have. All this adds months and tens of thousands of dollars to the transaction—and none of that increases the value of the house. You're spending money on verification because we operate in a *trust economy*.

Blockchains eliminate all of that. It replaces the trust economy with an *authentication economy*. Because data on a blockchain is permanent, we don't need to trust its legitimacy. It simply is, innately. The reason: as a *distributed* record, multiple parties (every computer on the network) has an identical copy. All the records are linked in such a way that no single person is the sole holder of the record, and therefore, no one can tamper with the record (they'd have to tamper with every copy of the record that exists everywhere, and they'd have to tamper with every copy at the same time).

Let's return to our Excel spreadsheet. Imagine entering data about yourself in cell A1. In cell B1 you'll find the deed to your house, and in cell C1 is information about the buyer. Each cell is a block. Within each block is data. And the three blocks are linked together in a chain. A *blockchain*.*

Because the data have been verified and are linked together, the transaction can be completed nearly instantaneously—as quickly as you buy bananas at the grocer. That means you instantly qualify for

---

* See? This stuff really isn't all that complicated.

FIGURE 2.1

the mortgage. No need for title searches or insurance. No escrow payments. You eliminate months of delay, and you save thousands of dollars in fees. You are able to move into the house the same day the sales contract is accepted.

It is impossible to overstate how transformative this is for global commerce. It's also incredibly disruptive—because if you're the settlement attorney or the title insurance company, you've just become as obsolete as the maker of horse-drawn buggies.

In fact, blockchains eliminate all middlemen, the *intermediaries* who are between buyers and sellers. Thanks to blockchain tech, we don't need any of them anymore. Stockbrokers, attorneys, insurance agents, ticket resellers—everyone who processes paperwork to help buyers and sellers execute transactions is likely to be out of work. We're talking about 10 million white-collar workers in the United States, representing 21% of our GDP.*

---

* For a list of exactly which jobs are going to be eliminated by 2035, see chapter 14 of *The Truth About Your Future*.

The Features of Blockchain

We've seen just one example so far of the transformational power of this new technology. And we've only just begun. Blockchain's capabilities are extensive, thanks to its many features. These include:

1. **It's decentralized.** There's no single point of potential failure. No single location or individual can threaten the network— either maliciously or through incompetence.

2. **No collusion.** By being decentralized, it is extremely difficult for manipulation to occur.

3. **Transparency.** Everyone has equal access to all records. It's the democratization of information.

4. **No preferential authority.** There is no hierarchy as with centralized systems.

5. **Immutability.** Once created, a record can't be deleted, copied, or altered.

6. **Limitless.** We can append to existing records and provide new information endlessly.

7. **Open-sourced software.** The program is not only viewable and auditable by anyone, but it can also be changed only by consensus. No dictators, no CEOs.

8. **Low transaction costs.** The technology is inexpensive to use, making it more accessible to more people worldwide.

9. **Greater speed.** Time is the one commodity we all have in equal amounts and which we cannot replace, so being able to complete transactions faster is one of blockchain's key features.

10. **Anonymity.** In many cases, you can post data onto a blockchain and execute transactions while maintaining your privacy.

The Benefits of Blockchain

There are thousands upon thousands of commercial applications for blockchain technology. DLT lets governments and businesses operate at higher speed, with greater safety, at lower cost, and with more transparency. Let's look at some of the key uses.

Consumer Purchases

In 2020, $4.2 trillion in merchant transactions, representing 14% of all global commerce, occurred over the internet. Most of those transactions involved credit cards; Visa and MasterCard typically charge merchants about 2%, American Express and Discover, 3%. That's about $100 billion per year in fees, which merchants pass along to consumers in the form of higher prices.

Visa

Amex

Blockchain technology allows consumers to skip the credit card infrastructure and transmit money directly to merchants. This provides massive cost savings to consumers but poses an existential threat to credit card companies.

Remittances

Every year, $4 trillion moves from one country to another. It's not just big corporations that move money globally. Ordinary people do, too: migrant workers send about $500 billion from one country to another—usually to family members living back home—according to the World Bank.

To send money to another country (called a *cross-border transmittal*) via the world's banking system, you use SWIFT, the Society for Worldwide Interbank Financial Telecommunication network. More than 11,000 banks process over 35 million of these transactions every day, and each transmittal takes up to five days to process, and costs an average of 6.7% of the amount being sent (and up to 20% in some sub-Saharan countries). And if it's Friday night, you'll have to wait until

Monday morning to tell your bank to initiate the transfer. (And let's hope Monday isn't a holiday.)

With blockchain technology, you can transfer money 24/7/365. Your recipient will receive it within minutes, and possibly in seconds, and the transaction will be virtually free—saving consumers and businesses $268 billion a year. Payment processors such as Western Union could become obsolete.

Corporate Financing

Hundreds of governments (including the Royal Bank of Canada, Bank of Thailand, the European Investment Bank, and the World Bank) and corporations (including HSBC, Goldman Sachs, Société Générale, and Santander) have sold bonds via blockchains. Doing so cuts underwriting costs 35%, says German fintech firm Cashlink, and lets the investors receive higher yields.

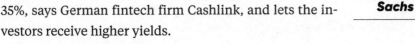

Goldman Sachs

Foreign Trade

Companies doing business outside their home country face significant financial risks because of routine delays in the banking system. When you use local currency to buy a product, the overseas merchant must convert your currency into its currency. The longer that conversion takes to occur, the greater the risk of price fluctuations. There are also substantial fees to convert currency, even if you can do it quickly. It's bad enough when you're spending a few grand on an international vacation. Imagine spending several billion dollars on corporate purchases. The losses can be enormous.

Blockchain technology can solve both problems. Transfers occur in real time, eliminating foreign-currency exchange-rate risk and alleviating cash-flow concerns. With blockchain, currencies can be exchanged within seconds at comparatively little cost, a huge savings in both time and money.

Programmable Money, aka Smart Contracts

When you send money to someone via a blockchain, they receive it almost instantly. But perhaps you don't want them to. Maybe you want to pay them only if or when they fulfill a promise—such as delivering your pizza or, say, upon a certain date, time, temperature, weather, political or sporting-event outcome, or some other condition. With smart contracts, your money is sent but not received until all conditions are satisfied—using a blockchain as an escrow account.

Ethereum

Smart contracts could alter how commerce is conducted on a global scale. Complex agreements in finance, manufacturing, real estate, and more can be executed with greater transparency, efficiency, safety, and compliance—protecting buyers from the risk that sellers won't deliver on their promises.

Micropayments

One issue preventing many industries from success is the inability to make payments in tiny amounts. In 2020, Bob Dylan sold the rights to his music catalog to a publishing company. What if that company decided to sell those rights to investors? It'd be cool to own a share of "Mr. Tambourine Man"—just imagine getting your cut of the royalty every time the song is played on the radio or Spotify!

The problem is that your cut would be tiny. Dylan's 600+ song catalog sold for a reported $400 million. Each song is therefore worth an average of about $667,000. Say the songs are sold for shares priced at $1,000 each—that's about 670 shares of "Mr. Tambourine Man." When the song is played on the radio, it earns a 9.1 cent royalty. If it plays 12 times a year, each of those shares would be entitled to a payment of $0.0016. Like I said, your cut would be tiny.

Not only is there no currency for an amount this small (pennies are only two decimal places of a dollar), the cost of distributing that payment would dwarf the payment itself. The stamp alone to mail the check is 55 cents, and let's not forget the cost of the check and the labor to issue and record it. It's economically impossible to make payments of such tiny amounts.

But that's only because the smallest denomination of the dollar is the penny, which goes to just two decimal places. But digital money (being bits and bytes, ones and zeros) can be fractionalized into far tinier units. It's easy, therefore, to make digital money that's a mere one-hundred-millionth of a coin. That's already been done—as we'll learn in chapter 8. And, its being digital, no postage is needed to send it. As a result, blockchain technology makes micropayments possible, further boosting the potential for e-commerce globally.

Indeed, 17% of the world's adults who lack bank accounts—300 million people worldwide—own a cell phone, and that's all you need to access digital assets. New technology is providing unprecedented access to money for billions of people.

Supply Chain Management

Supply chain refers to the movement of goods from the factory to the consumer. That chain is long, starting with raw materials and parts that are obtained or built and sent to a factory, then constructed or assembled, delivered to a wholesaler, then to a retailer, and ultimately to the consumer. It's expensive for manufacturers to order all those parts and track them and the finished products.

Thanks to shared records, available for the first time via distributed ledger technology, we can monitor the processing of goods and services as they flow through the supply chain. Within the DLT model, every party in the chain becomes interconnected. Traders, freight forwarders, inland transporters, ports and terminals, ocean carriers, as well as customs, FDA, law enforcement, and other authorities, all work within one secure system. Everyone shares real-time information, which captures shipping milestones, cargo details, trade documents, customs filings, sensor readings, and more. Because it's trustless, the system fosters collaboration by digitizing and automating business processes integral to global trade.

Consider the fishing industry. The Norwegian Seafood Association is using a blockchain created by IBM to track salmon as they are bred, caught, stored, and shipped. At the grocer, consumers can scan each fish's QR code to see when the fish was farmed and how long ago it left the sea. In turn, the fishermen can prevent fraud and reduce waste.

Or consider luxury watches. Some of the most prestigious watch-makers in the world, including Vacheron Constantin, Ulysse Nardin, and Breitling, are using blockchain technology to track every watch they manufacture. This allows buyers to authenticate each watch's provenance from the factory to the retailer—and guarantee authenticity through changes in ownership. Louis Vuitton is doing the same for its luxury handbags.

Virtually every industry can find similar value and benefit by deploying blockchain technology. At present, most companies have not yet engaged. But application of blockchain technology is almost certain to grow exponentially; Xerox invented the commercial fax machine in 1964, but fax machines weren't ubiquitous in corporate offices until the 1980s. It won't take nearly as long for blockchain technology to become equally commonplace. Health-care records, financial transactions, educational reports, environmental information—the list of data that can be placed on a blockchain is endless, and companies and governments have a tremendous economic incentive to do so.

Truly endless? You bet. We've talked about the supply chain in terms of manufactured products. But we could easily extend that conversation to the financial services sector, whose product is . . . money. All those ledgers at every bank and brokerage firm? They're really just warehouses of financial data. Imagine transitioning all that data to a blockchain. Know what you'd have? All the world's business records of commercial activity, at every point in the supply chain, in a single database. Everyone could track each transaction, regardless of how many intermediaries were involved. We'd have open access and transparency in a way that has never been possible. Until now. *That* is the real promise of distributed ledger technology.

Self-Sovereign Identity

Rather than Facebook having, owning, and being able to use all your personal information without your knowledge or approval, and without any compensation to you, blockchain technology lets you control your personal identity and information. You get to grant access to your digital self as you choose, and you can be compensated for doing so.

The Most Important Benefit and Use of All

It's easy to dismiss blockchain technology as a fad, a novelty, a toy, a choice. When considering it, most Americans—indeed, most people throughout the developed world—can reasonably ask, "What's the point?"

After all, we're all fine without it, thankyouverymuch. Our banking system operates well (even though we like to complain about it). We can sign leases and purchase agreements that let us get products now merely by promising to pay later. We can easily borrow money to buy houses, cars, and furniture. Got no money today? No problem, as we can just charge daily expenses to our credit cards. And the money in our bank accounts? That's safe—we never fret that the bank might close or that our government might confiscate our money.

For sure, if you're reading this book, odds are high that you don't need blockchain to make your life better. Your life is pretty good as it is.

Life is equally good for 5.6 billion other people around the world, too. But 2 billion people (including 6% of US households) aren't so fortunate. They are all *unbanked*, meaning they lack sufficient funds to open a bank account. As a result, they enjoy none of the benefits that you and I take for granted.

Consider credit. Without credit, you likely can't attend college, drive a car, or buy a house—and forget about making purchases that require a credit card (such as an online purchase). Without credit, businesses can't invest in factories, pay for research or product development, or easily finance the distribution of their products. Indeed, without access to credit, the global economy would be severely hampered.

But here's the fascinating part. Of the two billion people who are unbanked, the Pew foundation says 60% of them have a smartphone—which they can use to obtain and hold digital assets. That lets them create a transaction history of their income and purchases, which lets lenders determine their creditworthiness. And microlenders—those willing to lend as little as $25—can reach them. Suddenly, access to credit becomes available, without the involvement of banks.

A great example of this is M-Pesa, launched in Kenya in March 2007 (*M* stands for "mobile"; *pesa* is Swahili for "money"). Today, 96% of Kenyan households use it. It's also available in Albania, the Democratic Republic of the Congo, Egypt, Ghana, India, Lesotho, Mozambique, Romania, and Tanzania.

M-Pesa lets customers securely receive and store money and pay bills. No bank account is required; all you need is a basic mobile phone (smartphone users can download an app). The Kenyan government says M-Pesa has significantly reduced street robberies, burglaries, and corruption common in cash-based economies. It has also allowed the creation of "smart meters," prepaid devices that let low-income households pay for electricity and water on a pay-as-you-go basis. M-Pesa is also used to pay for food delivery to 100,000 refugees, eliminating middlemen and thus reducing the cost of distributing aid, while creating employment opportunities for people in refugee camps.

All this explains why, of Americans who know what a digital currency is, only 18% are supportive of having our government create one, compared to 42% of those who lack bank accounts. It also explains why 32% of Nigeria's population owns bitcoin (making it the world's number one country for crypto adoption, according to Statista), why El Salvador declared **Stastista** bitcoin legal currency (and why Panama, Ukraine, and Paraguay plan to do so, as well), why Cuba formally adopted bitcoin for use by its citizens, and why the greatest user of bitcoin per capita is

Vietnam (where 21% of adults own bitcoin), the Philippines (20%), Turkey (16%), Peru (16%), and India (9%).

Blockchain offers the best avenue ever invented to eliminate poverty globally, raising the standard of living for billions of people and growing the worldwide economy, which helps everyone on the planet. Without question, this is blockchain's biggest promise and its most important benefit and use.

As exciting as all these benefits are, keep in mind that, for now, those benefits are largely just promises. Few applications are in use, with relatively few users. As you evaluate the investment opportunities that we'll cover in part 3, remember that business fundamentals still apply. Is the company providing a service that customers want? Is the deployment of blockchain solving a real problem—or is it just a marketing gimmick? Use the same caution you would use with any potential investment.

Chapter 3

How Blockchain—and Bitcoin— Came to Be

Most give the credit for conceiving blockchain technology to Satoshi Nakamoto, who wrote a white paper describing the idea in 2008.* Actually, we can thank Scott Stornetta and Stuart Haber. They met at Bell Labs. Scott holds a PhD in theoretical physics from Stanford; Stuart has a PhD in computer science from Columbia. They coauthored pioneering papers describing their concept in 1991 (receiving the 1992 Discover Award for Computer Software). Of the eight citations in Satoshi's 2008 white paper, three reference Scott and Stu's work.†

Why, then, is Satoshi so much more famous? Because Satoshi solved the problem that prevented blockchain technology from working.

The Problem of Double Presentment

Say Grandma sends you a $50 check for your birthday. You'd like to spend that money, but no one will accept the check as payment. They don't know if the check is real or whether Grandma really has fifty bucks in her account to cover it. (There's that *trust* thing again.) So, you deposit the check into your bank account and wait for it to clear. You then withdraw the money so you can spend it.

Not so long ago, you had to go to the bank and physically hand

---

* No one knows who Satoshi is. Many believe Satoshi is an individual; others think Satoshi is the name of a group of people who collaborated to invent Bitcoin.

† Scott is a member of my faculty at the Digital Assets Council of Financial Professionals, where he teaches some of the online, self-study courses that financial professionals take to attain their Certificate in Blockchain and Digital Assets.

Grandma's check to the teller. Goodbye, check; hello, increase in your bank balance. Then, in 2009, USAA became the first bank to accept a photograph of Grandma's check. You simply snapped a picture with your phone and emailed the photo to the bank.

But wait. You're still in possession of the physical check. What's to stop you from walking into the bank branch and depositing the check after you send in the photo? By making two deposits with the same check—once by phone, once in a physical branch—your account would have $100, not just $50. Make a quick withdrawal before the bank realizes what you've done, and you've doubled your money.

That's a crime, of course; F5, a cybersecurity firm, says banks lose $1.7 billion annually to this scam, called *double presentment fraud*.

This problem could exist with blockchains, too. What if two copies of the same deed are posted? What if two people each claim to be buyers or owners of the same house?

Satoshi solved the problem. Essentially, Satoshi's innovation places a time stamp and encryption on every block of data that's placed onto a blockchain. Once done, everyone knows the information is reliable because it has been authenticated. No trust is required.

The Introduction of Bitcoin

Okay. Fine. You get it. You need to use blockchain technology to cryptographically authenticate data. But why the need for bitcoin?

The answer is simple. Satoshi called this new blockchain *Bitcoin*. And to submit a block of data onto the chain, you need a means of conveyance. Satoshi named it *bitcoin*.* The bitcoin is to the Bitcoin network what chips are to a casino. If you want to play poker, you must convert your dollars into chips. The chips are your means of conveyance—you use them to play the games. When you're done, you can convert your chips back into dollars. Ditto for blockchain: if you want to put blocks

---

* I'd have preferred a different word instead of lowercasing the same word, to help avoid confusion, but Satoshi didn't ask me for my opinion.

of data onto the chain, you must use coins that are native to the system. Satoshi invented them, and instead of calling them dollars, pennies, chips, tokens, or shares, Satoshi called them bitcoin.

So, if you want to engage with Satoshi's blockchain, you must use bitcoin. It has its own ticker symbol (BTC) just like publicly traded stocks.

What Motivated Satoshi to Fix That Banking Problem by Inventing Bitcoin?

In 2008, the world was mired in a global credit crisis. Mortgage lenders had provided loans to people who couldn't repay them, and when millions of those homeowners defaulted, the lenders lost all their money.

The biggest lender, Countrywide Financial, collapsed along with IndyMac Federal Bank and Washington Mutual Bank. The government nationalized Fannie Mae and Freddie Mac. Bear Stearns folded, then Lehman Brothers. The government rescued Citigroup, then arranged for Bank of America to buy Merrill Lynch, which was facing bankruptcy. Meanwhile, Wells Fargo bought Wachovia, as Goldman Sachs and Morgan Stanley became bank holding companies subject to the

Ford

Bank of America

Federal Reserve. The Reserve Primary Fund, the nation's oldest money market fund with $60 billion in assets, "broke the buck," becoming the first such fund to lose money (thus creating a "run" on Wall Street). Finally, Congress passed the $700 billion Troubled Asset Relief Program to bail out Ford, GM, and Chrysler—as well as AIG, the biggest insurance company in the world.

All this was shocking and unprecedented, and it occurred with incredible velocity. TARP helped avoid economic collapse, but a new fear arose: that the massive influx of currency into the economy and the resulting surge in federal debt would lead to runaway global inflation.

Satoshi was fed up. There had to be a better way for our global financial system to operate, no? So, in December 2008, during the depths of the financial crisis, Satoshi released a nine-page white paper, "Bitcoin, a Peer-to-Peer Electronic Cash System."* In the paper, Satoshi described the problem:

> *The root problem with conventional currency is all the trust that's required to make it work. The central bank must be trusted not to debase the currency, but the history of fiat currencies is full of breaches of that trust and that notion is the issue.*

What did Satoshi suggest as the solution? You don't have to read the white paper.† Instead, just read the title. Let's focus on its exact words.

Bitcoin The title's very first word was the introduction to Satoshi's brand-new invention. The name is a clever combination of *coin* (referring to money) and *bit* (referring to computer bits and bytes, the basis of data).

Peer-to-Peer This means "between you and me." When using bitcoin, there is no intermediary, nobody between buyer and seller. That's rarely the case in the world's current financial system, where there's almost always an intermediary.

Electronic Satoshi created a system designed to work in the digital age, using the internet. Importantly, paper is not involved—unlike with fiat currencies.

Cash This new electronic system provides a way to move cash from one person or entity to another.

---

* You can read it at bitcoin.org.

† Even though I just told you to.

System That's what Bitcoin is—a complete, self-contained system for allowing all this to function.

———————

In short, Satoshi's white paper showed how a digital currency could serve as an alternative to the paper currencies issued by the world's central banks.

Now you know why Satoshi created bitcoin. But how does it work?

Chapter 4
How Blockchain Works

We'll start with data. Suppose you have a document, anything from a short text to a doctoral dissertation. Maybe you have a simple banking record showing that you owe your brother $10.

Whatever the data is, we're going to convert it to a *hash*. A hash is a string of computer code that represents the data. These strings can be long, and if just one character in the original document is changed, it produces a completely new and different hash value, linked to the prior one. That, for instance, is how a property's deed is linked to the seller, then linked to the buyer.

The links on a blockchain are secure and unbreakable, and they are widely distributed among all those computer nodes worldwide. Together, the links form a single record, something the crypto community calls the *single source of truth*.

Importantly, any sort of record—not merely financial transactions—can be placed onto a blockchain.

By the way, I could tell you that a collection of blocks linked together in a chain are not necessarily linked linearly. The Hedera Hashgraph, for example, is a newer, more complex (and far superior, some say) blockchain than Bitcoin. So what? The key takeaway for you is that linking the blocks together—however that's done on a blockchain—is what guarantees the blocks' integrity.

Speaking of steering wheels, gas pedals, and brakes, there's one other essential part of your car: the key. Without it, you can't gain entry to the car or start the engine. Blockchains have keys, too; each is called a digital signature.

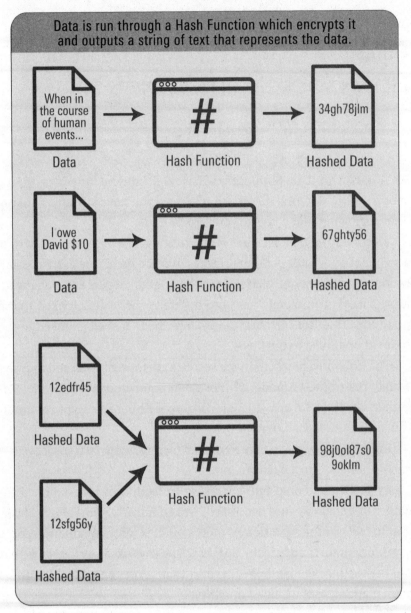

FIGURE 4.1

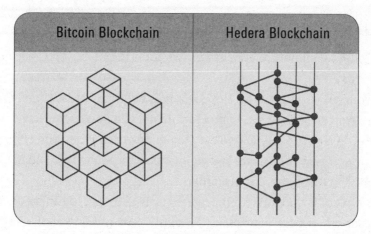

FIGURE 4.2

By this time in our journey, blockchain technologists reading this book are probably bald—because they've pulled their hair out in frustration over my extreme simplification in describing how DLT works. But, ahem, pardon me, Techie, this is a book for consumers and investors; it's not a College 301 programming course, and it's not meant to help anyone get a job as a blockchain software engineer.

So, dear reader, let's you and me stick together, while Techie grabs an ice-cold IPA (paying in bitcoin, of course) and chills. Everything you're reading here is accurate, albeit simplified. You're getting the essentials, so you're fluent enough in this new ecosystem to be able to decide if you want to participate—and if you choose to do so, how best to go about it.

In other words, I'm teaching you how to drive a car—and that means showing you the accelerator and brake pedals and the steering wheel; we are not exploring the principles of the internal combustion engine.

Public and Private Keys

Each digital signature consists of two identifiers—a *public key* and a *private key*.

Your private key is the Hope Diamond of passwords. Hugely valuable. Irreplaceable. It's assigned to you (no, you don't get to select your own) and is very long, so don't try to memorize it. When you engage in a transaction, your private key generates your public key, and it's your public key that's shared with others.

Think of it this way: Your private key is like your log-in credentials that let you access your email account. Your public key is like your email address, which you share with others. You share your private key with no one, ever.

It is essential that you keep your private key private. It's the only way you can retrieve your digital assets from a distributed ledger. If you lose your private key, you lose access to your digital assets forever. And if someone learns your private key, they can steal your digital assets.

Sound scary? Afraid your private key might get lost or stolen? I've got a solution for you—in chapter 16.*

Public vs. Private Blockchains

We've been talking so far about public blockchains. They're *permissionless systems*—because you don't need anyone's permission to join or participate, and no one can be excluded or censored.

But some blockchains are private. Each is operated by a company and thus known as a *permissioned system*, because the company operating it verifies your identity before letting you use it. In 2019, JPMorgan Chase launched the JPM Coin, becoming the first global bank to launch its own blockchain. The JPM coin lets the bank's customers make instantaneous payments, 24-7, across borders.

But to get access to JPMorgan's system, you must complete the

---

* Stay tuned!

bank's KYC/AML procedures. These Know Your Customer and Anti–Money Laundering laws are designed to help the government fight terrorism, drug dealing, and tax evasion. Banks and brokerage firms are required to know whom they're doing business with—and to alert regulators and law enforcement if they suspect something's amiss.

JPMorgan would be shut down by banking authorities if it facilitated transactions with people it didn't know. But the Bitcoin network lets you maintain your privacy. Some people even call this Bitcoin's best feature. Although people have your public key, they don't know who you are.*

---

* Now you know why ransomware attackers often demand bitcoin in payment.

PART TWO

Understanding Bitcoin and Other Digital Assets

Chapter 5
How Bitcoin Works

Satoshi launched the Bitcoin blockchain on January 3, 2009. The first block written to the ledger is called the Genesis Block* or Block 0 (and, yes, it's still there for you to see).

The Genesis Block quotes a London newspaper's headline: "Chancellor on Brink of Second Bailout for Banks."

What's noteworthy about the Genesis Block is that it's not financial. It's just text, which is ironic for a system known for being digital money. While that text is widely regarded as a criticism of the world's central banks (the reason Bitcoin was being invented), the fact that the first block wasn't money shows the true value of blockchain technology: it can serve as a repository of *data*.

But Satoshi's paper didn't emphasize data or blockchain; it emphasized money. Digital money. Thus, everyone reading the paper focused on money and bitcoin. It would be six years before serious attention would be paid to blockchain, the underlying technology that allowed bitcoin to exist.

---

* A great example of the crypto community's effort at creativity with its new lexicon. The reference, of course, is to the first book in the Bible, Genesis, and to the common use of the term *genesis* to mean the origin or beginning of something.

Where Is Bitcoin Stored?

You know that when you deposit money into your bank account, your bank maintains a record of your deposit on its ledger system. That's a closed, or *centralized*, ledger—it's available only to your bank and you. The bank spends lots of money on massive data centers to store all its data.

But who operates the blockchain Satoshi built? Satoshi isn't a company and has no customers. So, how does it work?

Recall that Bitcoin is distributed ledger technology. For now, focus on *distributed*. The Bitcoin ledger is not centralized like Bank of America's. Instead, it is *decentralized*—distributed across millions of computers around the world. As a result, no company, government, or individual (including Satoshi) controls it.

Instead, the Bitcoin computer network operates worldwide on the internet. Every computer on the Bitcoin network is called a *node*. The nodes hold the data.

How Do We Know That Data on the Nodes Are Authentic?

Simply stated, you post a block of data onto the Bitcoin network. Someone on the network uses their computer to verify the data; the process takes about 10 minutes. Once verified, the block of data is added as a new block on the blockchain. Once there, it is permanent and always available for all to see.

Why Would Anyone Bother to Authenticate My Data?

When I post data onto the network, I need someone to verify it for me. To entice you to do that, Satoshi created an incentive: when you add my data to the blockchain, you get paid. It's called a *block reward*. Getting the reward proves that you've done the work to verify my data.

The block reward doesn't give you dollars. Instead, you get *bitcoins*.

When Satoshi launched the Bitcoin network in 2009, data validators received 50 bitcoins for every block they verified. Fifty sounds like a lot, but back then, bitcoins were inexpensive to mine, had no apparent price, and could not be converted into anything practical. So those 50 bitcoins weren't anything you'd have considered valuable.

But computer programmers enjoy tinkering with new ideas. So instead of playing a video game, they said, "What the heck, let's play with this new Bitcoin network." At first, it was easy to collect block rewards. After all, there weren't many people trying to earn them.

Today, millions of people worldwide vie for block rewards; the competition is fierce.

Mining

Solving the required complex math equations to decipher a block is called *mining*.

How can you improve the odds that you'll win the block reward? It's like an auto race: the best driver with the fastest car is most likely to win. So, even though you can mine bitcoin with an ordinary desktop computer, you should consider getting a really fast computer.

Bitcoin mining computers cost about $12,000. In fact, buy thousands of them and link them together to further increase your computational capabilities. *Computer farms* operate all over the world, each vying to be the first to solve each block's unique cryptographic puzzle—and thus win the block reward.

I mentioned that the block reward back in 2009 was 50 bitcoins. No longer. That's because, about every four years, a *halvening** occurs: the block reward is cut in half. Halvings occurred in 2012, 2016, and 2020—

---

* Or *halving*. Bitcoiners use both terms. I'll let linguists settle the argument.

Mining Farm

Riot Blockchain's bitcoin mining farm in Rockdale, Texas.

Photos courtesy of Riot Blockchain

reducing the block rewards from 50 to 25, then to 12.5 and currently to 6.25 bitcoins. On the next halving—in January 2024—the block reward will become 3.125 bitcoins. The reward will be halved again in 2028 and again and again until the last of the bitcoins are mined in 2140.

Due to this, many are bullish on the price of bitcoin. If the block reward is cut in half, the price must double for miners to maintain their level of compensation. Bitcoin's price *has* always risen after each halving. Will that pattern persist? No one knows (past performance is no guarantee of future results), so decide for yourself.

2009: Bitcoin Miners initially received Block Rewards of 50 bitcoin	Block Reward cut to:
2012: First Halving	25.000 bitcoins
2016: 2nd Halving	12.500 bitcoins
2020: 3rd Halving	6.250 bitcoins
2024: Next Halving	3.125 bitcoins

FIGURE 5.1

Proof of Work vs. Proof of Stake

Mining is referred to as PoW, or *Proof of Work*. It's all part of the "authentication" nomenclature—by solving the complex computations, the Bitcoin blockchain cryptographically authenticates each transaction. "Trust" is not required.

But PoW isn't the only way to authenticate a blockchain's data. You can also do it via PoS, or *Proof of Stake*.

Staking evolved because of a criticism about PoW: it operates on sheer brute strength—i.e., your computing power. The more computers you have and the faster your machines, the more likely you'll win the block reward. But all that computer gear guzzles electricity (more on that later in this chapter). PoS avoids that problem (and the criticism that goes with it).

The PoS protocol is like a raffle. If there are 5,000 raffle tickets and you buy only one, your odds of winning are 1 in 5,000. But if you buy a thousand tickets, your odds of winning are one in five. So, the more coins you have in a PoS blockchain—the more you have at *stake*, get it?—the more likely you'll win the block reward. The PoS protocol therefore encourages people to buy coins; theoretically, the price rises as more and more coins are bought.

PoW and PoS are the two most common processes (called *consensus* *mechanisms*) for verifying data on a blockchain. But they aren't the only ones. Others exist, too (such as Proof of Space and Time), and more get invented regularly. But none of the other methods are yet common and thus are not worthy of conversation here.*

How Many Bitcoins Will Be Created?

Unlike dollars, which the Federal Reserve prints in never-ending quantity, only 21 million bitcoins will be produced—from the first in 2009 to the last in 2140. Of these, about 18.5 million have been created so far, and about 4 million are presumed lost.

LOST?!

Yeah. Stuff happens. Remember, bitcoin had no agreed-upon price back in 2009 and 2010. Only a small group of computer techies were playing with the network, getting worthless "rewards" for their time. Many of those programmers lost interest and quit, deleting their files, and their bitcoins with them. Others got new computers (and threw away their old ones). Still others suffered hard-drive crashes or simply forgot their private keys.

Easy come, easy go. With no price ascribed to bitcoin, no one back then really "lost" anything of value.

Miners aren't the only ones competing on the blockchain. Users are, too. If you want your transaction verified ahead of others, you'll pay a transaction fee so miners will serve you first. (This is sometimes called a gas fee—as in, the more gas you apply, the faster you go. Meaning, the more you pay, the quicker your transaction is verified.)

As block rewards continually get halved, transaction fees will become increasingly important to miners. It assures that validations will be paid even when there's no more bitcoin to earn as a reward.

---

* You're welcome.

One individual, who now works on Wall Street, told me that in early 2010, shortly after he graduated from MIT, a former roommate invited him over, saying, "You've got to see what we're doing." On arrival, finding his former roommate and three others mining bitcoin, he asked, "What's that?"

Over the next weekend, the five of them mined day and night, accumulating 250 bitcoins. By Sunday night, the guy was exhausted. "We just spent two days and nights wasting our time, collecting this worthless nothing!" he proclaimed. "We're all just wasting our time!"

They all quit. They shut down their computers and destroyed their files—and their bitcoins along with it. "If we'd continued," the guy told me with a wry smile, "today, we'd all be billionaires."

There are hundreds of stories like this one, of people who gave up before they realized what they were giving up. Others, though, know full well what they've thrown away—such as England's James Howells, 35, who told the world in 2021 that, eight years earlier, he accidentally put into the trash a hard drive containing 7,500 bitcoins. He asked the town council for permission to search its garbage dump, even offering the town 25% of the bitcoin if he finds them. At this writing, the council has refused, citing environmental concerns.

Then there's Stefan Thomas, a San Francisco computer programmer, who stored bitcoin worth $300 million on a portable hard disk—and then forgot the password. (Remember, this is a decentralized ledger system; there's no company offering you a FORGOT PASSWORD button to bail you out.)

Finally, there's the sad case of billionaire Mircea Popescu, 41, widely reported to be one of the world's largest owners of bitcoin. In 2021, he drowned off the coast of Costa Rica. News reports said no one in his family or business circle knew his private key. If true, the billion dollars he reportedly owned in bitcoin is lost forever.*

As shocking as these tales are, they're nothing new. The Treasury Department says $3.1 trillion of US dollars have been lost or destroyed—including $3 billion worth of pennies produced since 2014.

Types of Wallets

You know what a wallet is. You've got one in your pocket or purse!†

Apple

Amazon

PayPal

Venmo

You keep your money in your wallet. Likewise, you store your digital assets in a digital wallet. Duh.

Okay, fine, but where do you get a digital wallet? They're provided to you by the apps you use. When you establish a PayPal or Venmo account, for example, they create a wallet for you that holds the money you place on their app. Google, Walmart, Apple, Android, Samsung, and many others all provide digital wallets for their users.

If you open an account with a digital assets exchange, it will put the money you deposit into a digital wallet, too. (A digital assets exchange is like a stock exchange. More on this in chapter 16.)

A digital wallet is known as a *hot wallet* because it's connected to the internet. That's important because if you don't have an internet

---

* This isn't a book that talks about estate planning, so go read one that does: *The Truth About Money.*

† See? You really do know more about this subject than you realized.

connection, you can't access the app or instruct it to move money into or out of your wallet.

That's also the problem with hot wallets, though: they are connected to the internet. That makes them risky because a hacker could gain access to your wallet and steal its contents. To solve that problem, you can create or obtain a *cold wallet*. These are not connected to the internet and therefore are safe from online hackers.

Lots of vendors sell cold wallets for about $100, and they're easy to use. They look like (and actually are) flash drives, the kind you use to store data you created on your desktop or laptop computer. Cold wallets are meant to hold your digital coins and tokens, so they come with encryption (private passwords that only you know). If someone steals your cold wallet, they won't be able to access the contents.

Of course, you could use any flash drive; there simply won't be any encryption. Or you could simply write your private key on a sheet of paper—then store that paper somewhere safe and secure.

Cold wallets are safe from online hackers, but not plain ol' thieves who break into houses. And there's the risk of losing it, forgetting where

"You know, you can do this just as easily online."

you stored it, or forgetting its password. Remember the guy who stored his bitcoin on an encrypted drive and then forgot the code?

The final problem with cold wallets is that the money stored there isn't spendable. When you're ready to sell your digital assets or use them to buy goods or services, you must upload the coins to your app's hot wallet. Transferring coins from hot wallets to cold wallets and back again can be tedious and time-consuming. It does, however, reduce hacker risk because your coins are in the hot wallet only long enough for you to execute transactions.

To mitigate the hassle factor, some apps offer *warm wallets*. Your coins are maintained in a hot wallet, but you set instructions limiting where the coins can be sent. This is effective only if you send money to the same wallets (other people or vendors) all the time.

There are two solutions to all this. The first is to open an account with a digital assets exchange. They'll provide you with both hot and cold wallets; you simply tell them how many of your coins you want to place in each one. (You can easily move coins between them anytime.)

The other solution is to put your money into a fund instead of coins directly. It's like buying a stock fund instead of buying individual stocks. Many funds invest in digital assets; some are available to anyone with a traditional brokerage account, while others are available only to accredited investors (read: rich people. More on them in chapter 16).

Some funds invest in a single digital asset, while others buy a basket of coins, providing more diversification. All funds charge fees, which you should compare to the trading costs you'll incur at exchanges. We'll talk more about all this in chapter 16.

The First Known Commercial Use of Bitcoin

Let's return to those early bitcoin miners. They were receiving 50 bitcoins with each block reward, and while it was cheap and easy to win and accumulate them, there was no way to determine what they were worth.

Cold Wallet Hardware Devices

BC Vault
bc-vault.com

BC Vault is a cold-storage cryptocurrency wallet that stores the users' private keys on a secure hardware device. Every BC Vault ships pre-loaded with a private key, encrypted the same way as every other wallet on the device. This private key corresponds to a public address that owns 1.0 BTC.

BitBox
shiftcrypto.ch

BitBox is Swiss-made hardware and software for easy storage of your digital assets.

BitLox
bitlox.com

BitLox has the ability to use the security of the ultimate hardware wallet coupled with the absolute privacy of a "Darknet"-based access tool. BitLox can be used with TOR-based access.

Coldcard
coldcard.com

Coldcard is an ultra-secure, open-source, and hardware wallet that is easy to back up via an encrypted microSD card. Your private key is stored in a dedicated security chip. MicroPython software design allows you to make changes.

CoolWallet
coolwallet.io

CoolWallet is a credit card-sized Bluetooth hardware wallet that supports various tokens, including bitcoin, Ethereum, Litecoin, XRP, ERC20 and many more.

D'CENT Biometric
dcentwallet.com

D'CENT Biometric protects customer digital assets through D'CENT Hardware Wallet, a combination of software and hardware security solutions.

ELLIPAL
ellipal.com

ELLIPAL Titan is a complete network-isolated offline cold storage. The ELLIPAL cold wallet gives full protection against remote and online attacks.

For an up-to-date list, complete with hyperlinks, visit the
DACFP Yellow Pages
at dacfp.com

Cold Wallet Hardware Devices

KeepKey
shapeshift.com

KeepKey is a cold-storage wallet that has no operating system. PIN and passphrase protection guard against unauthorized use. You get customizable transaction speeds and limitless wallet addresses on one device. KeepKey is owned by ShapeShift, a digital assets platform that enables customers to buy, sell, trade, track, send, receive, and interact with their digital assets.

Keystone
keyst.one

Keystone offers staking a high-end cold storage wallet for advanced users (Cobo Vault), and custodial services for institutional investors, with support for more than 30 coins and 700 tokens.

Ledger Nano X
ledger.com

Ledger Nano X can be optionally and temporarily connected via cable to a Mac or Windows device so you can buy, sell, exchange, stake, lend, and otherwise manage 1,500+ tokens. The optional Live Ledger mobile app manages the wallet via Bluetooth; wireless connectivity is otherwise blocked.

NGRAVE
ngrave.io

NGRAVE ZERO is 100% air-gapped and non-WiFi/Bluetooth/NFC, with no USB internet connectivity to prevent online attacks. Instead, it uses a one-way QR code to relay information. The stainless steel case is fire-resistant.

Opendime
opendime.com

Opendime is a small USB stick that allows you to spend bitcoin. It connects to any USB so you can check your balance.

For an up-to-date list, complete with hyperlinks, visit the
DACFP Yellow Pages
at dacfp.com

Cold Wallet Hardware Devices

Prokey prokey.io	Prokey hardware wallet is an offline, cold-storage, and secure device that keeps your private key offline and protected, while enabling you to receive, store, and sign transactions to send digital assets like bitcoin, Ethereum, Litecoin, Tether, and more.
Secalot secalot.com	Secalot is a hardware cryptocurrency wallet. It's a small USB dongle that features OpenPGP smart card, U2F authenticator and a one-time password generator.
SecuX secuxtech.com	SecuX technology provides military-grade Infineon SLE Solid Flash CC EAL 5+ Secure Element. Its cross-platform operation includes SecuX web and mobile apps for 1,000+ digital assets for up to 500 accounts.
Trezor trezor.io	Trezor is the world's first bitcoin hardware wallet. The Trezor One and Trezor Model T cold wallets each support more than 1,000 coins, have an easy-to-use LED interface that's compatible with Windows, Mac, and Linux, and have several security features, including PIN entry, passphrase entry, and device recovery.

For an up-to-date list, complete with hyperlinks, visit the
DACFP Yellow Pages
at dacfp.com

To find out, software developer Laszlo Hanyecz offered to buy two Papa John's pizzas with bitcoin. He found a willing participant on May 22, 2010. On that date—today affectionately known as *Bitcoin Pizza Day*—Laszlo completed the world's first commercial transaction using bitcoin.

The two pies cost $14. The number of bitcoins required to complete the transaction?

Ten thousand.

At $50,000 each, those 10,000 bitcoins would be worth $500,000,000. Five hundred million dollars.

Those were very expensive pizzas.

Other Ways to Receive Coins

Mining and staking aren't the only way you can obtain coins. There are other ways, too.

Forks

I'm not referring to the tool you use to eat spaghetti. Rather, it's what happens when developers working on a blockchain disagree about how the tech should operate. And, no, I don't mean that one of them exclaims, "Fork you!"

When creating Bitcoin, Satoshi open-sourced the software code so other developers could improve it. Changes can't occur without consensus, but sometimes, consensus can't be reached. For example, some developers began to lament Bitcoin's slow speed (it takes 10 minutes to verify each block of data). If we change the code, they said, we can make Bitcoin faster. But making it faster, others noted, weakens its security.

Unable to attain consensus, the developers agreed in August 2017 to split Bitcoin into two parts, called a *fork*. It's similar to what happens when a major corporation does a spin-off, turning a division into a separate, stand-alone company.*

When corporate spin-offs and crypto forks occur, existing owners keep what they have. They also get some of the new entity. In the case of the 2017 fork, all owners of BTC received some BCH, the new *Bitcoin Cash* coin. Bitcoin Cash was then altered to provide greater speed. (Today, BCH is nearly 17 times faster than BTC.)

---

* Note: the tax treatment of forks is *not* similar to that of spin-offs. More on that in chapter 20.

Converting BTC into both BTC and BCH is called a *hard fork* because there are now two blockchains instead of one. In a *soft fork*, both coins—old and new—use the original blockchain.

Bitcoin Cash

Bitcoin SV

In case you're wondering, no, the BCH hard fork did not resolve the developers' dispute. Further disagreements led to another hard fork—this time from BCH to BSV (for Bitcoin Satoshi Vision). BSV promises to adhere strictly to Satoshi's white paper. It's 128 times faster than BTC, and proponents say it offers a better user experience, lower costs, and greater security. (At this writing, BTC is the largest digital asset; BCH is 19th largest and BSV is ranked 51st—suggesting that people haven't fully bought into the improvements purportedly created by the forks.)

There have been hundreds of forks involving many coins over the last decade, so the above are just a couple of examples. By the way—and this is a big by-the-way—there's a tax implication to forks, and we'll cover that in chapter 20.

Airdrops

Another way coins get created is via an *airdrop*. The term is based on the phrase *helicopter money*, which came into use in 2008 when the federal government pumped (dropped from the sky, so to speak) $700 billion into the economy to combat the credit crisis.

Here's what happens. You create a new, better-than-bitcoin protocol. To get people to use it, you create coins and send them to people who have certain other coins—perhaps coins that are similar (but in your opinion, inferior) to your coin. It's like a new band trying to get noticed—it books a gig at the local pub and mails free tickets to every house in the neighborhood.

Airdrops are indeed often just marketing gimmicks. To receive the coins, you sometimes must do something, such as follow a certain Twitter account. And, yes, there are tax implications when receiving airdrops (chapter 19).

Concerns About Bitcoin's Involvement with Illicit Activity

Criminals, terrorists, and rogue nations love executing financial transactions without revealing their identity. A major feature of bitcoin is anonymity. So, bad guys are naturally attracted to it.

bitcoin

Imagine being able to buy and sell drugs, guns, and stolen credit cards without having to move money through the banking system! That's what the illegal internet site Silk Road facilitated in 2011.

The FBI shut down Silk Road in 2013. In 2021, after hackers demanded $4.4 million in bitcoin from Colonial Pipeline, the FBI got most of Colonial's money back within two weeks. And when hackers stole $611 million in digital assets from the Poly Network, the thieves returned almost all the money they took within days. How were these crimes solved and money recovered so quickly? Because digital assets leave digital footprints. (All it took was for Poly Network's CEO to issue a tweet saying he knew the hacker's computer and email addresses. Poof! The money was promptly returned.)

I'm not suggesting that there's no risk to owning digital assets. Many custodial platforms have been hacked, including Mt. Gox, Bitfloor, NiceHash, BitFunder, and Bitstamp. From 2014 through 2020, the US Securities and Exchange Commission took 87 enforcement actions involving blockchain and digital assets, including fraudulent securities offerings, fraud related to cryptocurrency trading, failure to properly disclose compensation, and Ponzi schemes involving bitcoin. That's an average of 15 cases per year.

But that's out of more than 700 SEC enforcement actions annually, meaning crypto comprises only 2% of the SEC's cases. Likewise, a 2021 report by Chainalysis found that criminal activity represented only 0.15% of all cryptocurrency transaction volume. This directly contradicts Treasury Secretary Janet Yellen's assertion in 2021 that digital assets "are used mainly for illicit financing." Indeed, Jake Chervinsky, general counsel of Compound Labs, told *Forbes*, "Her statement is demonstrably false."

Let's remember that there have been frauds in every asset class: stocks, bonds, oil, gold, real estate, art, and more. Nobody suggests shutting down those markets. Every innovation, sadly, is attended by evildoers—it's an unavoidable accoutrement.

And it's always been that way. The very first publicly traded security in the United States was Alexander Hamilton's issue of federal bonds to repay the debts that the colonies had incurred during the Revolutionary War. Hamilton's plan leaked, and the bonds were quickly mired in the first-ever investment fraud: insider trading. (Insiders bought the bonds from veterans for pennies on the dollar, knowing Hamilton would soon redeem them at par.)

Ever since we've had investments, we've had investment fraud. Just as the invention of the automobile led to auto thefts.

Data from the United Nations proves the silliness of criticizing bitcoin because of illegal activity. The UN estimates that routine money laundering and other illicit activity is 2% to 5% of global GDP. So rather than banning bitcoin because a tiny bit is used nefariously, shouldn't we eliminate all fiat currencies first, since they're used improperly to a far higher degree?

Concerns About Bitcoin Mining's Impact on the Environment

Maybe you want to buy bitcoin, but you've heard that it's "bad for the planet." You can go ahead and buy bitcoin—and feel good about it—because the "bad for the planet" claim is simply wrong.

The assertion is nothing but a distraction, typically touted by people who don't believe bitcoin is a good investment idea. (We'll cover *that* question in part 3.)

Since detractors haven't been able to stop people from buying bitcoin or stopping bitcoin's price from rising, they've latched on to this other tack: guilt. "Bitcoin is bad for the planet!" So what? Smoking, alcohol, and gambling are all bad for you, too, but we haven't outlawed them. Instead, we merely regulate them. Bitcoin can be handled the same way.

Or maybe bitcoin needs no such handling. Maybe it's not bad for us like smoking, alcohol, and gambling. Let's explore this, starting with the complaint that bitcoin mining consumes as much energy every year as Argentina.

Argentina?

I checked. That assertion is apparently correct. But it's also correct that Argentina doesn't use much energy: it ranks dead last among the world's 30 largest industrialized countries.

And before you get all worked up about Bitcoin's energy usage, you might want to get upset about cars. The US Energy Information Administration reports that transportation is the world's biggest energy hog, consuming 25% of the world's energy. But the Bitcoin network's energy consumption is less than 0.5%, according to the Cambridge Centre for Alternative Finance. So, if you're willing to drive a car, ride a bus, or sit on an airplane, you shouldn't have any problem buying bitcoin.

Cars didn't always consume so much energy. They used little in 1920, when the auto industry was still new. As the automobile's popularity rose, so did its energy usage.

It's the same with Bitcoin. Ten years ago, Bitcoin used little power. That it's using a lot of energy today reflects growing demand. It's a sign of success. Some argue that cars at least have commercial uses, but as we've seen, Bitcoin has valuable commercial uses, too.

So instead of beating up Bitcoin, let's beat up something that's a bigger energy hog—an energy hog that is all the worse because it has no useful purpose at all. I'm talking about all those always-on devices in your house: your TV, coffeepot, Alexa, and that stupid clock on your oven.* Those devices consume 344 million kilowatt-hours of electric-

---

* Why do ovens need clocks, anyway?

"We made three billion dollars mining Bitcoin, minus our electricity bill—that comes to $1.61."

ity in the United States annually and spew 250 million tons of carbon dioxide into the air—4% of all US greenhouse gas emissions, according to the Natural Resources Defense Council. In the United States alone, those devices consume as much energy as all bitcoin miners in the entire world! So, before you tell bitcoin miners to shut down, you might want to tell people to unplug their TVs every night.

And if you really want to eliminate energy waste, tell everyone to stop playing video games. A 2020 study found that video gamers consume 46% more energy than the world's bitcoin miners.

Emissions, Not Energy

Those who complain about Bitcoin's energy consumption are forgetting one important point: It doesn't matter how much energy you use. What matters is how much carbon dioxide you kick into the atmosphere.

Nearly 80% of the energy used by the transportation industry is provided by petroleum, natural gas, and coal. Their use emits massive amounts of carbon dioxide, which is bad for the planet. But 73% of Bitcoin's energy consumption is carbon neutral. The Cambridge Bitcoin Energy Consumption Index shows that miners mostly use hydropower, solar, wind, or geothermal energy. Only 38% rely on coal. As a result, the journal *Joule* reported in 2021, Bitcoin's annual global emissions are about equal to those of the city of London, rather than the entire country of Argentina.

Imagine Ford saying that although it takes a lot of energy to make cars, drivers use no energy to operate them. If only that were so. But it is so with Bitcoin: almost all of Bitcoin's energy usage is consumed by mining. Once coins are mined, the energy required to buy or sell them is minimal.

All that said, Bitcoin's energy usage isn't zero. We do need to get there, and everyone in the crypto community knows it. That's why, as noted by the *Harvard Business Review*, many have signed the Crypto Climate Accord (comparable to the Paris Climate Accords), which advocates for reducing Bitcoin's carbon footprint.

Miners might do more to solve the world's energy crisis than any other industry. Why? Because they have the greatest motivation to do so. For most industries, materials and payroll are their biggest expenses. But the #1 cost for miners is the price of energy. That gives them a big incentive to lower their energy costs—and that, in turn, motivates them to seek cheaper, alternative energy sources. Many mining companies, for example, have moved their facilities to locations where they can take advantage of renewable energy sources, such as wind farms and hydropower. No doubt other industries will use whatever solutions the Bitcoin network comes up with.

I don't share the view that bitcoin should be banned because it's bad for the environment. But if you feel that way, then simply don't buy bitcoin. Buy Proof of Stake coins, instead. Problem solved.

Biggest Proof of Stake Coins by Market Cap	
Coin	**Issuer**
ADA	Cardano
ALGO	Algorand
ARDR	Ardor
ARK	Ark
DCR	Decred
EOS	EOS
HBAR	Hedera Hashgraph
HIVE	Hive Token
ICX	ICON
LSK	Lisk
ONT	Ontology
QTUM	Qtum
RUNE	THORChain
STEEM	SteemROSE
TOMO	TomoChain
TRX	Tron
TOMO	Tezos

ADA

Algo

FIGURE 5.2

Chapter 6
Who Uses Bitcoin?

We've come a long way since Laszlo paid 10,000 bitcoins for a couple of pizzas. Bitcoin's annual transaction volume now exceeds $1.5 trillion—more than twice as much as PayPal and six times more than Discover. No wonder that, at this writing, bitcoin's market cap is bigger than JPMorgan, MasterCard, UnitedHealth, Home Depot, and The Walt Disney Company. Yet, Bitcoin has no offices, no employees, and no shareholders. It's truly revolutionary.

Companies began offering credit cards linked to bitcoin in 2021; instead of getting cash back or airline points when you use the card, you get bitcoin—and Visa says its customers have already spent more than $1 billion on bitcoin-rewards cards. MasterCard, too, offers "safe and secure experiences for customers and businesses in today's digital economy," while PayPal lets its 325 million users buy bitcoin on its platform and use it to make purchases with the 24 million merchants connected to the app; the company says nearly 20% of its users have done so.

AXA, the third-largest insurance company in the world, now allows customers to pay in bitcoin due to "growing customer demand," noting that "bitcoin makes payments easy." Online travel agency Travala says it has booked 10 million trips, with 70% of its customers paying with bitcoin. United Wholesale Mortgage lets homeowners make mortgage payments in bitcoin.

Retailers aren't the only ones accepting bitcoin. Politicians are, too. The Federal Election Commission lets candidates accept political contributions in bitcoin. Wharton Business School lets students taking a class in digital assets pay their tuition in bitcoin and Ethereum.

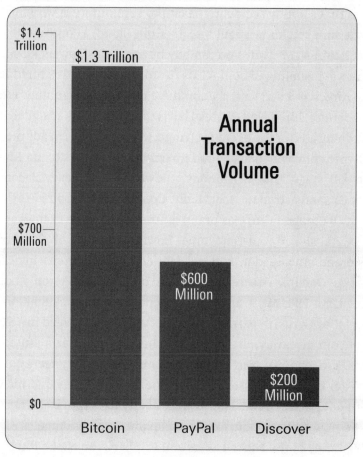

FIGURE 6.1

Thousands of charities and nonprofit organizations also accept donations in bitcoin.

Who Owns Bitcoin?

At this writing, 200 million individuals own bitcoin, including 24% of American adults, according to Crypto.com. Coinbase is the most popular free app in the Apple Store. Another 63% of adults call themselves "crypto curious." People are getting involved because they're hearing so much about it.

And that's not by accident; the crypto community is working hard to make sure you know about bitcoin. Coin Cloud, a company that installs bitcoin ATMs (yep, you can buy bitcoin at a sidewalk kiosk, and Walmart is installing bitcoin ATMs in stores nationwide), hired Spike Lee to direct and star in a TV commercial. CoinFlip, another bitcoin ATM operator, hired Neil Patrick Harris to appear in its ads. Alec Baldwin is doing ads for the eToro exchange. Matt Damon is in ads promoting Crypto.com, which also hired mixed-martial artist Ronda Rousey, basketball star Carmelo Anthony, snowboarder Lindsey Jacobellis, rapper CL, and astronaut Scott Kelly. Competitor FTX hired two-time NBA MVP Stephen Curry as brand ambassador, while exchange Voyager Digital signed four-time Super Bowl champion Rob Gronkowski as its brand ambassador. Pop star Mariah Carey is promoting crypto exchange Gemini. Green Bay Packers quarterback Aaron Rodgers, a three-time NFL MVP, along with rapper Megan Thee Stallion and singer Miley Cyrus, in partnership with Cash App, engaged in a $1 million bitcoin giveaway on Twitter and Instagram. After a fan caught the 600th touchdown pass thrown by Tampa Bay Buccaneers quarterback Tom Brady, Brady sent the fan one bitcoin. Brady and his wife, supermodel Gisele Bündchen, bought equity in crypto exchange FTX and are now ambassadors for the company. The Los Angeles Staples Center, home of the NBA's Lakers and Clippers, the NHL's Kings, and the WNBA's Sparks, is now Crypto.com Arena. (The company paid $700 million to secure the naming rights for 20 years.) The Dallas Mavericks have partnered with bitcoin exchange Voyager, while the NBA and WNBA made Coinbase its exclusive crypto sponsor in a multi-year deal. Restaurant giant Landry's (owner of Bubba Gump Shrimp, Morton's The Steakhouse, the Rainforest Cafe, and dozens of other brands) has a loyalty program that gives you $25 in bitcoin when you spend $250. Adidas is partnering with Coinbase ("probably nothing," Adidas joked in a tweet). Burger King is partnering with Robinhood Crypto, giving away bitcoin, Ether, and Dogecoin. Burger King even launched its own digital asset in Russia, called WhopperCoin. AMC Theaters is promoting that it now accepts bitcoin, Ethereum, Bitcoin Cash, and

Bitcoin ATM

© Adobe Stock printed with permission

Litecoin—and reports that 14% of its moviegoers are paying for online tickets via these digital assets.

And all this isn't just happening in the US; it's worldwide. In India, for example, 70% of the television ads appearing during the Cricket World Cup promoted crypto companies.

Schwab

All this publicity, supported by huge increases in the price of bitcoin and other digital assets, has created a seemingly unstoppable force. Coinbase, a publicly traded online exchange for digital assets, now has more account holders than Charles Schwab. And Schwab reported in 2019 that among the top ten holdings of its millennial customers was the Grayscale Bitcoin Trust (which we'll learn about in chapter 16). Indeed, Schwab said, millennials own more bitcoin than they do shares of Berkshire Hathaway, Disney, Netflix, Microsoft, or Alibaba.

Voyager Digital

Grayscale

Bank of New York

Bank of New York Mellon, the nation's oldest bank (established by Alexander Hamilton in 1792) now provides custody services for bitcoin and other digital assets. Amazon is operating a digital currency project

Digital Asset Banks

Anchorage Digital Bank
anchorage.com

Anchorage Digital Bank is the first national digital asset bank in the United States. As a federally chartered Qualified Custodian, it maintains client funds, holds securities, and enables RIAs to meet federal custody obligations. Account holders can stake and lend digital assets under Anchorage's custody governance blockchain protocols.

Avanti Bank & Trust
avantibank.com

Avanti Bank & Trust is a Wyoming bank built to connect digital assets with the legacy financial system. Avanti is a custodian of digital assets that can meet the strictest level of institutional custody standards.

Kraken
kraken.com

Kraken is the first digital asset exchange to obtain a bank charter in Wyoming as an SPDI. Kraken Bank customers can bank seamlessly between digital and fiat currencies, and move assets from their bank account into their investment and trading portfolios.

Silvergate Bank
silvergate.com

Silvergate Bank is a Federal Reserve member bank and the leading provider of innovative financial infrastructure solutions and services for the growing digital asset industry.

For an up-to-date list, complete with hyperlinks, visit the
DACFP Yellow Pages
at dacfp.com

in Mexico. JPMorgan, Goldman Sachs, Bank of America Merrill Lynch, and MassMutual all offer bitcoin to their customers. Uber accepts bitcoin as payment.

The Office of the Comptroller of the Currency has begun approving banks to accept and custody digital assets. In 2021, OCC approved the first digital asset bank, Anchorage Digital Bank.

Community banks and credit unions are serving retail investors, too. Through a partnership with NCR (the cash register company formed in 1884) and NYDIG, a digital assets investment firm, 24 million bank customers from 650 banks (40% of all financial institutions in the United States) can trade bitcoin on their phones.

And we mustn't leave out the kids. Dozens of summer crypto camps teach children as young as age five how to mine bitcoin. Parents can do it, too; all you need is Norton antivirus software. Click a button, and your computer will mine for bitcoin whenever you're not using it, allowing you to earn money simply by having your computer turned on.

Ordinary consumers aren't the only ones getting involved. Goldman Sachs says 24% of its wealthy investors and 10% of its institutional clients are trading digital assets, too—and that another 20% are interested in doing so. JPMorgan says 10% of its institutional clients are now trading digital assets.

Every major firm is busy helping its clients buy digital assets. Morgan Stanley offers a bitcoin investment fund, Citigroup has a digital assets group, Bank of America Merrill Lynch lets clients trade bitcoin futures via its digital assets research team, State Street Global Advisors has a digital asset fund services division. Fidelity serves institutional clients via Fidelity Digital Assets, and Franklin Templeton has a digital assets division as well.

Fidelity

Fidelity Digital Assets

University endowments are also buying digital assets,

including those of Harvard, Yale, MIT, Stanford, Dartmouth, and the University of North Carolina. Germany's 4,000 pension funds and endowments, which manage $2.1 trillion, got government approval in 2021 to invest up to 20% of their assets in digital assets. (If they all invest the legal limit, $400 billion will flow into bitcoin and other digital assets.) US pension funds are already investing, including the Houston Firefighters' Relief and Retirement Fund, and the Fairfax County (VA) Employees' Retirement System and the Police Officers Retirement System.

Vanguard

BlackRock

ARK

Franklin Templeton

Marathon Digital

Micro-Strategy

PayPal

CNBC*

Skybridge

Billionaires, too, own digital assets, including Paul Tudor Jones, Stanley Druckenmiller, Ricardo Pliego, Bill Miller, Ray Dalio, George Soros, Mark Cuban, Tim Cook, Peter Thiel, and Bill Gurley.

Corporations are buying digital assets as well: PayPal, Square, MicroStrategy, TIME, MassMutual, and Tesla. CNBC's Jim Cramer says it's "almost irresponsible for companies not to own bitcoin" as part of their corporate treasury reserves.

Lots of fund managers invest in bitcoin, too, including those of Renaissance, Ruffer, Guggenheim, Bridgewater, BlackRock, SkyBridge. The Motley Fool does, too.

Bitcoin has become so commonplace that it's now the first question asked on your tax return. IRS Form 1040 asks, "At any time during the year, did you receive, sell, send, exchange, or otherwise acquire any financial interest in any virtual currency?" That's the IRS's way of saying it knows lots of Americans own digital assets but aren't reporting their transactions to the government—or paying the taxes due.

---

* I also appear frequently on CNBC and CNBC.com.

Chapter 7
Why Are There So Many Coins?

Satoshi invented bitcoin in 2009 to replace fiat currencies. One coin for one purpose: an electronic cash system.

Turns out, though, that bitcoin has some limitations. For example, its price fluctuates—a lot. Bitcoin's average daily price movement is 3%, or three times more than the stock market. Volatility is bad for a currency, so someone created Tether, the first *stablecoin*, a digital asset whose price is meant to equal that of the US dollar or some other fiat currency. (More on stablecoins in chapter 8.)

Someone else realized that Bitcoin takes a long time (seven seconds) to verify each transaction. Visa processes 1,700 transactions per second (that's 150 million per day). That led to Litecoin, which processes 56 transactions per second—a lot faster than Bitcoin, but still much slower than Visa.*

Another thing. Bitcoin transactions are processed immediately, which might not be what you want to happen. Ethereum's introduction of smart contracts lets you control the timing of your transmittals.

Okay, we've just identified three legitimate reasons why Bitcoin isn't enough and why Tether, Litecoin, and Ether were introduced. Add a few more solutions, innovations, and improvements, and you can justify the need for maybe a dozen or so coins.

Yet, CoinMarketCap lists 11,233 coins and 393 exchanges where you

---

* The faster you go, though, the weaker your security. US consumers lost $11 billion to credit card fraud in 2020, according to the Nilson Report, and Visa says it finds an average of 140,000 instances of malicious software on its servers every month. The Bitcoin network, by contrast, has never been hacked.

can buy them. And more coins emerge every day. Many coins are gimmicks, some are scams (more on that in chapter 13), and a bunch are sheer marketing ploys, designed to capture consumer attention and money. And lots are merely brand extensions.

The other day, I went to the Levi's website to buy a pair of jeans. The site asked me to select my preferred fit and provided these options: Taper, Straight, Slim, Athletic, Relaxed, Skinny, Bootcut, Original, Loose, So High, or Western. Then I was asked if I wanted 501 jeans, or 502, 505, 510, 511, 512, 513, 514, 517, 527, 531, 541, 550, 551, 559, or 569. And did I want black, blue, brown, dark wash (whatever that is), green, gray, or khaki? Wait, we're not done. Do I want material called Sustainability, WaterLess, Organic Cotton, Sustainably Soft with TENCEL, Lyocell, Cottonized Hemp, Recycled Polyester, Recycled Cotton, or Repreve, and do I want my jeans stretched or nonstretched, and distressed or not distressed? I also had to choose the style: Chino, Cargo, Cropped, Hi-Ball Roll, Jogger, or Western. And do I want 100% Cotton, All Seasons Tech, Custom (oh no!), Eco Ease, Hemp, Flex, or Selvedge? Finally, do I want a button or zip fly?

Levi's

Heinz

I had the same problem buying a bottle of ketchup. Heinz offers tomato ketchup in a variety of sizes, sure, but also:

- No Artificial Sweeteners
- No Salt Added
- No Sugar Added
- Sweetened Only with Honey
- With a Blend of Veggies
- Hot & Spicy Blended with Tabasco Pepper Sauce
- Jalapeño Blended with Real Jalapeño
- Sriracha Blended with Sriracha

© sheilaf2002 / Adobe Stock printed with permission

If you thought Satoshi's invention of bitcoin in 2009 would forever serve as the only digital money we'd ever need (or end up with), well, keep that in mind when you spill ketchup on your jeans.

The Digital Asset Universe

The digital asset ecosystem is complex and ever growing. The World Economic Forum places all coins into one of four categories; I've seen others describe as few as two and as many as seven. Sheesh.

My goal is to help you get an idea of the types of protocols and coins that exist, partly for comprehension but also for investment consideration. So, I'm going to provide you with four categories. The first two match WEF's approach:

- *base layer protocols* (the root blockchain networks that allow for the creation, transfer, and storage of digital assets)
- *second layer protocols* (which are built on the base layer and provide additional features and capabilities)

The next two describe a variety of products and applications that let consumers, investors, and businesses interact with the base and second layers. They are:

- financial
- nonfinancial

Base Layer Protocols

Also called the *native layer*, this is where it all starts. All digital coins begin as a protocol; each is named by its creators. Satoshi created the Bitcoin protocol. Vitalik Buterin created the Ethereum protocol, and Jed McCaleb conceived the Ripple protocol, to cite a few examples.

Each protocol creates a digital asset to operate on its platform—sort of like saying, "I'm going to build a highway, and then I'm going to manufacture cars to drive on it." The highway is the blockchain, the coin or token is the vehicle for operating on it, and the protocol sets the rules that those coins must follow.

Each creator gives their blockchain a name. They also name their coin. Satoshi wasn't terribly clever, giving the name *bitcoin* to both the blockchain and the coin. Ethereum's coin is Ether, while Ripple's is XRP. And so on.

Amazon

Disney

And just as stocks have ticker symbols—AMZN for Amazon, F for Ford Motor Company, and DIS for The Walt Disney Company—digital assets get tickers, too. BTC for bitcoin, ETH for Ether, and XRP for, uh, XRP. So, you end up with three descriptors for each protocol—the blockchain, the coin, and its symbol, as in Bitcoin, bitcoin, BTC or Ethereum, Ether, ETH.

Major Base Layer Protocols

Arweave   arweave.org
The project's primary goal is to ensure that vital historical and cultural information is never lost, censored, or altered. Arweave's token (of the same name) rewards those who store data, so those who host apps on the network don't have to worry about technical maintenance or ongoing hosting costs; once their code is deployed, it will last forever.

To preserve historical information, Arweave partners with such institutions as the Internet Archive to secure records. Files can be stored for a one-time fee and content can be uploaded and shared anonymously. Arweave launched in 2018.

Avalanche   avax.network
Avalanche bills itself as the fastest smart contracts platform in the blockchain industry, and has the most validators securing its activity of any Proof of Stake protocol. It can handle more than 4,500 transactions per second.

Bitcoin   bitcoin.org
The first blockchain.

Bitcoin Cash   bitcoincash.org
Bitcoin Cash lets you send money to others for less than a penny and stores savings securely with no middlemen. BCH is also private; there is no transaction history like those of bank accounts. More than 11 million BCH transactions occur monthly and more than 300 million since its inception in 2017. Dozens of exchanges let you buy, sell, and hold BCH.

cUSD   celo.org
cUSD is a stablecoin that tracks the value of the US dollar. Celo's goal is to serve the unbanked. cUSD launched in 2020 and already has 27,000 wallet addresses and 15 million cUSD in circulation. More than a million transactions have been processed. The platform is supported by the Alliance for Prosperity, a group of 100+ organizations devoted to improving the lives of the world's underserved and unbanked people.

For an up-to-date list, complete with hyperlinks, visit the
DACFP Yellow Pages
at dacfp.com

Major Base Layer Protocols

EOS eos.io

Bitcoin's price rises as more people use it. The EOS Public Blockchain has a different model: it locks up EOS tokens to reserve CPU bandwidth (the time to process a transaction), bandwidth (the size of a transaction in bytes), and RAM (the storage of data in bytes). Essentially, EOS tokens own digital real estate; when you lock your tokens, you reserve a portion of the total available resources. You can pay a small fee to power your account long enough to execute your transactions or deposit idle tokens to receive a percentage of the fees generated by the entire EOS blockchain. Depending on your usage level, you might collect more fees than you pay to power your account.

Ether ethereum.org

Ethereum pioneered "smart contracts." It is a programmable blockchain, meaning you can dictate the terms of transfers of the ether coin. Ethereum's network of thousands of computers tracks the status of each contract; anyone can audit them on Ethereum's public ledger, which is maintained by the Ethereum Foundation, a not-for-profit organization. To grasp the scale, consider this: Microsoft employs 40,000 software developers. By contrast, there are more than 200,000 developers programming on the Ethereum blockchain.

Filecoin filecoin.io

Filecoin's mission is to decentralize cloud storage by letting users choose from thousands of geographically distributed storage providers. You obtain storage space by paying in Filecoins, giving those with extra storage space an incentive to share it. Filecoin launched in October 2020; within three months, thousands of miners had committed 1.3 exabytes of storage (enough to hold 650x all the data stored in US research labs). More than 100 applications have been built on Filecoin to date.

Litecoin litecoin.com

Bitcoin's use as a money transfer platform is limited by its ability to process transactions. Litecoin was invented to solve that problem. It confirms blocks eight times faster than bitcoin.

For an up-to-date list, complete with hyperlinks, visit the
DACFP Yellow Pages
at dacfp.com

Major Base Layer Protocols

MobileCoin   mobilecoin.com
MobileCoin is designed for use as digital cash on your phone. Most transactions complete in less than ten seconds. Mobile messaging apps like WhatsApp, Facebook Messenger, and Signal can integrate with a MobileCoin wallet. Each transaction is cryptographically protected. MobileCoin is not available to US users because payments are private.

Neo   neo.org
Neo is "the most feature-complete blockchain platform" for building decentralized applications, supporting decentralized storage, oracles, and domain name services. It was the first public smart contract platform founded in China, by Da Hongfei and Erik Zhang in 2014, making it a pioneer in the early blockchain industry. Today, Neo has developers worldwide contributing to core development, infrastructure, and tooling, including alumni from Microsoft, Facebook, Amazon, Samsung, Dell, Seagate, and others.

Stellar   stellar.org
The Bitcoin network was created solely to trade bitcoin. By contrast, Stellar digitizes all forms of money, allowing the global financial system to operate on a single network. It's also faster and cheaper than other blockchains (its ledger is verified and updated every five seconds). It launched in 2015 and has processed 450 million+ operations by 4 million+ accounts.

Stellar's digital currency is the lumen, required only to initialize accounts. After that, transactions can be in any currency. For example, digitized dollars can be used by people worldwide without the need for a US bank account. Ditto for all fiat currencies. In fact, you could use Stellar to issue a token for any asset—from corn bushels to an hour of your time as a consultant.

Stellar tokens can be seen, held, and traded by any user, but are highly configurable. And unlike other payment systems, Stellar lets a user send one currency and have the recipient receive another—essentially exchanging money in a single transaction. Cowrie, Settle, Tempo, Finclusive, and many other coins operate on Stellar.

For an up-to-date list, complete with hyperlinks, visit the
DACFP Yellow Pages
at dacfp.com

Major Base Layer Protocols

Tether   tether.to
Tether is a stablecoin, tied to the US dollar, euro, and the offshore Chinese yuan. Tether is the most widely integrated digital-to-fiat currency in use today.

Tez   tezos.com
Tezos launched in 2011 and pioneered the Proof of Stake protocol. The platform lets users create smart contracts and build decentralized applications that cannot be censored or banned by third parties. Stakeholders can also participate in network upgrades by evaluating, proposing, or approving amendments without hard forks. Tezos can represent stocks, gold, real estate—even votes in presidential elections.

XRP   ripple.com
The RippleNet network can connect hundreds of financial institutions worldwide via a single interface, allowing money to move faster, cheaper, and more reliably. By using XRP, financial institutions don't need to pre-fund accounts in destination currencies to facilitate cross-border payments. Payments settle in about three seconds; the network can handle 1,500+ transactions per second at a cost of just $0.0003 each.

RippleNet is available in 55+ countries on six continents, with payout capabilities in 70+ countries. Dozens of companies have signed contracts for its On-Demand Liquidity, including MoneyGram, Azimo, Santander, American Express, CIMB, Siam Commercial Bank, SBI, and HDFC.

Zcash   electriccoin.co
Zcash transactions can be transparent, although users can opt to shield their information partially or fully, providing transaction-level privacy. Zcash is an open-source project backed by Electric Coin Company and the Zcash Foundation.

For an up-to-date list, complete with hyperlinks, visit the
DACFP Yellow Pages
at dacfp.com

Second Layer Protocols

Developers continue to seek ways to improve blockchain networks. They want to accomplish three goals:

1. **Decentralization**, meaning the network (not an individual, corporation, or government) is responsible for the assets;

2. **Security**, meaning the network cannot be breached or its data copied, changed, deleted, stolen, or rendered inaccessible; and

3. **Scalability**, meaning that what you can do for 10 people you can do for a billion people.

The effort to achieve all three goals is called the *trilemma*, a term coined by Ethereum founder Vitalik Buterin. It's easy to build a blockchain that achieves one or two of these goals, but extraordinarily difficult to provide all three.

Bitcoin and Ethereum, for example, were designed with a focus on decentralization and security (neither is owned by anyone and neither

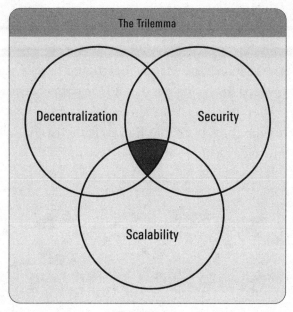

FIGURE 7.1

has ever been hacked), but they provide these features at the expense of scale. (Ethereum can process only fifteen transactions per second, and Bitcoin is even slower, at seven transactions per second. Visa, by contrast, can process 24,000 transactions per second, but is controlled by a corporation and has been hacked many times.)

The trilemma stymies base layer protocols. So, developers created a framework on top of the base layer. The base layer thus provides security and decentralization, while the secondary layer provides speed and scale.

The first and best-known example is the Lightning Network, which sits on the Bitcoin blockchain. Invented in 2015 by Joseph Poon and

Bitcoin

Bitcoin Cash

Bitcoin SV

Ether

Thaddeus Dryja, the Lightning Network completes transactions faster and cheaper because it doesn't require the full computation and settlement of Bitcoin's Proof of Work effort. It does this via *off-chain* transactions—so-called because the transactions aren't executed on a blockchain.

To understand this, think of life in a casino, where the casino is a blockchain. You walk in and convert your dollars to chips (the casino's digital coin). That's an *on-chain* (meaning, on the blockchain) transaction—you need the dealer's permission to exchange your dollars for chips, and the casino records the transaction. But once you're at the poker table, you and other players swap chips freely and often—and the casino pays no attention to these *off-chain* (meaning, between parties) transactions. Only when you convert your chips back into dollars is the casino involved, and that's the only trade recorded on the blockchain.

On-Chain Transaction

Off-Chain Transactions

FIGURE 7.2

Major Second Layer Protocols

Aave   aave.com
One of the first decentralized lending protocols, Aave lets you lend or borrow money using dozens of digital assets. More than $25 billion in assets reside on the platform.

Bancor   bancor.network
Bancor Protocol instantly converts tokens at fair and predictable prices. It decentralizes automated token swaps on Ethereum and across blockchains, using smart contracts to create automated market makers (called AMMs, liquidity pools, or bonding curves). It is thus an alternative method to the "bid and ask" or "order books" approach that plagues traditional exchanges.

Bancor Protocol continually shows exchange rates for all tokens in real time, and any token can be added to the network by anyone anytime—not just financial institutions and large investors. Since its launch in 2017, liquidity pools for hundreds of tokens on the Ethereum blockchain have been added to the Bancor network. More than $2 billion in token-to-token conversions across tens of thousands of wallets have occurred.

Cardano   cardano.org
Cardano is built on the Ouroboros protocol and uses the Haskell programming language for unparalleled security and stability.

Chainlink   chain.link
Ethereum's smart contracts require information that is sometimes off-chain. Without it, they can't function. Chainlink solves this problem by securely connecting smart contracts to reliable external data sources and systems. The token LINK powers Chainlink. It can be traded for fiat or digital currencies.

Compound   compound.finance
Compound exists on top of the Ethereum blockchain. Any asset you obtain via Ethereum can be deposited into Compound, where you'll earn interest. You can also post the asset as collateral to obtain loans 24/7 from anywhere in the world. Compound thus creates a new credit market with interest rates based on supply and demand.

For an up-to-date list, complete with hyperlinks, visit the
DACFP Yellow Pages
at dacfp.com

Major Second Layer Protocols

Etherisc   etherisc.com
Etherisc is the first insurance protocol built on the Ethereum blockchain. It ensures that policy terms are permanently coded into smart contracts, with payouts immediately and reliably executed. Licensing requirements are limiting growth; approaches are being tested to scale programmable risk protection without the requirement of insurance licenses.

The Graph   thegraph.com
The Graph is an indexing protocol. The data can be shared across applications so anyone can query with a few keystrokes. Before The Graph, teams used proprietary indexing servers. Now data is stored and processed on open networks with verifiable integrity.

Lightning Network   lightning.network
Lightning aims to make bitcoin faster and cheaper so bitcoin can become the primary payment network for the internet. With Lightning, sending and receiving bitcoin is as simple as sending and receiving a photo.

Settling a bitcoin transaction is virtually instantaneous. And its cost is inconceivably small: just 0.0000001 satoshi. You could thus execute 100 million Lightning trades for the cost of a single satoshi.

For an up-to-date list, complete with hyperlinks, visit the
DACFP Yellow Pages
at dacfp.com

Chainlink

Uniswap

MetaMask

There are other scaling approaches, too, such as *sidechains* and *childchains*. A sidechain is a blockchain that's attached to, but faster than, a parent blockchain. Rootstock and Liquid are two examples. A childchain is a blockchain that operates on the original blockchain rather than next to it. Plasma is one example. Childchains are thus dependent on their host's (parent's) blockchain, while sidechains are not. Childchains are as secure as their parent chain; sidechains are not.

Major Second Layer Protocols

OMG   omg.network
The network's goal is to enable real-time, peer-to-peer transfer and payment of digital assets—and not just digital assets, but also other intangible forms of value, such as loyalty points. OMG sits on top of the Ethereum blockchain network, allowing applications to operate faster and cheaper without compromising Ethereum's security. OMG can perform thousands of transactions per second at one-third the cost. OMG's token is distributed across 678,000 addresses, making it one of the most widely distributed tokens in the Ethereum ecosystem.

SushiSwap   sushi.com
A rival to Uniswap (see below), it debuted in August 2020.

Uniswap   uniswap.org
One of the biggest projects on Ethereum is Uniswap, a decentralized exchange (more on this in Chapter 10). Since 2018, the protocol has supported $20 billion in volume traded by 250,000+ unique addresses across 8,000+ assets and secured $1 billion+ in liquidity, deposited by 49,000+ liquidity providers.

For an up-to-date list, complete with hyperlinks, visit the
DACFP Yellow Pages
at dacfp.com

Financial Products and Services

Satoshi created Bitcoin so people could freely move money around the world. You think that was creative? Wait'll you read about these next innovations. All are built on top of the base and second layers of blockchain technology.

Bitgo

Major Blockchain Applications of Financial Products and Services

Binusu binusu.com
Uganda's 42 million people have only 6 million bank accounts—but 23 million mobile money subscribers. However, mobile money suffers from high costs, slow transactions, and limited features and services. Binusu lets Ugandans borrow, lend, save, invest and trade, using a custom blockchain trading the BNU, a stablecoin pegged to Uganda's currency, the shilling. Binusu thus delivers noncustodial financial services to merchants and consumers outside the banking system. Binusu's interest rate is the lowest in Uganda, and its merchant services enable real-time settlement.

BitGo bitgo.com
BitGo serves institutional clients; in 2018 the BitGo Trust Company became the first independent, regulated custodian built for digital assets. Its security platform is used by hundreds of exchanges and institutional investors and in the digital asset space. BitGo now offers secure storage of digital assets, prime services (which aggregate lending, borrowing, trading, clearing, settlement, and other capital markets services in one managed account), and portfolio tools, including tax solutions, to help users manage their holdings. Developers and institutions can easily integrate BitGo's offering into their own applications. The firm has 350+ institutional clients in 50 countries and processes $15 billion+ in transactions monthly. That's 20% of all Bitcoin transactions.

Cowrie cowrie.exchange
Nigeria's currency is not globally traded, making cross-border payments slow and expensive. Cowrie lets Nigerians transact around the world efficiently and cost-effectively with digital tokens backed by the Nigerian naira.

Deutsche Bank cib.db.com/solutions/securitiesservices
One of the world's ten largest financial institutions, Deutsche Bank is developing a fully integrated custody platform for institutional clients and their digital assets, an all-in-one easy-to-use platform that ensures safety for clients via institutional-grade hot/cold storage with insurance-grade protection.

For an up-to-date list, complete with hyperlinks, visit the
DACFP Yellow Pages
at dacfp.com

Major Blockchain Applications of Financial Products and Services

LocalBitcoins localbitcoins.com
LocalBitcoins lets people from different countries exchange their local currency into bitcoin, making the global economy accessible worldwide. LocalBitcoins is available on every continent and has been used in 8,000+ cities. The biggest volume involves the Russian ruble and Venezuelan bolivar. Unlike exchanges and centralized trading sites, LocalBitcoins lets users negotiate with each other, making the process customizable, fast, and suited for exchange rather than speculation.

MetaMask metamask.io
MetaMask provides a secure, easy-to-use Ethereum wallet that lets users interact with thousands of websites and smart contracts with one login—providing more use cases than any other solution, including payments, trading and DEX swaps, decentralized financial services, gaming, art collecting, international transactions, self-sovereign identity, authentication, and more. Two-thirds of MetaMask Mobile users are outside North America and Europe, mostly in unbanked markets.

PayPal paypal.com
The payments company wants to expand the adoption of digital assets by its 346 million consumers and 26 million merchants in 200+ markets to around the world. Its goal is to let buyers pay with bitcoin and let transactions settle in fiat currency. At this writing, users can buy, sell, and hold Bitcoin, Ethereum, Litecoin, and Bitcoin Cash.

Rally rally.io
Rally lets influencers, athletes, and creators with millions of followers launch and manage their own digital coins to fuel fan engagement. Once created, coins can be bought or earned by fans, building a decentralized community. Its "no-code" tools let any creator launch a coin without any technical knowledge or advanced understanding of digital assets.

For an up-to-date list, complete with hyperlinks, visit the
DACFP Yellow Pages
at dacfp.com

Major Blockchain Applications of Financial Products and Services

Ripio   ripio.com

In 2019, the Central Bank of Argentina limited monthly US dollar purchases to $200 and introduced a 65% tax to avoid massive draining of reserves. Ripio, the leading digital assets firm in South America, lets Argentinians save money and earn interest via products that are compliant with local regulations but not affected by purchase limits and taxation. The platform lets users deposit and withdraw Argentine pesos 24/7, and easily buy, sell, and store digital assets.

SuperRare   superrare.co

SuperRare makes art accessible to anyone with an internet connection. Each artist issues a certificate of authenticity for the work, letting patrons track provenance.

XBT Provider   coinshares.com/etps/xbtprovider

In 2015, CoinShares' Bitcoin Tracker became the first bitcoin-based security available on a regulated exchange, making it easy for investors to buy digital assets via traditional securities exchanges.

For an up-to-date list, complete with hyperlinks, visit the
DACFP Yellow Pages
at dacfp.com

Nonfinancial Applications and Services

If you're impressed by the financial field's creativity, you'll be doubly impressed when you read about some of the innovations offered by those outside the industry.

Major Blockchain Applications and Services Outside the Financial Industry

CryptoFund   cryptofund.unicef.io
UNICEF launched CryptoFund in October 2019 to receive and disburse bitcoin and ether as a means of funding start-ups in emerging or developing economies that are using innovative technologies to solve local challenges. Transferring digital assets to start-ups can be done in a few minutes at virtually no cost, compared to traditional methods that involve several intermediary banks, take days to complete, and cost as much as 8% of the money being transmitted.

World Food Programme   innovation.wfp.org/project/
Winner of the 2020 Nobel Peace Prize, the World Food Programme is the world's largest agency delivering humanitarian cash. The agency has distributed billions of dollars to tens of millions of people in dozens of countries. Giving cash to those in need is often the most effective and efficient way to distribute humanitarian assistance while also supporting local economies. However, in many areas where WFP operates, financial service providers are often insufficient, unreliable, or unavailable. In others, refugees cannot open or access bank accounts.

To solve these problems, WFP uses a digital assets network to distribute money via mobile phones. Beneficiaries control how and when they receive and spend the cash—in retail shops, at ATMs, via mobile money, and more. For example, $25 million was transferred to refugees via 1.1 million transactions, including 106,000 Syrian refugees in Jordan. Using blockchain technology, WFP cut its bank transaction fees by 98%.

For an up-to-date list, complete with hyperlinks, visit the
DACFP Yellow Pages
at dacfp.com

Chapter 8

Are Digital Assets Money?

Satoshi's intent was clearly for bitcoin to be treated as money, a "digital currency" that replaces all fiat currencies. Did Satoshi's dream become reality, and if not, will it ever?

To answer that question, we must first answer this one: What is money? Let's explore this concept so you can decide if bitcoin or any other digital assets meet (or will ever meet) the definition—or if it even matters. This will help you decide if you want to own any digital assets and, if so, which ones.

What Is Money?

Money has served a core coordinating function of society for centuries. Money lets us efficiently facilitate transactions, so we don't have to rely on the inefficient *barter system*.

If you give your neighbor a quart of milk in exchange for a cup of sugar, that's bartering. Records show it was used by Mesopotamians, Phoenicians, and Babylonians as far back as 6000 BC—long before currency was invented.

Bartering is a hassle, though, because you must carry that milk with you until you find someone who has some sugar. An easier method of exchange was needed—and that's what introduced the concept of money. Instead of carrying the milk, I can carry small pieces of paper, metal, or some other item. When you tell me you have some sugar, I can give you the paper in exchange for it. Later, you can give the paper to someone who gives you milk.

Money makes life efficient. You don't have to receive milk at the very moment you give me sugar. You can carry and safeguard money more easily than milk. And the paper is interchangeable for anything—you don't have to own what the person with milk wants.

Our ancestors used all sorts of items as money, including animals, crops, shells, metal, paper, salt, even large rocks.

Milk is milk, and assuming it's fresh, there's little difference between one quart and another. So, it's easy for people to agree on how much milk is required to obtain a cup of sugar. But if I want to give you coins for your sugar, how many coins will you demand?

You'll want to know who created the coin. And that was the first problem. In the early days of money, anybody could create it—just like anybody could milk a cow. Since individuals and businesses created their own money, a lot of it proved worthless. As a result, people were reluctant to accept money as payment—returning us to the problematic barter system.

To give everyone confidence that the coins were worth accepting, governments began declaring that they and only they would be permitted to print money. Governments are more stable and have the authority (thanks to their armies) to enforce their rules. The problem, though, is that governments come and go, and there's always more than one.

Rai Stone

People living in the Yap Islands of Micronesia used stones as money. Called rai, their diameter ranged from about 1.5 inches to 12 feet (and weighing 8,800 pounds). The big ones were too difficult to move, so ownership was maintained via oral history. You can still find these stones on the islands—as well as in museums worldwide.

© Adobe Stock printed with permission

In America, for example, all 13 colonies issued money. But Massachusetts currency didn't have the same value as Pennsylvania currency, nor was there broad agreement about what those relative values were.

This isn't a book on economic history, so I'll skip the details, but you know how it all turned out: in the United States, the federal government is now the sole issuer of money, and as it says on every dollar bill, that currency is valid for all debts, public and private. Other governments also print currencies for use within their borders, with many refusing to accept those printed by others. The US dollar, though, is accepted by pretty much everyone in the world.

But those US dollars are still being printed on paper.* The Trea-

---

* Actually, the material is 75% cotton and 25% linen—part of the government's anticounterfeiting efforts.

"How will you be paying? Crypto, Venmo, Zelle, electronic fund transfer, credit card, check, cash, precious metals, brightly colored shells or livestock?"

sury Department's Bureau of Engraving and Printing prints 4.2 billion pieces every year, in values ranging from $1 to $100.

Sure, carrying money in your wallet is a lot easier than carrying milk. But the money is still a hassle—especially if you have a lot of it. Want to walk around with hundreds of thousands or millions of dollars in your pocket or purse?

So, people soon decided that they needed a place to store their money—and that led to the introduction of banks. At first, you made cash deposits at your local bank and it stored your money in its vault. But no longer. Today, your deposits are made electronically; local banks have little cash on hand. (In Sweden, banks require advance notice, and they charge a fee, if you want to withdraw physical cash.)

And yet, the Treasury Department keeps producing paper money.

We've digitized almost everything else—from photos to health records to deeds—so it was inevitable that somebody would figure out how to digitize money. That somebody wasn't the Federal Reserve, the World Bank, or the International Monetary Fund. It was Satoshi Nakamoto. Go figure.

But is bitcoin truly money?

"Oh, there's nothing really wrong with our marriage.
We'd just like to figure out a way to monetize it."

Defining Money

To answer that question, let's ascertain what qualifies as money. *Money* is usually characterized by three key functions:

1. store of value

2. unit of account

3. medium of exchange

Let's look at each.

Store of Value

You're confident that each dollar in your wallet will maintain its value. Thanks to this confidence, you're willing to receive a dollar today even though you don't plan to spend it for days—or decades. In the meantime, you can easily store your money and retrieve it anytime. None of that is true for milk, which decomposes over time and thus doesn't hold its value.

Money, though, isn't a perfect store of value because its purchasing power also diminishes over time. That's because of inflation. In the United States, the Federal Reserve's goal is to reduce the value of the currency by 2% per year. As a deliberate matter of policy, you can expect that each dollar in your wallet will be worth only 98 cents a year from now.

If losing two cents a year is annoying, consider countries with far less stable governments and economies. Venezuela's inflation rate in 2021 was 2,300%—meaning groceries you'd buy in the morning for $100 would cost $300 that night. In 2021, you needed 400 billion Venezuelan bolivars to buy what you could buy with a single US dollar.

It is safe to say that if your currency is not a store of value, it is not money.

Unit of Account

Money can be used to describe the relative value of goods and services, and assets and liabilities. This lets us put a price on something and compare it to something else.

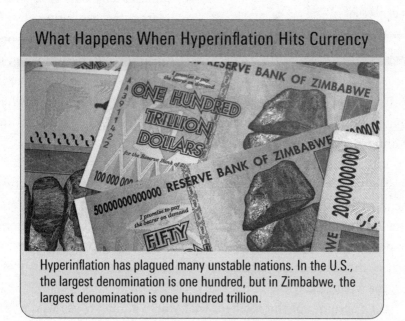

What Happens When Hyperinflation Hits Currency

Hyperinflation has plagued many unstable nations. In the U.S., the largest denomination is one hundred, but in Zimbabwe, the largest denomination is one hundred trillion.

When we see that one car costs $30,000 and another costs $100,000, we immediately understand their relative values. Without money as a common denominator, it would be virtually impossible for society to transact commerce.

Medium of Exchange

Money is an intermediary; it facilitates the exchange of goods and services. Without its use as a medium of exchange, we're forced to rely on the inconveniences of a barter system.

Does bitcoin satisfy these three definitions?

Yes, according to these three characteristics, bitcoin is money.

But some argue that there's more to consider. Bitcoin, they say, can't be regarded as money because it isn't backed by anything tangible, such as gold or silver. That argument doesn't work—for the simple reason that US dollars aren't backed by gold or anything else, either.

	U.S. Dollar	Bitcoin
Store of Value	✔	✔
Unit of Account	✔	✔
Medium of Exchange	✔	✔

FIGURE 8.1

US dollars have value because the two parties using it in a transaction agree there is value. And they agree on what that value is. The parties have confidence in the currency and thus are willing to use it. They have trust in the currency.

Is there similar agreement, confidence, and trust with bitcoin?

Not to a level that matches the agreement, confidence, and trust people have for the US dollar. Perhaps, as bitcoin becomes used more, the level of agreement, confidence, and trust in it will grow. Millions of people worldwide already believe that bitcoin is money—because it passes the three-characteristic test above—and perhaps someday everyone will agree.

Let's assume for the moment that you're among those who agree that bitcoin is money. Does that mean bitcoin is also currency?

Defining Currency

Currency is the physical representation of money. So, as we ask whether bitcoin is money, we must also ask if bitcoin can be considered currency.

Currency has six characteristics:

1. durability

2. portability

3. divisibility

4. uniformity

5. limited supply

6. acceptability

Let's examine each so we can decide if bitcoin passes the test.

Durability Currency must be strong enough to survive repeated use. Livestock and produce don't meet this test, but dollar bills and coins do.

Portability Currency must be easy to transport and use. Dollar bills are easily portable; barrels of oil aren't. Tiny quantities of gold are portable, but large amounts are not.

Divisibility Currency must be reducible to small denominations. Dollars can be reduced to pennies. Gold bars can be cut into ounces or grams—even divisible down to the atom if you have the right equipment.

Uniformity Each unit of currency must have the same value as each other equivalent unit, regardless of when the unit is created. Each dollar, for example, has the same value as every other dollar.

Limited Supply For money to maintain its value, its currency must be scarce. The Federal Reserve maintains strict control over the issuance of US dollars to prevent excessive supply from entering the marketplace. As we've seen with Venezuelan bolivars and Zimbabwean dollars, excessive issuance of currency sharply reduces money's value.

Acceptability Currency must be generally accepted by a population for the exchange of goods and services. US dollars are accepted worldwide, not just in all 50 states.

Does bitcoin satisfy these six definitions?

Durability Digital assets are extremely durable because they are bits and bytes—software code never degrades or evaporates. The ones and zeros that comprise our electronic age can last forever.

Portability Digital assets are completely portable. Because the data is stored on the internet and accessed via apps on your phone, your digital assets are always with you. You always have immediate access, and you can transmit your digital assets to others within seconds.

Divisibility The smallest denomination for bitcoin is the *satoshi* (*sat* for short); each is worth 0.00000001 bitcoin. One hundred million satoshis equal one bitcoin.*

Uniformity Bitcoins are like dollars and gold; each is the same as all the others. That's not true for livestock, fruits and vegetables, houses, or cars.

---

* For this reason, it doesn't matter how high bitcoin's price becomes. The price is already so high that most people can't afford to buy one. Instead, people buy satoshis—part of a bitcoin. (Similarly, no one has enough money to buy Apple, so they buy part of Apple—a single share—and because single shares of Apple are now expensive, you can buy a fraction of a share for just $5.) In the future, people won't refer to bitcoins. They'll refer to satoshis.

Limited Supply Unlike dollars—where supply keeps growing because the government keeps printing them (especially during financial crises)—bitcoin has a limited supply. Only 21 million bitcoin will ever be produced.*

Acceptability Bitcoin is increasingly being accepted as a means of payment. Tens of millions of merchants worldwide accept bitcoin as payment via PayPal, and governments (starting with El Salvador) have started to designate bitcoin as official currency alongside their fiat currencies. But acceptance is not yet universal.

Many people (including me) believe that bitcoin's limited supply helps its price rise. It's the classic *supply versus demand* economic theory, which we'll cover in chapter 11. Admittedly, that could interfere with bitcoin's being money, because if you are convinced the price will rise, you won't want to spend any on groceries. You'll hoard it instead. In fact, there's a name for such people: *HODLers*—as in Hold On for Dear Life. Also called Diamond Hands, because as the saying goes, diamonds are forever.

Bitcoin clearly possesses all the characteristics of currency, except perhaps for acceptability. So, does bitcoin qualify as currency? I'd guess it depends on whom you ask, and what country you're in. Eventually, the answer will become a clear yes or no. In the meantime, it's your call.

---

* Limited supply is not always a feature of digital assets. Some allow for an unlimited quantity. (Dogecoin, for example, has more than 130 billion in existence, and 5 billion more are being added annually—one of many reasons investing in Dogecoin is both stupid and dangerous. More on this later.)

	U.S. Dollar	Bitcoin
Durability	✔	✔
Portability	✔	✔
Divisibility	✔	✔
Uniformity	✔	✔
Restricted Supply	✔	✔

FIGURE 8.2

A Better Digital Currency Than Bitcoin

One of the biggest concerns about bitcoin's use as a currency is its volatility. How can you have confidence in a currency whose price fluctuates constantly, often dramatically?

Enter stablecoins. We were introduced to Tether in chapter 7. It and all stablecoins claim to do what bitcoin can't: provide a stable price. If true, it would enable them to truly serve as digital currency. So, let's look at stablecoins more closely.

Stablecoins

Unlike bitcoin and other digital assets whose prices are "whatever investors say they are," the price of a stablecoin is the same as the currency it's meant to replace—thus eliminating volatility.

Say you buy $100 worth of a US stablecoin. The sponsor uses your money to buy one hundred US dollars, thus creating a one-to-one ratio of coin-to-dollar. In practice, that makes using the stablecoin exactly the same as using US dollars.

Why bother with the stablecoin, then? Why not just use dollars as we always have?

Simple: Dollars operate within the federal financial system. You need a bank account to store them, and you can only send money by following its rules—which, as we learned in chapter 2, are time-consuming and costly. By contrast, you can transfer stablecoins 24/7/365, virtually free.

Well, there are two issues with stablecoins, the second a result of the first. The first, as noted, is that stablecoins don't necessarily conform to federal banking laws. Banks are required to maintain a certain amount of capital, for example, but stablecoins have no such obligation. They also aren't required to adhere to Anti–Money Laundering, tax compliance, or other rules. And there's no FDIC to protect you.

Some stablecoins are pegged to the US dollar. Others are pegged to the euro or yen—or a basket of many fiat currencies.

Other stablecoins are pegged to a commodity, such as gold, silver, or oil. Some are even backed by an algorithm, which controls supply and demand to stabilize their coins' prices.

And, yes, there's a stablecoin that's backed by—you guessed it—other digital coins.

- SUPPLY
- DEMAND
- RUMOR

BUSINESS 101

"The price of a stock will fluctuate on these three factors..."

That leads to the second problem. While all stablecoins say they are pegged 1:1 against their chosen currency, no law or regulation requires them to do so. Therefore, as you might predict, questions have been raised about the assets that are purported to be backing some stablecoins.

Consider Tether. It's the largest stablecoin and claims that all its deposits are backed exclusively by the US dollar. But the SEC says much of Tether's assets are instead held in US Treasurys, bank CDs, commercial paper, corporate bonds, and municipal debt. Those assets are not as safe as US dollars. (Tether and Bitfinex paid a $41 million fine to the Commodity Futures Trading Commission in October 2021 for falsely saying its digital tokens were fully backed by US dollars.)

The government is worried because investors and consumers have placed $120 billion into stablecoins. A slew of federal agencies are working on the issue, including the President's Working Group on Financial Markets, the Federal Reserve, the Office of the Comptroller of Currency, and the Financial Stability Oversight Council. Might stablecoins be regulated or even banned? That answer will be in this book's sequel.

But isn't the government being rather silly? I mean, why do they object to stablecoins? In concept, they're a better choice than our current financial system—which takes too long (five days) and costs too much (6.7% on average) to move money cross-border. It even takes a week or more to move money *within* our border (try sending a check to someone who lives in another state and see how long it takes for that check to clear after it's deposited). And if you wire funds, you incur those wire fees. And all this assumes you have a bank account in the first place. Our current system might have been defendable 50 years ago, but today, given current technological capabilities, our system is severely outdated.

So instead of fretting over stablecoins and the fact there's no regulation and fears of insufficient backing, why doesn't the government just create its own stablecoin?!

News flash: they're going to.

Central Bank Digital Currencies

Before the end of this decade, you'll be earning, receiving, using, and storing *digital dollars*. They'll be the same as the dollars in your pocket or purse, issued by the Federal Reserve and backed by the full faith and credit of the federal government of the United States.

To understand why and how this is happening, let's take a step back and look at how governments (alone or in partnership with neighboring nations) issue currency.

The process begins simply enough: The government hires a bank. The bank prints the currency and distributes it to other banks. As part of its charter, the bank is responsible for the nation's monetary policy. This includes setting interest rates and determining how much currency it'll distribute throughout the country. The bank even has regulatory authority over other banks, such as telling them how much cash they must hold relative to their deposits (which impacts their profit potential). And the bank that gets this government charter has a monopoly on all these rights; no other bank in the country has the same authority.

Clearly, it's a sweet deal. You might think that every bank in the country vies for the chance to be selected. But, nah, that's not how it works. Usually, governments just invent a new bank and grant all those powers and responsibilities to it. Because this bank is so important, so central, to the nation's economic system, it's called a *central bank*.

Virtually every government in the world has a central bank. There's even an association of them, called the Bank for International Settlements. Currently, 63 of the world's 179 central banks are members.

All the central banks work similarly. And of all the customs they have in common, one in particular (for our purposes here) is noteworthy: they all still print their currencies.

Seriously?

Yeah, even in today's digital age, they still do it the old-fashioned way. Even you, as an ordinary citizen, are managing your money in a more advanced way than central banks. You receive your paycheck, pension, annuity payment, and Social Security benefits via electronic bank deposit. You pay bills with credit and debit cards, and you send and receive money via digital apps such as PayPal, Venmo, and Zelle. You don't even bother to pay most bills manually; you just put them on autopay so you don't have to fuss with them. You file your tax return, pay your taxes, and receive your tax refund electronically, too.

You do much of your shopping online. And when you're in a store, you merely wave your phone at the cash register. You can't remember the last time you paid for something in cash. You might even have stopped carrying cash since there's no need for it.

Yet the government keeps printing it.

All that printed cash comes with problems. One is the sheer magnitude of the effort. The US Bureau of Engraving and Printing spends more than $1 billion a year printing 5.8 billion bills ranging from $1 to $100. That money must be secured, delivered to local banks, and protected from counterfeiting. And every year, a lot of it is destroyed—which incurs still more costs.

Even the cash itself creates problems. The first involves terrorism and drug cartels. Crooks and terrorists don't pay for drugs or bombs with Visa or MasterCard. They use cash. In 2007, for example, US and Mexican authorities seized $200 million in cash in a drug bust. Rogue nations and terrorist organizations largely support themselves via the illicit use of cash.

The other problem is tax evasion. When you pay the babysitter $50,* you probably don't issue an IRS Form 1099—and it's equally unlikely that the babysitter reports the income on their tax return. Ditto for the home builder who says that new roof you want costs $25,000, but it'll be just $20,000 if you pay in cash, thus allowing the roofer to "forget" to report the income to the IRS—saving maybe $10,000 in taxes. How big is the problem? Well, IRS Commissioner Charles Rettig says unpaid taxes amount to $1 trillion a year—equal to the federal government's entire pre-Covid budget deficit. In other words, Congress doesn't need

---

* With Venmo or PayPal, right? Anyone still using cash? Anyone? Bueller?

to raise tax rates on law-abiding taxpayers; it just needs to collect the taxes that aren't being paid by tax cheats.

For sure, from a law enforcement and tax compliance perspective, printed currency is dangerous and harmful. But a solution now exists: digital money.

Digital money can severely impede—if not outright eliminate—terrorism funding, illegal drug dealing, and tax evasion. That's because digital money leaves a digital footprint. Every electronic transaction can be tracked—and while that might annoy privacy advocates, it downright panics criminals.

This is why digital assets are here to stay: governments love 'em. And that's why every central bank in the world is investigating or developing CBDCs—*central bank digital currencies*. The Bahamas has already launched theirs, called the sand dollar. (The Bahamian currency is called the dollar.) The island's government realized that hurricanes often force local banks to close for weeks—preventing residents from accessing their money at the very moment they need lots of it. The sand dollar allows the island's economy to function even when the banks can't.

The Bahamas isn't alone. China is experimenting with a digital yuan, as is Russia with a digital ruble and Japan with a digital yen. Nigeria launched its digital currency in 2021, Brazil and Switzerland are doing so in 2022, Sweden in 2023. The central banks of Australia, Malaysia, Singapore, and South Africa are testing a joint CBDC with the Bank for International Settlements; the central banks of Hong Kong, China, the United Arab Emirates, and Thailand are doing the same.

Here in the United States, the Federal Reserve Bank of Boston is working with the Digital Currency Initiative at the Massachusetts Institute of Technology to identify the benefits and challenges of a digital dollar. Boston Fed Assistant Vice President Robert Bench calls the project's potential "immense." Meanwhile, the Federal Reserve has hired its first Chief Innovation Officer. Lael Brainard, vice chair of the Fed's Board of Governors, said in July 2021, "It is essential that the Federal Reserve remain on the frontier of research and policy development regarding CBDC," noting that "the dollar is very dominant in international payments, and if you have the other major jurisdictions in the world with a CBDC offering, and the United States doesn't have one, I just can't wrap my head around that. That just doesn't sound like a sustainable future to me."

Others agree. A July 2021 paper by the Bank of England notes, "New forms of digital money would be the latest innovation in an evolving landscape for how payments are made in the economy. They could contribute to faster, cheaper and more efficient payments and they could potentially enhance financial inclusion. New forms of digital money could potentially offer benefits in terms of cost and functionality. There could also be potential gains from a shift to a more market-based financing. It is also possible they could enhance the transmission of monetary policy." The following month, European Central Bank President Christine Lagarde said, "We need to make sure that we do it right—we owe it to the Europeans." And the central banks of Japan, Canada, and South Korea have all released white papers extolling the benefits of CBDCs.

All told, 80% of the world's central banks are exploring CBDCs, according to BIS, which projects widespread usage around the world by 2025. No wonder 76% of finance professionals worldwide surveyed by Deloitte in 2021 agreed that digital assets "will serve as a strong alternative to, or outright replacement for, fiat currencies in the next 5–10 years." A study by Deutsche Bank reached the same conclusion, saying cryptocurrencies could replace cash by 2030.

The Facebook Threat

But let's not kid ourselves. Central banks are not planning to launch CBDCs solely because of their advantages. They're launching CBDCs because they're petrified of what might happen to them and their governments if they don't.

Their fear was made clear in 2019 when Mark Zuckerberg announced that he'd formed a nonprofit organization in Switzerland that would launch the stablecoin Libra (now called Diem). Pegged to the world's leading fiat currencies, Diem would be available only to users of Meta Platforms–owned apps like Facebook, WhatsApp, and Messenger, and they could use Diem to send money to each other and to buy products on Facebook Marketplace, which competes with Amazon, Walmart, Craigslist, and eBay.

Facebook has nearly 3 billion users worldwide. That's nearly half the planet's population; two-thirds of all people with an internet connection have a Facebook account. If everyone in the world could now instantly buy anything and send money to anyone using a privately created currency that operates outside government purview or control, well, why would anyone have any use for dollars, pounds, or euros anymore? One world, one currency—all controlled by one guy, Mark Zuckerberg.

Instantly, governments worldwide freaked out. Within minutes of Zuckerberg's announcement, French Finance Minister Bruno Le Maire said France would not allow Diem in the European Union, citing threats to its monetary sovereignty. Japan immediately began investigating Diem and its potential impact on Japan's monetary policy and financial regulation. And officials from 26 central banks quickly convened to discuss Diem.

In the United States, a phalanx of US regulators and legislators howled within hours of Zuckerberg's announcement. US Representative Maxine Waters, chair of the House Financial Services Committee, hauled Zuckerberg to the Capitol for hearings and later sent Facebook a letter demanding that it stop development of Diem, citing privacy, national security, trading, and monetary policy concerns. Federal Reserve Chair Jerome Powell told Congress that the Fed had "serious concerns" about Diem, and President Donald Trump tweeted that if Facebook wanted to proceed, it "must seek a new Banking Charter and become subject to all Banking Regulations." On October 19, 2021, US Senators Richard Blumenthal, Sherrod Brown, Brian Schatz, Tina Smith, and Elizabeth Warren wrote to Mark Zuckerberg demanding that he "not bring Diem to market."

And authorities didn't stop there. Congress went after Visa, PayPal, MasterCard, and Stripe, too, forcing them to explain what they would do if Diem was launched.

In the face of so much resistance, Zuckerberg has . . . killed Diem. He initially tried to placate government officials by moving the non-profit from Switzerland to the United States, but Congress was non-plussed. So, Zuckerberg sold Diem to Silvergate Bank for $182 million in cash and stock (not bitcoin).

Despite their machinations, the world's governments know they can't stop this. Sure, they might stop Meta—but only because Meta is a big company with other business interests it wants to protect. But another player could come along that doesn't have such vulnerabilities. The internet is everywhere, and blockchain technology allows for organizations to be created with no central location or authority (more on these DAOs—decentralized autonomous organizations—in chapter 10), making it challenging for governments to stop or even just regulate them.

So, sure, CBDCs offer wonderful benefits for everyone—governments, businesses, and consumers alike. But the world's central banks are motivated to create their own digital currencies because they know that if they don't, someone like Mark Zuckerberg will instead, eliminating them and the world's current financial system.

If you can't beat 'em, join 'em.

Thus, the central banks are joining 'em. And when they do, a new question will arise: If the government provides us with digital currency, will we still need stablecoins?

Do CBDCs Threaten Bitcoin?

Regulators don't have to ban stablecoins. They could simply render them unnecessary—by creating their own. Indeed, a digital dollar issued by the Federal Reserve ought to be far more popular with businesses and consumers than a stablecoin invented by some private entity. The marketplace will decide, but there's no doubt that the Fed's CBDC will be the stablecoin to beat.

If CBDCs win the stablecoin war, what does that mean for bitcoin? Do CBDCs pose an existential threat for bitcoin and other digital assets like it—either because governments will ban bitcoin (like they might ban stablecoins) or because consumer interest will fade (and bitcoin will simply die off, worthless) as everyone chooses the Fed's CBDC?

I don't think either scenario will occur. Bitcoin's prospects as currency remain intact, demonstrated by El Salvador's decision to make it official currency (with Panama, Ukraine, and Paraguay following suit at this writing). But even if bitcoin is not widely regarded as currency, it's still not a threat to central banks—unlike Diem.

The reason? While there might be debate as to whether bitcoin is a digital currency, there is no debate that it is a digital asset. And digital assets don't threaten the Fed. As proof, consider that there are already lots of digital assets—airline miles, gift cards, loyalty points, and more—and they haven't scared any central banks. Sure, bitcoin and other digital assets face issues with price, availability, security, and privacy, but those can easily be regulated—just as the stock and bond markets have been regulated.

That also explains why interest in bitcoin will not fade. The prices of all assets fluctuate, and this attracts rather than repels investors. You can't get rich buying currency, but you can get rich buying stocks, real estate, and baseball cards. If people think they can make money buying bitcoin and other digital assets, they'll keep buying them.

Therefore, the emergence of CBDCs by governments around the world enhances rather than diminishes bitcoin's legitimacy. The issuance of a digital dollar is the blunt admission by the federal government that digital money works and has features and benefits that paper money lacks. This is an implicit endorsement of blockchain (the technology that will be used to launch and manage all CBDCs) and, thereby, all digital assets.

Thus, you'll be able to buy a digital currency, issued by the government with a stable value, or a digital asset, issued by others with prices that give you the opportunity for wealth creation. These two will peacefully coexist.

Gold vs. Bitcoin

We can't leave a chapter that talks about money without talking about gold. Not because gold is money, but because some people insist that it is. These "gold bugs" believe gold is the only true money—and that stocks, bonds, real estate, and all other assets are not worth owning.

But bitcoin adherents believe bitcoin is better than gold. Some actually refer to bitcoin as "digital gold."

Well, for gold enthusiasts, them's fightin' words. And for sure, gold adherents offer lots of reasons for owning gold:

- Gold has been a store of value for 5,000 years—offering confidence other assets can't match.
- Gold is a real physical asset. It's not merely a piece of paper representing something else.
- Gold protects against inflation and geopolitical uncertainty.
- Gold has many commercial uses because it is inert; doesn't tarnish or corrode; requires no lubrication, maintenance, or repair; can be melted and easily made into wire, hammered into micro-thin sheets, or alloyed with other metals; conducts electricity; and is nonallergenic. Gold is most frequently used in jewelry, but it's also used in electronics, the space program, and health care (including dentistry and treatment for rheumatoid arthritis and cancer). Since gold has long connoted excellence, prizes and medals are often made of it.
- Gold mining has been declining since 2000, while demand has grown. The supply/demand thesis argues that gold's price will rise.

- Gold is not positively correlated to stocks or bonds, making it an excellent addition for portfolio diversification.

- There are many ways to buy gold—bullion, gold coins, stocks of gold mining companies, gold futures contracts, and gold ETFs.

I'm not terribly impressed by the above list. Gold's history is irrelevant; it's the future that counts.

As for geopolitical uncertainly, well, if the world collapses, it won't be gold you want, but bullets and whiskey. As for the benefit of being a physical asset, a million dollars is about 35 pounds of gold. Try lugging that around all day.

Also, gold is not necessarily an effective inflation hedge. Over the past hundred years, gold prices sometimes rise with inflation. But, other times, they fall. You simply can't be confident that gold will protect you from inflation.

Let's also remember that gold dealers, prices, and fees are not regulated, and that the prices of gold mining stocks often deviate from gold's price. It's true that gold never vanishes or expires, but that also means its supply grows every year—requiring rising demand just to prevent the price from collapsing.

So, am I telling you not to own gold? Not at all. Instead, I believe the "gold versus bitcoin" debate is silly. The two asset classes have nothing in common, and the words *bitcoin* and *gold* should never appear in the same sentence.

This entire debate is a manufactured contortion by zealots (on both sides) who believe the only way they can be right is if everyone else is wrong. The truth is, you don't need to choose between the two. If you are a disciple of portfolio diversification (a concept we'll explore in chapter 14), you should own both!

Chapter 9
Tokens

Uh-oh, here comes another new word . . . *tokens*. But fear not, because you're already familiar with them and how they work. You just don't realize it yet.

Tokens are small, physical representations of something intangible. For decades, you needed a token to ride on New York buses and subways. You use tokens to play games at many amusement parks. A "token gesture" is a small act representing your feelings—as in handing a rose to your love.

Note the word *small*. It's key. Consider buying a large pizza. You can't eat it all, so you slice the pie into eight pieces. Each piece is a slice, a *share* of the pie.

Ditto for stocks. Wouldn't it be cool to own Amazon? Unfortunately, Amazon is worth $1.6 trillion—and you don't have that much money. No worries—you can buy a tiny slice of the company—a *share*, just like our pizza pie—and you'll own some of Amazon. The more shares you buy, the more of the company you own.

In the crypto world, they don't sell shares. Sometimes they sell *coins*, as we've seen. But in other cases, they sell *tokens*. Same thing as shares and coins, just a different (third) name.

Let's look at digital assets that are issued in the form of tokens.

Utility Tokens

The word *utility* refers to something that is useful. Airline mileage points are an example of utility tokens—each point has a value, and if you accumulate enough of them, you can exchange them for something useful, like an airplane ticket or hotel room.

Utility tokens are valid only for the intended use. You can't use your airline miles to ride the subway, and you can't use subway tokens to fly to Paris.

New companies, called *start-ups*, often issue utility tokens. Say you're launching a new business. You will soon have a nifty new product to sell, but it's not yet ready. Without a product, you can't attract customers—or their money. But you need their money now, to help you finance development of your product. Since you can't yet sell a product, you sell customers a token—the right to get your product when it becomes available. "Buy my token today," you tell prospective customers, "and in the future you can exchange it for my product."

Utility tokens are not investments or securities like stocks and bonds, any more than subway tokens are. Their prices are set by the issuing company and aren't expected to fluctuate (although they might if the start-up issues only a few and lets recipients resell them). Instead, people generally buy utility tokens because they want the product you're promising to deliver, and they want to be among the first to get it. Or, in cases where the product will be made in limited supply, they want to be able to buy one before they sell out.

You're taking a risk when you buy a utility token because the issuing company might never release the product or, by the time it does, you might not want it. In the meantime, there's probably no way you can sell your token. It's like buying a concert ticket where you must hope that the event does eventually occur and that you will really be able to go—because if not, you probably can't sell your ticket and the event promoter won't provide a refund if the concert is canceled.

Be careful when buying utility tokens.

Security Tokens

The name is a misnomer because this type of token has nothing to do with cybersecurity. Instead, the name is a (poor, inaccurate) reference to federal securities law. Therefore, these tokens should be called securities tokens, not security tokens.

But (sigh) since the crypto community uses the wrong phrase, so must we. Let's move on. (Grumble.)

Security tokens are an online representation of a real, physical asset. You know that a deed represents ownership of a house, and a stock certificate represents ownership of a company. Likewise for a security token: it represents ownership of an asset—an asset identified by whoever issued the token.

But security tokens are not merely a new age way for companies to issue stock. Rather, these digital assets can be used to raise capital and provide liquidity for *any* asset—including those that have, historically, been highly illiquid.

Can you think of an asset that is worth a lot of money but notoriously difficult to sell? You got it: *real estate.*

It would be cool to own, say, the Empire State Building. But the building is worth $2.3 billion. That's not only a problem for you (since you don't have that much cash in your checking account) but for the building's owner. When it wants to sell, it must find buyers with verrrry deep pockets.

Blockchain to the rescue. The owner of the building could tokenize the property—issuing security tokens just like Apple issues shares. Each token would represent part ownership of the building, and if the tokens are priced affordably, millions of investors could buy them— and then easily trade them among themselves, just as they do with stocks.

This isn't science fiction. The first tokenized real estate deal was completed in 2018—a $30 million luxury condo building in lower Manhattan. More recently, in 2021, Dubai real estate company Arms & McGregor International Realty launched the Mideast's first real estate tokenization platform, using tokenization infrastructure provider Blocksquare.

Real estate is the most valuable asset class in the world—$280 trillion, according to Savills World Research, or roughly three times more than the global stock market—and all of it can be tokenized, creating a massive new asset class for investors. And by doing so, one of the

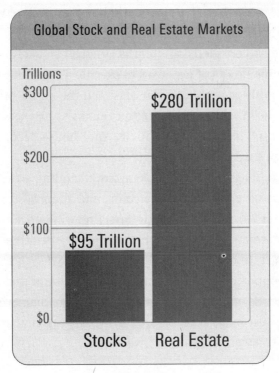

FIGURE 9.1

world's largest but illiquid assets can become as easily tradable as stocks.

Imagine being able to tokenize your home. Why would you want to? Well, if you're like most homeowners, your house is your largest asset. Say it's worth $1 million. You're in retirement and you need additional income to support yourself. You could sell your home, but you don't want to move. You could get a mortgage, but it's difficult to qualify for one during retirement. Besides, you don't want to be saddled with the monthly payments.

So, tokenize the house instead. Slice the deed into 100,000 pieces, or tokens, each priced at $10. Then, sell as many of the tokens as you want. Sell some now, sell some later—whatever you wish. Buyers will be investing in real estate—your real estate. And they'll be able to sell their tokens to other investors on the blockchain. You can even buy the tokens back if you want; their value will be based on the then-current value of the house and supply/demand.

Real estate is considered an illiquid asset; it can take a long time to sell, and you incur lots of expenses to execute a transaction. And that transaction is all-or-nothing—you must sell the entire property (you can't merely sell the dining room). But thanks to blockchain technology, you *can* sell just the dining room. Your house becomes a liquid asset, just like stocks and bonds.

Any physical asset could be tokenized, including artwork, collectibles (such as baseball cards, rare coins, and stamps—tax aspects of this in chapter 20), antiques, exotic cars, fine wine, royalties and performance contracts (the money that actors, artists, athletes, and authors earn over time). Sellers get liquidity and buyers get access to new investment opportunities—and unprecedented ways to create astonishing new levels of portfolio diversification, more than ever before.

Exciting! Just make sure, before buying any token, that you evaluate it just as you would any other investment.

Governance Tokens

We've seen that disagreements among developers could cause a coin to fork. But which developers get to vote on those decisions?

Some protocols answer the question by issuing governance tokens. One token = one vote, so the more tokens you collect, the more say you have over that particular blockchain.

Think about that for a moment. When a company is facing a decision, the board—sitting around a conference table at corporate headquarters—votes. That's a centralized structure. Everyone knows who is voting and where the voting is taking place.

But when hundreds of thousands of developers and users around the world place votes about a decentralized blockchain, who is in control? Nobody; the organization is operating autonomously. And where is the voting occurring? Nowhere and everywhere simultaneously.

This organization is thus called a *decentralized autonomous orga-*

nization, or DAO. These entities already hold more than $8 billion in assets, according to tracker DeepDAO; *MoneyWeek* has declared the 2020s "the decade of the DAO." Some call DAOs the next big thing in digital assets. Personally, I think they are the next, next big thing. The next big thing (coming sooner) is . . .

Non-Fungible Tokens

To understand what a non-fungible token is—and why I'm calling it the next big thing—you must first understand what a fungible token is.

Fungible means identical and interchangeable. Dollar bills, for example, are fungible. Say I lend you a dollar and you pay me back next week. The dollar you give back to me does not have to be the same bill I gave you, because all dollar bills are the same. They're fungible. Mileage points you get with your Visa card are fungible, too, as are casino chips. We casually exchange fungible tokens, shares of stock, currencies, and other assets, because each is the same as every other. Ditto for bitcoin, Ether, and XRP—every coin and every token is fungible.

Except when they are not. When tokens are not fungible, meaning not the same, they are, duh, *non-fungible tokens*, or NFTs. Every NFT is unique. Like paintings by Picasso, no two are alike.

An NFT is a digital asset that represents real-world objects such as art, music, and video game items. Like other digital coins and tokens, NFTs are created on a blockchain. (While several blockchains allow for their creation, as of this writing, the Ethereum blockchain is the most widely used. NFTs are bought and sold using the native blockchain coin, in this case Ether.)

Attention to NFTs started in February 2021 when Christie's auctioned a digital image created by Mike Winkelmann, an artist living in Charleston, South Carolina. He goes by the name Beeple. His NFT sold for $69 million. The buyer obtained the legal right to the digital image—but that's all it is, an image. The artwork doesn't exist in the real world. The buyer can't hang it on a wall, only view it on a phone.

Why would someone buy art that can't be hung on a wall?

For the simple reason that you don't look at your wall very often. You look at your phone with far greater frequency. Doesn't it make sense to have your art with you so you can look at it anytime you want?

Okay, that makes sense. But millions of other people can view Beeple's artwork, too, not just the buyer, because the image is readily available for everyone to see on the internet. (Go ahead. Google it.)

Wait—what exactly did the buyer buy?

Bragging rights, partly. But also, the buyer bought the legal claim to be the one and true owner of the asset (digital though it may be) and, therefore, to have the right to sell, license, or distribute it as they wish. Including the right that everyone else posting the image cease and desist or suffer the pain of legal consequences.

Whether you're nodding in understanding or shaking your head in disbelief and disapproval, recognize that total worldwide sales of non-fungible tokens exceeded $13 billion in 2021; in 2020, it was less than $30 million. More than four million people now buy and sell NFTs every day. They're popping up everywhere, with issuers vying for buyers' attention. When Coinbase created its NFT platform in 2021, more than 900,000 people signed up—on the first day.

The National Basketball Association has become one of the most successful issuers of NFTs, with virtual trading cards called NBA Top Shots. These are collectible cards, much like the baseball cards traded by kids for generations—except that these new cards exist only on the internet. The NBA initially created 2,500 packs priced at $999, with 10 cards per pack. The packs were offered on a blockchain and sold out in minutes. Today, you can buy, sell, and trade the cards on the Top Shot website. NBA Top Shot has had $700 million in sales in less than a year; a quarter of a million people log on to the site every day. And Dapper Labs, the firm that built Top Shot for the NBA, is valued at $7.6 billion.

Although a LeBron James NFT sold for $300,000, it's not the exclusive domain of rich people; there have been three million trades of less than $50 each. It's so popular that the NBA has also launched cards

for the WNBA, and Major League Baseball and the National Football League have followed suit, along with European soccer clubs.

Why would anyone want to buy trading cards that exist only in digital form? Lots of reasons. Because the cards are digital, they can feature video as well as photos. They aren't restricted to the small three-by-four-inch size of physical trading cards—allowing them to offer far more content, including hyperlinks to other sites. They can't be lost, damaged, or stolen. And ownership of NFTs can come with rights and benefits to buyers that physical cards may not have—such as first rights to other products, including game tickets, or special access to the athletes. And because the cards trade exclusively on a blockchain, traders know exactly who prior owners were because the complete history is viewable. This publicly available provenance can boost a card's value (just as a house can be worth more if it was once owned by a celebrity).

Best of all, traders know that the cards they're buying are authentic and not fake, thanks to the immutability of blockchain technology.

Fake sports memorabilia is a huge problem; the FBI says 50% of all sports memorabilia on the market is fraudulent, and Chubb, the giant insurance company, says other experts put the figure closer to 80%. But NFTs can't be duplicated or forged.

A famous early example of NFTs is CryptoKitties. These aren't real cats; they exist digitally, trading on the Ethereum blockchain. There have been three million transactions of CryptoKitties, totaling $39 million; the highest price ever paid for one is $120,000. Another outfit is called the Bored Ape Yacht Club.* Ten thousand unique digital apes, each an NFT. The average ape sold for $3,600 in July 2021, up almost 1,600% from the launch just three months earlier. More than $60 million has been invested, sorry, wrong word, *spent* on these NFTs.

Everybody, it seems, is creating NFTs, including Katy Perry, Rob Gronkowski, Floyd Mayweather, Porsche, Mattel, the *New York Times*, McLaren, and Jay-Z. Visa launched an NFT program to help artists join the digital art space. The Associated Press issued NFTs called "Unique Moments"—digitized photos and newswires based on AP's reporting on historical moments of the last century, including Japan's World War II surrender, Nelson Mandela's inauguration, and the discovery of Pluto. Film director Quentin Tarantino auctioned seven NFTs, each featuring an uncut scene from *Pulp Fiction*. Mark Cuban's Dallas Mavericks gave NFTs as rewards to fans who attended home games. The *Economist* published an issue featuring crypto on the cover—then sold an NFT of it for $420,000. The Rolling Stones sells tokenized versions of their music, bundling virtual and real-world merchandise. McDonald's conducted a sweepstakes giveaway of McRib-themed NFTs. State Farm rolled out an augmented-reality treasure hunt, letting consumers find NFTs. Campbell's, Pizza Hut, Taco Bell, Clinique, American Eagle, Charmin, and Pringles all hosted NFT-related promotions in 2021.

James Allison, a professor who, while at Berkeley, won the Nobel Prize for his work on cancer immunotherapy, digitized his research pa-

---

* Ya gotta love these names.

pers and turned them all into digital art, then sold the work as an NFT—the scientific equivalent of digitizing Mickey Mantle's rookie baseball card. Berkeley did the same for Jennifer Doudna, another of Berkeley's Nobel winners (for CRISPR technology). Sir Tim Berners-Lee invented the World Wide Web in 1989. He wrote the code but never patented his work. So, he converted the code into an NFT, and the auction house Sotheby's sold it for $5.4 million.

The New York Times

USA Today

The Economist

It's not just people and companies who are into NFTs. So are charities. NFT for Good raised $80,000 for antiracism causes by selling NFTs. Noora Health auctioned an NFT for $5 million. Alex's Lemonade Stand sold NFTs of artwork drawn by children with cancer. Merriam-Webster auctioned the definition of *NFT* and donated the proceeds to Teach For All. Macy's sold 9,500 NFTs of classic balloons during its 2021 Thanksgiving Day Parade—NFTs based on classic parade balloons, benefiting the Make-A-Wish Foundation. The World Wildlife Fund launched a "Non-Fungible Animals" series of NFTs, while StreetCode Academy auctioned "pNFTS" (philanthropic NFTs) to help minorities join the tech economy. Gannett, which owns *USA Today*, raised money for the Air Force Space and Missile Museum Foundation by selling an NFT of the newspaper Alan Shepard delivered to the moon. Leukemia and Lymphoma Society, Save the Children, the Fred Hutchinson Cancer Research Center, and other charities all sell NFTs as fundraising activities. MLB, NHL, and NFL all conduct NFT auctions for charity.

People are now even buying and selling furniture, houses, and land that exist only as NFTs. SuperWorld mapped the planet and divided it into 64 billion plots, each 300 feet by 300 feet. You can buy any plot—the Eiffel Tower, Roman Colosseum, Empire State Building, your childhood home, you name it. If the plot is unclaimed, you pay 0.1 Ether (about $400 at this writing). If someone already bought the plot you want, you can buy it from them; you simply negotiate the price as people do in any market. Once you own a plot, you can sell it to others anytime, just as you can sell any asset you own.

Want to learn how to do this? Online games will teach you. Axie Infinity is a play-to-earn game. As you breed, battle, and trade digital pets called Axies, you earn NFTs and other rewards, and use your assets to buy virtual plots of land within the game. (One plot sold in December 2021 for $2.5 million.)

It's so easy to create NFTs that even a kid can do it. Ahmed, a 12-year-old coder who lives with his parents in London, created his own NFT collection called Weird Whales during the summer of 2021. His parents provided the $300 he needed to upload his NFTs onto a blockchain—and the entire collection sold out in nine hours. Ahmed has earned $5 million so far from both sales and resales (he earns a 2.5% royalty on every secondary sale). As of this writing, Ahmed is developing more NFT projects—and still doesn't have a bank account. Just a crypto wallet.

Electronic gamers are also engaged in NFT activity. And why not? Worldwide, people spend $160 billion a year to play (see sidebar). But that money is gone once you stop playing the game. Until now, that is. Burberry has made 100,000 NFTs of its clothing; players can buy the clothes and dress their avatar. And instead of these being worthless trinkets in the game, you own your Burberry NFT. Meaning, you can take it with you and wear it in other games. You can also sell it when you get tired of it.

Mythical Games is also making and selling NFT clothing for gamers. You can create your own clothes to use or sell. Mythical Games raised $120 million from investors, but you don't need massive capital to get started. It costs less than $1,000 to create an NFT, and some sites let you do it for free.

And instead of *spending* money to play, many gamers are *earning* it. Led by Axie Infinity, a battle-simulator game, gamers vie to earn Smooth Love Potion (the game's token). Substantial incomes can be earned. The game is particularly popular in the Philippines, where some people generate their sole income by playing the game. Other popular play-to-earn video games include:

- **CryptoBlades:** a role-playing game on the Binance Smart Chain where you can earn SKILL tokens by defeating enemies and conducting raids.

- **Cometh:** gamers explore the galaxy and mine tokens from asteroids.

- **Plant vs. Undead:** gamers earn PVU tokens by watering the virtual plants on other players' digital farms. They use tokens to buy real seeds and plants.

- **Zed Run:** gamers breed virtual racehorses using bloodlines and ancestry to create horses of various colors, strengths, and speeds. Good breeders can win thousands of dollars in prizes by racing their e-horses on digital racetracks.

Nearly 3 billion people worldwide spend $160 billion a year playing e-games online. They spend it on acquisition and subscription fees, avatars (digital versions of themselves to use while playing games), costumes and cosmetics, (because, after all, your avatar has to look good!), hints, weapons, and skill tools (to improve your gaming performance). 7 in 10 gamers pay for these purchases with credit and debit cards; only 3.2% pay with bitcoin or other digital assets. The growth potential for digital assets is therefore enormous—as is the threat to credit card companies.

Not Just a Silly Game

If this is all still sounding a little silly to you, that's because we've only talked about art, baseball cards, and video games. None of that *really* matters, does it?

Fair enough. So, let's try this: Soon, you'll be able to convert your passport into an NFT backed by blockchain technology. You won't have to carry the physical paper with you. Your passport is unique, and thanks to the blockchain, it is authenticated, can't be duplicated, copied, or erased.

Or, airports, airlines, and sporting events can issue NFTs as digital keepsakes. Instead of buying a T-shirt at a concert, you buy an NFT.

Or, Live Nation, the world's largest music event organizer, now sells concert tickets in the form of NFTs.

Or, the New York City restaurant Quality Eats created a cocktail in 2021 and an NFT of the secret recipe. It sold at auction for about $2,000. In addition to owning the recipe, the buyer gets a free drink on every visit to the restaurant. It's a smart business move—the restaurant gets two grand in cash up front and brings in a frequent diner who brags to friends about owning the recipe. The meal they purchase

Quality Eats

"I don't care how much I own—there's still something unsatisfying about digital Girl Scout Thin Mints."

each time upon coming in for a free drink costs a lot more than the cost of a free drink. Everyone wins.

Or, Masterworks buys art painted by Warhol, Banksy, Monet, and others. The company then tokenizes the paintings and sells the tokens. For the first time, millions of retail investors can own a piece of rare paintings.

In the digital world, everything can be tokenized, monetized, and democratized. The only requirement for participation is possession of a cell phone connected to the internet. No wonder the NFT market is exploding: in the third quarter of 2021, NFT trading volume hit $10.7 billion, a 700% increase from the prior three months. Morgan Stanley says the NFT market will be a $300 billion business by 2030, helping luxury brands increase their profits by 25%. All this explains why, according to *Economist*, venture capitalists invested $20 billion in blockchain and digital asset companies in 2021, seven times more than they did in 2020.

All this excitement is increasingly due to the *metaverse*. That's a broad term referring to virtual reality, a term that itself essentially means "video game." Players create an avatar, buy land, tools, skills, knowledge, and NFTs, and trade their possessions with other gamers. The metaverse is interconnected, with 3D virtual worlds operating 24/7 worldwide. It's a self-contained internet economy that encompasses both the digital and physical worlds.

And the metaverse economy is huge. Grayscale says it will generate $400 billion in annual revenue by 2025, and ultimately be a $1 trillion market. Now you're beginning to understand why Mark Zuckerberg changed his company's name from Facebook to Meta Platforms.

Want to buy some NFTs, perhaps to trade in the metaverse? Evaluate them like you would anything else you'd buy.

Simple Agreement for Future Tokens

Venture capitalists investing in decentralized projects (chapter 10) often buy equity of the enterprise by acquiring SAFTs—*simple agreements for future tokens*. The SAFT is a contract: the company promises to give the VC tokens in the future, should the tokens ever be issued. This is new, with many legal and tax questions unresolved—and thus at this writing, it's not yet a vehicle ready for use by everyday investors.

Chapter 10
Decentralized Finance, aka DeFi

When we talked about NFTs, we quickly realized that we couldn't understand non-fungible tokens until we first understood fungible ones.

Likewise with DeFi, or *decentralized finance*. To understand it, we must first understand what *centralized finance* is. The good news is that you already do: The financial services you use every day are provided by centralized companies—banks, brokerage firms, and stock exchanges. They have physical locations, lots of employees, and shareholders who own them. The company chooses whether to grant you permission to let you participate. You can't trade stocks unless the brokerage firm agrees to open an account for you; you can't open a bank account without the bank's approval.

Centralized companies thus have substantial power. But DeFi eliminates them—and their power. Amazing but true: banks, brokerages, and exchanges are no longer required. Everybody everywhere gets to engage without needing anyone's permission.

This is revolutionary.

The world of decentralized finance provides you with everything offered by traditional financial services companies—borrowing and lending, asset management, investment and insurance products. Everything is provided via *smart contracts* (which we learned about in chapter 2) on a blockchain.

To use a decentralized application, you obtain a hot wallet, such as one provided by MetaMask. Place a digital asset into it, such as Ether. That's it. You're ready to use any decentralized application. No log in. No username. No password. Nobody's permission required.

MetaMask

So, instead of buying stocks via a brokerage firm connected to the New York Stock Exchange (two centralized companies!) you go to a DEX—a *decentralized exchange*. The largest is Uniswap, which has processed more than $400 billion in transactions since its founding in 2018; each day it processes more than $350 million in trades. NYSE has more than 3,000 employees; Uniswap has 37. The NYSE was founded in 1792; Uniswap was founded by Hayden Adams in 2018, two years after he graduated college. Mind-blowing, huh?

Uniswap

NYSE*

Already, DeFi platforms hold more than $240 billion across multiple blockchains, according to tracking service DefiLlama, and venture capital and private equity firms have invested more than $70 billion in DeFi start-ups, according to DeFi Pulse.

But it's all still new, and thus risky to use. DeFi operates outside any regulatory framework—no SEC, CFTC, or FDIC to protect you. If there's a bug in the smart contract, the function might fail or execute erroneously—causing you financial loss. Gas fees (covered in chapter 5) can be $100 or more per transaction. And you can never be certain who's behind the curtain; the protocol PolyGaj, for example, manages $7 million; it was created by Gajesh Naik. He's 13 years old.

So before engaging, make sure you understand the technology— and the people behind the platforms you're planning to use.

Oracles

An *oracle* is software code that connects the digital world with the real, physical world. For example, what is the price of IBM stock right now? The New York Stock Exchange can tell you because that's where IBM trades. But blockchains have no idea. That's where oracles come in.

Oracles bring data from the physical world (called off-chain) onto a digital blockchain (on-chain). There are thousands of uses for oracles—

---

* I have equity in ICE, the parent company of the NYSE, and Bakkt, a digital exchange once owned by ICE.

"Didn't I just give you money for a start-up last week?"

supply chains and the movement of goods, the weather, the number of users in a particular ecosystem, political trends, legal agreements, and more. All that data can be brought into the digital world.

There are also *outbound oracles*. They tell a real entity outside a blockchain about an event that occurred on-chain, such as the total amount of money lent by a particular app, network, or protocol.

At this writing, Chainlink is the largest provider of blockchain oracles.

Chapter 11
Valuation and Pricing of Bitcoin and Other Digital Assets

It's the most common question I get, and understandably so: What is the value of bitcoin? It's essential that you know the answer so you can decide the potential for it to increase.

There's a problem with this question, however. Not with the question per se, but with the person asking it. You see, the question "What is the value of bitcoin?" mostly comes from critics who "demand to know" the value of bitcoin—because they have already decided that the answer is zero. These people huff and puff that bitcoin has no intrinsic value, no expected return (according to theories expounded by their economics professors), no utility, interest, dividends, or use. "*Humph,*" these people say to me, "bitcoin has no value!"

I never argue with them. It'd be pointless since troglodytes (like a certain investment manager I know) can't be reasoned with. Instead, I reply, "Bitcoin might not have any value. But it has one helluva price."

So-called experts have been telling me that bitcoin has no value ever since the word *bitcoin* entered their thick skulls. They said it had no value when it was selling for a few hundred dollars (its price when I first encountered it). They said it had no value when it rose to $20,000. They said it had no value when it fell 84% but was still priced at $3,000. They said it had no value when the price reached $60,000. And they still say today that it has no value.

Fine. It has no value. But its price has risen 87,000,000% since its inception. Bitcoin is the most profitable asset in history. So those ivory-tower, graduate-degreed money managers should abandon their hubris, lest history associate them with "experts" who said the Earth is flat.

Jamie Dimon, CEO of JPMorgan Chase, Hates Bitcoin

$812 — January 2014   Jamie said bitcoin is a "terrible store of value."

$400 — November 2015   Jamie said, "Bitcoin is going to be stopped."

$3,900 — September 2017   Jamie said, "Bitcoin is a fraud. It isn't going to work."

$3,900 — September 2017   Jamie said, "It'll eventually blow up. It's a fraud, okay?" — while threatening to fire his firm's traders who bought bitcoin.

$5,600 — October 2017   Jamie said, "If you're stupid enough to buy it, you'll pay the price one day."

$6,300 — October 2018   Jamie said, I don't really give a sh*t — that's the point, okay?"

$53,300 — May 2021   Jamie said, "I'm not a bitcoin supporter. . . . I don't care about bitcoin. I have no interest in it."

$54,800 — October 2021   Jamie said, "Bitcoin has no intrinsic value. I think it's a little bit of fool's gold."

$57,500 — October 2021   Jamie said bitcoin is "worthless." "My own personal advice to people is, stay away from it."

Jamie Dimon and Warren Buffett hate bitcoin. But not everyone in their ranks share such views. For example, James Gorman, CEO of Morgan Stanley, said in October 2021, "I don't think crypto's a fad, I don't think it's going away. . . . The blockchain technology supporting it is obviously very real and powerful."

So, you'll have to decide whom you want to listen to. For me, I choose to ignore people who say they "don't really give a sh*t" and who admit

Warren Buffett Hates Bitcoin

$450—March 2014	Warren said, "It's a mirage basically. The idea that it has some huge intrinsic value is just a joke in my view. I wouldn't be surprised if it's not around in ten or twenty years. It's not a store of value. It's been a very speculative kind of Buck Rogers–type thing."
$9,900—January 2018	Warren said, "We don't own any. We'll never have a position in them. Why in the world should I take a position in something I don't know anything about?" ,
$7,300—May 2018	Warren said, "Probably rat poison squared."
$6,900—August 2018	Warren said, "It will feed on itself for a while. It draws in a lot of charlatans. It will come to a bad ending."
$3,700—February 2019	Warren said, "Bitcoin has no unique value at all. It's a delusion basically."
$8,800—February 2020	Warren said, "Cryptocurrencies basically have no value and they don't produce anything. In terms of value: zero. Bitcoin has been used to move around a fair amount of money illegally. I don't have any bitcoin. I never will."

"I don't know anything about [it]." I find it more helpful to accept that the marketplace has indeed assigned a price for bitcoin and all other digital assets—even Jamie Dimon and Warren Buffett agree it has!—and therefore focus on the question that really matters: What will the future price be? After all, as with any investment, knowing whether the price will rise or fall would sure be helpful information!

Traditional money managers and investment analysts often contend that bitcoin is worthless by showing that their valuation techniques say so. Indeed, they often display their research to prove their point. The problem is that the methodologies they're using—the tried-and-true, well-established metrics applied to a variety of traditional asset classes (such as stocks, bonds, and real estate)—don't work when evaluating digital assets. That's because digital assets lack the inputs that other asset classes have. That's not a flaw of digital assets; what's flawed is the belief that the absence of those inputs must mean that bitcoin has no value.

Investment academics and practitioners routinely use three techniques to determine an asset's value. Let's look at them, and you'll see why it doesn't make any sense to apply them to digital assets.

Cost Approach

This technique basically states that the price of an asset should be equal to the costs incurred to build, replace, or procure it. That figure was fairly easy to estimate during bitcoin's early days when Laszlo's pizza purchase set bitcoin's price at seven one-hundredths of a penny.

An early bitcoin-related website looked at the amount of money needed to rent a computer to mine bitcoin and pay for the electricity to power it, then compared that cost to the amount of bitcoin you got from mining. That seems to make more sense, and it works when you're trying to figure out the proper price of Coca-Cola. But bitcoin isn't a product, and you're not trying to ascertain the price of the coin. What you want to identify is the cost of the entire network, and this "cost of mining" approach ignores the value of the Bitcoin ecosystem and its network. That's a pretty big omission, which is why it leads to a wildly errant (and low) valuation.

Market Approach

This approach values assets by comparing transactions to others with similar characteristics, adjusted for different quantities, qualities, or sizes. The Public Company Comparables Method compares data of similar publicly traded companies. This is obviously not helpful with digital assets, since none of them are public companies; they have no employees, headquarters, products, or sales.

The Precedent Transactions Method looks at companies that have been sold in a given industry and uses their *multiples* as the basis for setting a price for the company being valued. For example, say a hotel company has $10 billion in profits, and it is sold for $50 billion. That's a 5x multiple. So, if your hotel has $3 billion in profits, you should be willing to sell it for about $15 billion, using the same multiple.

The problem is that bitcoin isn't a company and doesn't have revenues or profits; there's nothing to base a valuation on, rendering this approach moot. But instead of realizing that, many market analysts insist that this proves that bitcoin has no value.

Discounted Cash Flow

This is an effective tool when you know or can make reasonable assumptions about future cash flows, discount rates, and terminal value, but it isn't reliable for assets that don't generate cash flows—like bitcoin.

As you can see, these techniques don't provide accurate information when applied to digital assets. Despite that, many financial analysts and investment managers persist in using them. So, when the techniques fail to produce valid data, they simply say, "Bitcoin has no value," instead of saying, "We need a better valuation method."

The latter is what participants in the digital asset field have done. They've developed or applied other approaches to help them determine the proper price of bitcoin and other digital assets. Each approach is worthy of a college-level course, so I'll just provide short summaries here (partly to introduce you to the concepts, and partly to avoid boring you to death).

Market Substitute and Utility Value

Satoshi's intent in creating bitcoin was clear: it was to be an independent peer-to-peer payment system. In other words, bitcoin was designed to be money. If that is its sole utility, then its entire value must be based on that function. Some believe the value of bitcoin can thus be compared to other "store of value" assets that it would theoretically replace, such as gold.

If bitcoin were to be an alternative to gold, its price would have to be set at a level comparable to gold's. So, let's do that and see what answer we get.

The World Gold Council estimates that 190 million metric tons of gold have been mined throughout history (and are still accounted for). Assuming a price of $2,000 per ounce, the total value of the world's gold is $13.4 trillion.

That must therefore also be the value of all the world's bitcoin, this theory goes. Since a total of 21 million bitcoin will ever be mined, the price of each bitcoin—if it's priced comparably to gold—should be $639,000.

But wait. We know that only 18.5 million bitcoins have been mined so far, and about four million of them are considered lost. That leaves 14.5 million bitcoins—meaning the actual price of each existing bitcoin should be $926,000.

Remind me, what's the actual price of bitcoin today?

As you can see, the *market substitute and utility value* approach suggests that the price of digital assets will rise dramatically as investors realize that current prices are below actual values.

The Velocity of Money

You've got a dollar bill under the mattress. How fast is it moving?

Well, duh, it's not moving at all. It's just lying there, under your bed. Zero velocity. But say you hand that dollar to a merchant in payment for a product. The merchant hands the dollar to a wholesaler, to buy

"Ya know, 'DUH' can be a very hurtful word!"

more goods. The wholesaler gives the dollar to the manufacturer to buy more products, and the manufacturer uses the dollar to buy raw materials from a supplier.

The movement of money through an economic system is referred to as the *velocity of money*. As the number of transactions in a given period rises, the velocity of money increases—and the higher the velocity, the faster the economy is growing.

Apply this to bitcoin buyers. Are they using bitcoin to buy and sell goods and services? Or are they acting as HODLers? Under this theory, if you believe bitcoin's use as a financial transaction tool will rise over time, you're arguing for an increase in its price.

Network Value

This valuation approach is based on Metcalfe's Law, which states that the value of a network grows exponentially as the network adds users. The theory was conceived by economist George Gilder in 1993, but it was internet pioneer Robert Metcalfe (coinventor of Ethernet and co-founder of 3Com) who applied it to the users, rather than the devices, of a communications network.

Metcalf's Law holds that a network's value is proportional to the square of the number of the network's connected users. In simple terms, Facebook is worth a lot of money because it has a lot of users, and as the number of users rises, Facebook's value grows not linearly, but exponentially.

Remember, Bitcoin is a network. So, it's not surprising that those trying to value bitcoin have applied Metcalfe's Law to its price. The Network Value to Metcalf ratio, or NVM, divides the market capitalization of a digital asset by the number of active addresses squared.

Many regard this technique as more useful to compare one digital asset to another (or to itself over different time periods) than as a tool to identify a digital asset's intrinsic price. Furthermore, the ratio does not take into consideration each user's geography, frequency of activity, throughput, or other factors. For these reasons, I've yet to meet anyone who relies solely on this method. Instead, it's considered alongside other metrics.

NVT Ratio

Some bitcoin analysts look to the Network Value to Transactions ratio. This measures the value of a digital asset's network and the total dollar value of all the circulating units of the asset, to its value as a payment network (which is measured by the dollar value of the transactions settled on the asset's blockchain).

The NVT ratio helps signal how much the market is willing to pay for the transactional utility of a blockchain.

Stock-to-Flow Ratio

This metric is used to quantify the scarcity of an asset. The ratio is calculated by dividing the existing supply by the annual production growth.

Speculative Value

Valuation here is based on the hope that future investors will pay more for the digital asset than you're paying today. It's all a matter of supply and demand, this says.

––––––

That's six valuation approaches devised or deployed by the digital assets field. And there are plenty more.

Woobull.com offers this extensive list:

- **Bitcoin Price Models.** Various price models for bitcoin.
- **Bitcoin NVT Ratio.** Bitcoin's P/E ratio. Detects when bitcoin is overvalued or undervalued.
- **Bitcoin NVT Price.** Bitcoin's NVT price, useful to see the price supported by organic investment.
- **Bitcoin NVT Signal.** NVT ratio optimized to be more responsive, useful as a long-range trading indicator.
- **Bitcoin VWAP Ratio.** A useful signal for local and global market tops and bottoms using Volume Weighted Average Price.
- **Bitcoin MVRV Ratio.** A bitcoin under/overvaluation indicator based on realized cap.
- **Bitcoin RVT Ratio.** A volume-based variation of MVRV used to determine market tops and bottoms.
- **Bitcoin Mayer Multiple.** Trace Mayer's ratio to measure bitcoin price in relation to its historical movement.
- **Bitcoin Difficulty Ribbon.** A view into miner capitulation; typically signals times when buying is sensible.
- **Bitcoin Risk-Adjusted Returns.** Compares bitcoin ROI, adjusted for its risk, to that of other assets.

- **Bitcoin Volatility vs. Other Asset Classes.** Compares bitcoin volatility to that of other asset classes.

- **Bitcoin Growth vs. Other Asset Classes.** Compares bitcoin growth to that of other asset classes.

- **Bitcoin Held in ETFs and Corporate Treasuries.** Tracks bitcoin held in publicly accessible entities via shareholding.

- **Bitcoin Valuation Gain per Dollar Invested.** Dollar for dollar, how much bitcoin's price increases per dollar invested.

- **Bitcoin Network Volume.** The monthly volume of bitcoin moving between different investors on the network.

- **Bitcoin vs. Gold.** Compares the investment performance of bitcoin versus gold.

- **Bitcoin Volatility Trend.** This compares to FOREX; also traded volume.

- **Bitcoin Money Supply vs. USD.** Is bitcoin trending toward a world reserve currency?

- **Bitcoin Inflation Rate.** Track the historical annual inflation rate of bitcoin's money supply.

- **Bitcoin Monetary Velocity.** Is bitcoin trending toward payments or savings/investments?

- **Bitcoin Volume vs. Network Value.** Volume transmitted by bitcoin's blockchain tracks its network value closely.

- **Bitcoin SegWit Adoption.** Tracks the adoption of SegWit.

- **Bitcoin Network Throughput.** Bitcoin's throughput in transactions, payments, and USD value per second.

- **Bitcoin Congestion.** User-centric metrics tracking network congestion, e.g., payment fees, confirm times.

- **Bitcoin Hash Price.** Price per hash tracks the bitcoin's mining hardware capabilities over time.

- **Bitcoin Outputs per Tx.** Tracks how many outputs are packed into each bitcoin transaction.

I'm sure you're relieved that I'm not delving into the details of any of these. If you're interested in learning more about them, visit woobull .com. My point in listing them is to illustrate that smart and serious market participants—many of them current or former Wall Streeters—are working hard to determine bitcoin's price. To suggest that bitcoin has no value merely because a couple of other methods, created for unrelated asset classes, don't reveal a valid price doesn't mean there is no price.

The conclusion you should reach from this content is that while assertions might be correct that bitcoin has no intrinsic value, it certainly has a price.

PART THREE

Investing in Digital Assets

Chapter 12
Is It Too Late to Buy Bitcoin?

Bitcoin's price since inception is up 87,000,000%. It's impossible for that gain to recur. But, massive increases are still quite possible—especially when you compare the potential returns to those of other asset classes, which typically fall in the single digits or low double digits annually.

So, it's not the past that we should focus on, but the future. What might be the future price of bitcoin and other digital assets?

Many are predicting further massive growth, arguing that this emerging asset class is still in its early stages. Billionaire hedge fund manager Steve Cohen says, "While the [digital asset] market is now a $2 trillion asset class, we are still in the early stages of institutional adoption." Former Prudential Securities Chair George Ball calls digital assets "very attractive" and predicts "many people will be investing in this asset class." BlackRock CIO of Fixed Income Rick Rieder says bitcoin could rival gold as a primary store of value. His boss, BlackRock CEO Larry Fink, says, "Bitcoin is here to stay." And Niall Ferguson, professor of economic history at Stanford, says the best investment opportunity postpandemic is bitcoin.

JPMorgan strategists led by Nikolaos Panigirtzoglou say bitcoin could rise to $140,000. Tiburon Strategic Advisors predicts $150,000. Tom Fitzpatrick, global head of Citibank Technicals, says bitcoin will rise to $318,000. Guggenheim says it will reach $400,000. ARK Invest says $500,000. Forex Suggest says bitcoin will be $1 million by 2025. And Jurrien Timmer, Fidelity Investments' Director of Global Macro, says bitcoin's price will be $1 million by 2030 and $1 billion by 2038. (That's not a typo. One. Billion. Dollars.)

Small wonder that the Association of Governing Boards of Universities and Colleges says digital assets have "already produced hundreds of millionaires, a number of billionaires and may produce the world's first trillionaires within the next decade." The organization is enthused because those new 'aires will be asked to make large donations to university endowments.

Tiburon

In 2018, Inigo Fraser Jenkins bashed bitcoin. That was noteworthy because he's cohead of portfolio strategy for AllianceBernstein, a global investment manager with $631 billion in assets under management. But in 2021, in a research paper distributed to the firm's clients, Fraser Jenkins wrote, "I have changed my mind about bitcoin's role in asset allocation." His decision was spurred by a variety of developments, including the pandemic, changes in government policy, federal debt levels, and new diversification options for investors in the digital asset ecosystem. Bitcoin does have a role in asset allocation, he now says.

Much of the enthusiasm for bitcoin is due to the law of supply and demand. Sand is cheap because there's so much and few want it. Diamonds are expensive because they are rare but desired by many.

Bitcoin has scarcity, too, and as demand for it grows, so will its price. Consider this: There are 47 million millionaires in the world. If they all wanted to buy just one bitcoin, they wouldn't be able to. That's because only about 14 million bitcoin are thought to exist at present, and no more than 21 million ever will. If every millionaire starts clamoring with the others to buy bitcoin, the price will have to rise—perhaps significantly.

And what about everyday Americans? How many of them want bitcoin? In 2009, the answer was "nobody." By 2021, 24% of Americans owned bitcoin, and it's projected that by 2029, 90% will own it. What do you suppose might happen to the price of an asset when its supply is fixed but demand increases 530%?

It's early even among financial advisors. So far, only 14% of them have added bitcoin to client portfolios, according to *Financial Advisor*

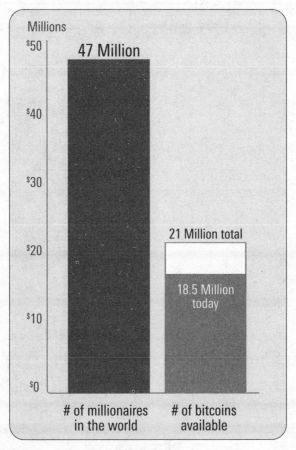

FIGURE 12.1

magazine—but another 26% say they plan to start, tripling the rate of engagement. If true, then one in two advisors will be recommending bitcoin and other digital assets by the end of 2022. Advisors control $8 trillion in investor assets, says Tiburon Strategic Advisors; if all those advisors place just 1% of client assets into bitcoin, $80 billion will flood into the market, an amount equal to 8% of bitcoin's market cap at this writing. If a sudden 8% increase in demand occurred for tickets to a concert, what do you suppose would happen to the price of those tickets?

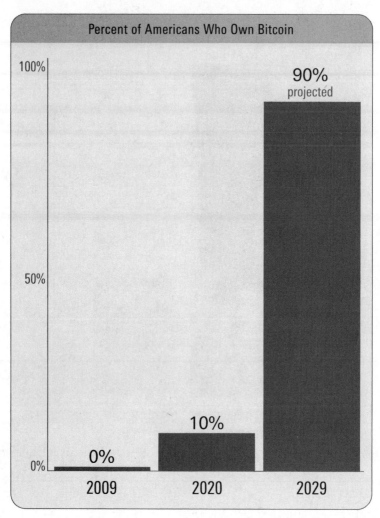

Source: Skybridge Capital

FIGURE 12.2

That's nothing. Surveys in 2021 by Ernst & Young and Intertrust found that 31% of hedge fund managers say they will add digital assets to their portfolios by 2023, investing an average 7.2% of their portfolios by 2025. Intertrust's survey suggests inflows of $312 billion, a surge equal to more than a third of bitcoin's total value at this writing.

It is too late? Hardly.

The financial advisors and wealth managers who recommend digital assets to clients are smart: they're going to share in the fee revenue generated by managing these assets. How much in fees? A total of $4.6 billion over the next 5 years, according to Broadridge Financial Solutions.

Chapter 13
The Risks of Investing in Digital Assets

Although many are enthused about the future prospects for bitcoin and other digital assets, we must admit that this is still an emerging asset class. No one knows what will happen—which means we must seriously consider the possibility that we could experience a massive and permanent market crash in the prices of digital assets.

Therefore, we must closely examine the risks of investing in this asset class. You must do that with any investment opportunity; we must always ask ourselves what we expect the return will be on our money and whether we will ever get a return *of* our money.

So, let's explore the reasons why prices of digital assets might fall . . . all the way to zero.

Market Manipulation

This risk applies to every asset class. Pump-and-dump schemes, front-running, and insider trading are common problems in the investment world, and digital assets are not immune. Worse, many digital assets are not securities in the view of the SEC. Therefore, also, behavior that would violate securities regulations occurs in the digital assets world.

Business and Commercial Failure

Digital assets don't materialize on their own; they are invented by entrepreneurs. An idea might be great, but turning it into a successful business that operates efficiently, profitably, and at scale is another matter entirely. You might be investing in something that fails in the marketplace.

Technological Obsolescence

Remember the Sony Betamax? It was crushed in the marketplace by VHS video recorders—which were themselves destroyed by Netflix. Lotus 1-2-3 was overtaken by Microsoft Excel. Encyclopaedia Britannica was outdone by Wikipedia. The great innovation of today that is disrupting the marketplace could be rendered worthless by the next great innovation—destroying the price of your investment.

Netflix

Microsoft

Wikipedia

Sony

Consumer/Investor Demand

Beware of Kevin Costner Syndrome—the belief that "if you build it, they will come." That only happens in the movies. In real life, it takes a lot more than faith to build a successful company. Just because you open a store doesn't mean people will visit it—or buy anything when they do.

Consider how many ads you see every day. Companies try hard to get your attention, and the most successful ones don't necessarily offer the best products; often, they simply have the best marketing.

Will the digital asset you're buying gain traction because it solves a business or consumer problem? Or will it be ignored or quickly forgotten?

Regulatory Intervention

The digital assets field continues to be controversial. Some governments have banned them entirely. Others ban certain practices. Others limit who can buy and what they can buy.

Reflecting the rapid evolution of this space, many governments frequently change their minds—creating havoc for the crypto community. You must acknowledge that the federal or state government could outlaw your investment or impose onerous taxes or reporting requirements. All these actions could have an adverse impact on the price of your investment.

51% Attack

A local bank branch is a tempting target for bank robbers because so much money is in the vault. That's the risk of centralized systems—and it explains why so many companies have been hacked: the location of each company's network is known and can thus be targeted.

But blockchains are decentralized; it's like a bank having each dollar bill scattered in vaults all over the world. How could a hacker track them all down and steal them? Impossible.

That's a key reason why members of the crypto community are so confident about their activities: blockchains are unhackable. Indeed, in Bitcoin's entire history, it's never been hacked.

It's not impossible, though. There is one way a hacker could do it. It's called a 51% Attack. To take control of a blockchain and steal its data (and assets), a hacker would have to control the majority of the network's nodes.*

With millions of nodes scattered around the world, it's "considered" impossible for the bitcoin network to be hacked. Perhaps we ought to say "damn near impossible" or "virtually impossible" or "hell, instead of worrying about a 51% attack, find something else to be worried about."

There's a reason for such dismissiveness: the Bitcoin network is so large—with more than 11,500 nodes worldwide, according to the site Bitnodes.io—that it would cost $5.5 billion in hardware alone for

---

* Although a majority is technically 50.1% and not 51%, calling it a 50.1% attack is cumbersome, so we go with the (slightly inaccurate) shorthand. Cut us some slack, people.

a hacker to gain control of 51% of them, based on 2021 hash rates. A hacker with that much money probably doesn't need any more, though you do need to worry about rogue governments. (Many believe rogue governments such as North Korea love bitcoin because it lets them skirt the economic sanctions imposed by the United States and other nations. So maybe we ought to be more worried about the CIA conducting a 51% attack than Kim Jong Un.)

Anyway. Just because the Bitcoin network is considered "too big to hack" doesn't mean that's true of all blockchains. Indeed, some *have* been victims of 51% attacks—made possible because they're much smaller. BSV suffered a 51% attack on August 4, 2021. Earlier attacks hit Bitcoin Gold, Ethereum Classic, Verge, and others. In every case, coins were stolen before the attack was repelled, causing substantial losses for investors.

Bottom line: the smaller the network or the newer the coin or token, the greater the vulnerability to 51% attacks. Keep that in mind when deciding which digital assets to buy—and how much of your money to place into them.

Advances in Quantum Computing

Throughout this book—including in the above section—we've been taking a rather cavalier attitude about the impenetrability of bitcoin's private key. The keys are so long (256-bit numbers composed of letters and numerals) that there are 10^{77} possible permutations. It's simply impossible for any computer to crack the code, and that's why hackers instead go after that silly 4-digit PIN you use at the ATM.

According to stackexchange.com, it would take the world's fastest supercomputer 0.65 billion billion years* to crack a single bitcoin address. So, there's not much to worry about.

---

* No No that's that's not not a a typo typo. I really did mean 650,000,000,000,000,000 years. Just didn't want to have to type all those zeros. Now look what you've made me do.

Until quantum computing reaches the marketplace. It's the next major advance in computer science and widely expected to become commercial by 2030. How major an advancement? Say you wanted to find one piece of data from a database of one trillion items. It would take today's supercomputers 10,000 years to find the data you're seeking. A quantum computer could find it in 200 seconds. The implication, many cybersecurity experts fret, is that bitcoin's private keys will easily be hacked.

Should you worry? That's up to you, but I'm not concerned for two reasons. First, if these new machines will be able to hack the Bitcoin blockchain, blockchains would be the least of our worries. I'd fear instead the security of our nation's power grid, water systems, air traffic control—and our nuclear arsenal.

"These bitcoins things are backed by
technology and the internet!
What could possibly go wrong?"

Second, if hackers could use quantum computers to crack private keys (and our nukes), don't you think that bitcoin developers (and the Defense Department) will use quantum computers to create new cybersecurity systems that protect against such hacks? Let the bad guys build a 10-foot ladder. We'll build a 12-foot wall.

If I'm wrong, and quantum computing does destroy all digital security systems, well, game over. Nothing would be safe in that scenario—everything will be hacked, including your bank and brokerage accounts, pension fund, Social Security check, insurance policy, annuity, credit card, and more.

That's why I'm not worried. You might as well worry about asteroids hitting the planet. If it's gonna happen, it's gonna happen. And if it happens, there ain't nowhere to hide.

Don't avoid digital assets over this fear. Even if you're not hacked, everyone else will be—leaving you in the same dismal position as if you were also hacked. Find something else to worry about, and don't use this one as a reason not to invest.

Rogue Custodians

When's the last time you thought about air? It's probably been a while—because it's ever present and in vast quantity. You give this no thought because none is needed. Yet it's vital to your life.

That's what custody is to your financial life—a hugely important, integral part of your personal finances. So integral, so automatic, so certain, that you probably don't even realize you're completely dependent on it.

But it wasn't always this way. Today's custody structure is the result of fixing problems we've encountered for centuries—and only seriously dealt with in the past 90 years.

What is custody? It's the legal term for someone holding and being responsible for something that is someone else's. (If you die, who will get *custody* of your minor children? See—you know this term better than you thought.)

After we got past the barter era, people started receiving currency when selling products and services. As people became successful, they began amassing lots of currency—and that posed a problem. How do you keep it safe?

You could hide it under your mattress or bury it in the backyard— but it could be lost, stolen, or destroyed. You might simply forget where you put it, and if you died, your heirs wouldn't know where you stashed it. So, you put it in the bank, where it would earn interest and be safe.

Safe, that is, until Billy the Kid, Jesse James, Butch Cassidy, and other bandits of the 1870s and 1880s showed up. Banks suffered further robberies during the Great Depression, victims of John Dillinger, Bonnie & Clyde, Baby Face Nelson, Machine Gun Kelly, and other notorious outlaws. In every case, when robbers stole money from banks, they were stealing *your* money.

That caused many people to stop putting their money into banks. Without deposits, banks had little money to lend. Without funds to borrow, commerce couldn't grow, and the economy was stymied.

Eventually, Congress acted. It declared bank robbery a federal crime and granted the new Federal Bureau of Investigation the power to chase and arrest robbers regardless of which state they were in. Congress also created the Federal Deposit Insurance Corporation, insuring bank deposits to give consumers confidence that their money was safe, even if the bank itself wasn't.

Today, the Office of the Comptroller of the Currency, Federal Reserve, FDIC, CFPB, SEC, FTC, and other federal and state agencies all regulate banks—and conduct audits to make sure they are properly accounting for and safeguarding the money on deposit. Banks themselves engage in careful business practices, including extensive security systems (such as massive vaults) and internal audits to prevent and detect employee fraud.

Ditto for the securities industry. The SEC, FINRA, NYSE, CFTC, DOL, PBGC, and other regulators work hard to confirm that your cash and securities on deposit at brokerage firms, exchanges, and custodians are safeguarded. And SIPC insures your securities account much like FDIC insures bank accounts.

Today, the entire financial services industry does such a good job at custody that you give it no thought. You never even think about the risk that your custodian (the firm holding your account for you) might collapse or steal your assets. That's because there is indeed little risk. So instead of worrying about losing your money to custodial collapse or malfeasance, you merely need to worry about your investments collapsing due to market declines. (SIPC, for example, insures you against a firm's failure, not losses due to market crashes.)

Chapter 16 will show you how to choose a custodian. For now, be aware that when dealing with digital assets, your choice of custodian is as important as your investments.

Lost Passwords, Compromised Wallets, and Hijacked SIM Cards

You know the importance of cybersecurity and protecting your personal information. All those careful behaviors are especially important when dealing with digital assets because, by their very definition, everything you do with them occurs online—and therefore you are at constant risk of theft by cybercrooks. Safeguard your usernames, passwords, and PINs. Don't share, forget, or lose them. Watch out for thieves who use technology to illicitly access your wallets.

In particular, be aware of SIM card hijacking. Your SIM card is a removable memory chip in your smartphone. It stores information about you and connects your phone to your provider's network, so you can make phone calls and access the internet.

Thieves don't have to physically steal your phone to get your SIM card. Instead, all they need is your phone's PIN. If scammers have your PIN, they call your cell provider, pretend to be you, and convince them to change the SIM card linked to your phone number to a new SIM card and phone. That lets the crook take over your phone number—giving them access to all your online accounts, including the two-factor authentication codes you receive through text messages. That puts all your financial accounts at risk, including bank and brokerage accounts and, of course, your digital asset accounts and wallets.

Before you realize it—maybe you're in a meeting or asleep—the crooks access your email, social media, and financial accounts, change your passwords, and masquerade as you online.

So, is your PIN safe? Well, in August 2021, T-Mobile was hacked, exposing the Social Security numbers, driver's licenses—and, yes, PINs—of 50 million customers.

Fat-Fingered Trades

Ever hit the wrong key while typing? Of course you have. We all do it from time to time.* Usually, it's no big deal. But in the financial industry, there can be serious consequences. When Samsung was supposed to distribute $2.8 billion to employees as part of a profit-sharing plan, an employee accidentally ordered the distribution of 2.8 billion *shares*—more than the entire value of the company. More than $100 billion was sent out, causing the stock's price to fall significantly.

Fortunately, Wall Streeters are playing only with money, not people's hearts like cardiac surgeons do. So, in most cases, losses can be recovered. If you buy 100 shares when you intended to sell, you can often tell your broker to cancel the trade. If they can't (or won't), you can simply place an opposite trade to reverse the process. You might incur some commissions and suffer a bit of loss due to price fluctuations that occur while you're sorting everything out, but you're likely to get back most of your money.†

---

* Every few seconds, in my case. I'm an incredibly fast typist—more than 100 words a minute (top 1%)—but when you adjust for my typos, my speed falls to under 40, or below average. Took me four minutes to finish this footnote.

† If you're lucky, the market will move in your favor, and you'll actually profit from the error. That happened in France, when in 2018 a trader who thought he was practicing on a test platform entered real trades and made $11.6 million.

There's also insurance available to restore losses. Finally, government agencies, such as FDIC, SIPC, and PBGC, are there to protect savers, investors, and pensioners.

But none of that will help when you fat-finger a public key. Say you own both bitcoin and Ether, and you want to move the coins from wallets at one exchange to another. You must move your bitcoin from one bitcoin wallet to another. If you mistakenly send your bitcoin to your Ether wallet, either by mistyping the public key or coding the key into the wrong wallet, Your. Bitcoin. Will. Be. Lost. Forever. As in, Gone. Irrevocably. Irretrievably. Undoably.

When you trade or send crypto, t...y...p...e v...e...r...y
s...l...o...w...l...y a...n...d c...a...r...e...f...u...l...l...y
a...n...d t...r...i...p...l...e c...h...e...c...k
e...v...e...r...y...t...h...i...n...g y...o...u
t...y...p...e...d a...n...d I m...e...a...n
e...v...e...r...y...t...h...i...n...g b...e...f...o...r...e
y...o...u h...i...t t...h...e e...n...t...e...r
k...e...y.

Plain Ole Everyday Scams

Investment scams are far too commonplace. Crooks lurk everywhere, ready to trick you into giving them your money by promising outlandish returns with no risk. Criminals target stock, gold, and real estate investors—and people interested in digital assets. The Federal Trade Commission says consumers lost $164 million to crypto scams in 2021. So, be as careful when approached with an investment idea in this space as you would be with any other investment.

These risks show that you can't be cocky when investing in digital assets. A lot of this ecosystem operates outside the jurisdiction of regulators, allowing operators to function with impudence. And if there's a failure, there's no FDIC or SIPC to reimburse you.

Sometimes scams are hiding in plain sight. I'm talking about Dogecoin.

In 2013, two software engineers created Dogecoin as a joke. Even the name was a gag: it's the misspelling of *doggy*, leading to many mispronunciations of the name.

Dogecoin is not and was never intended to be a legitimate digital asset. Bitcoin has 500,000 times the computing power, and bitcoin is scarce, while Dogecoin's supply is unlimited. (Already, 113 billion dogecoins are in circulation and 14 million more are minted every day.) Scarcity allows bitcoin's price to rise, while Dogecoin's abundance makes its price far riskier.

Despite all this, Dogecoin's price has risen more than 40,000% since inception. In 2021, 62% of Robinhood's crypto trading was Dogecoin.

For many Americans, Dogecoin is their first awareness of digital assets. The problem is that Dogecoin has enjoyed growth for all the wrong reasons. It's not helpful when Elon Musk, the richest man in the world, touts Dogecoin in a way that looks to me like a pump-and-dump scheme. His actions, and those of many others, are worrisome because Dogecoin was intended to be a short-lived joke. There's no business use case, so it can't possibly be anything other than a fad.

Bitcoin is called "digital gold" by many. I'd call Dogecoin a "digital pet rock"—and like that 1970s fad, it will disappear. And when it does, a lot of people are going to get hurt. The scandal will be a stain that has the potential to interfere with the serious efforts undertaken by serious people who are working hard with regulators and legislators to legitimize the emerging digital asset class.

Dogecoin is dangerous, and it bothers me greatly that it's getting such attention, however fleeting that may prove to be.

Do not buy Dogecoin. Tell your friends and family not to buy it, and to sell it if they own it, and assure them that it has little in common with other developments in the blockchain and digital asset ecosystem.

You often hear people refer to crypto as the Wild West. It's even worse than that. As one crypto commentator told me, "It's not the Wild West. It's Lewis and Clark!" Therefore, it's vital that, while you focus on how to generate a return *on* your money, you do everything you can to assure the return *of* your money.

You wouldn't be crazy if you allowed the specter of failure to dissuade you from investing in digital assets. But before you reach that conclusion, read the next chapter—for it will show that the high risk of digital assets actually serves as the most important reason you should invest!

Sound crazy? Read on, my friend!

Chapter 14

The Risks Are the Reason for Investing in Digital Assets

Why invest in digital assets if it's risky? Because doing so will reduce your risk.

Huh?

Yeah, I know. That doesn't seem to make any sense. So, let me explain. Or rather, let Harry explain.

Modern Portfolio Theory

In the early 1950s, while a graduate student at the University of Chicago, Harry Markowitz discovered that investing in two risky assets is safer than investing in just one of them. His research was ignored for a long time, but others eventually realized how fundamentally important his ideas were—and in 1990 Harry received the Nobel Prize for what is now known as Modern Portfolio Theory. Today, Harry's work is the basis for professional portfolio management worldwide.

Harry, whom I've had the pleasure of meeting, was the first to realize that adding a risky asset to a portfolio can cause the portfolio's overall level of risk to decline. The key, he said, is *correlation*: if you own two assets and they both rise and fall at the same time—meaning they are *positively correlated*—you're no better off than if you owned just one of them. But if one of them rises while the other falls and vice versa—meaning they are *negatively correlated*—then your overall risk of loss is sharply reduced. And if you add a third asset that's riskier than the other two but isn't correlated with either of them, you not only reduce the overall losses of the total portfolio at any one time, you improve its overall returns (because the new third asset makes more money than the other two).

Thus, you get higher returns with lower risk.

Amazing. Profound. And worthy of the Nobel Prize.

To convert that academic research into practical application, all you must do is add an asset to your portfolio that's riskier than your other assets. And the riskiest asset available today is bitcoin.

And that, dear reader, is the investment thesis for this new asset class: *adding digital assets to your portfolio can help you obtain higher returns while actually lowering your investment risk*. Indeed, in a 2021 survey of financial advisors by Fidelity Digital Assets, 69% of financial advisors said the top reason they like digital assets is their low correlation to other asset classes, as shown in Figure 14.1.

Their reasoning is shown by the four metrics financial professionals commonly use to measure risk and return. Let's look at them.

Bitcoin's Correlation to Other Asset Classes is Very Low	
1.00 = Correlation	0.00 = No Correlation
Bonds	.25
Equities	.12
Gold	.07
Commodities	.00
Liquid Alts	.00

FIGURE 14.1

Sharpe Ratio

This measures the return earned per unit of volatility. This tool can help reveal whether your returns are due to smart decisions—or because you took excessive risk. (It refutes the "can't argue with success" theory.) You want a high Sharpe ratio because the higher the number, the better the risk-adjusted performance of your portfolio. *Portfolios with bitcoin have higher Sharpe ratios than portfolios without bitcoin.*

Sortino Ratio

This is a variation of the Sharpe ratio. It acknowledges that not all volatility is harmful (after all, no one ever complains about *upside* volatility!). So, the Sortino ratio measures only the downside volatility of a portfolio. Again, the higher the number the better. *Portfolios with bitcoin have higher Sortino ratios than portfolios without bitcoin.*

Standard Deviation

The ideal portfolio would generate the same returns all the time; they would never *deviate*. Only bank savings accounts do that—but their returns are very low. Stocks offer higher returns—but their returns fluctuate all the time, sometimes dramatically. If it's normal for an asset's returns to deviate, then that deviation becomes standard—hence, *standard deviation*. A bank account's standard deviation is zero; the S&P 500's is about 15%, meaning its return in any one year is typically 15% higher or lower than its average return. Thus, the lower the standard deviation, the better. *The standard deviation of portfolios with bitcoin is virtually identical to a portfolio comprised of 60% stocks and 40% bonds.*

Max Drawdown

This number reflects a portfolio's maximum loss. It's an indicator of downside risk over a given period. It only measures the largest loss, not the frequency of losses or how long it took to recover from each loss. It thus answers the question: "How much money can I lose?"—a key concern for most investors. Investments that have similar Sharpe ratios, Sortino ratios, and standard deviations could have vastly different max drawdown numbers. Obviously, the lower the number, the better. *Adding bitcoin to a 60/40 portfolio has little impact on this statistic.*

It must be noted that the correlation data discussed above reflects bitcoin's price performance from its inception through mid-2021. But when the stock and bond markets fell in late 2021–early 2022, bitcoin fell as well. Does this mean the correlation story has changed? It's too soon to say, but investors will want to monitor this situation closely.

Now that we see how adding a risky asset such as bitcoin to a portfolio helps to reduce the portfolio's overall risk, we're ready to tackle the next question: How much of your portfolio should you place into digital assets?

And, dang, by a great stroke of luck, that's the title of the next chapter!

Chapter 15

How Much of Your Portfolio to Place into Digital Assets

The previous chapter showed that adding bitcoin and other digital assets can lower your portfolio risks while improving your returns.

It's time, therefore, to consider the next question: **How much money should you invest in this asset class?**

Please don't answer that question in dollars. Instead, think in terms of percentages. That's because dollar values change constantly but percentages never do: Whatever the value of your accounts, you always have 100% of it.

In the past, when considering the boldfaced question above, you probably allocated your money among four major asset classes: cash, stocks, bonds, and real estate. Now there's a fifth: digital assets. So, yeah, the question is now a little more complicated.

It's like carving a pizza pie into five slices.* How big should each slice be?

Your answer comprises the *asset allocation* of your investment portfolio. Experienced financial advisors and investors know that the size of each slice must be material; otherwise, there's no reason for the slice to exist.

Consider this simple illustration, using just two asset classes: cash, earning 1% per year, and stocks, earning 10% per year.

A 100% cash portfolio would earn 1.00%. If we create a 99/1 cash/

---

* Oh, yes, you can.

stock allocation, our total return would be 1.09%. The difference is so small that there's no point putting any money at all into stocks; we might as well put everything in cash.

A 50/50 allocation would produce a return of 5.5%—five times more than cash—but that also requires you to invest half your money in the stock market (which is far riskier than having all your money in cash). This is the classic risk/return trade-off that all investors face.

Experienced financial advisors and investors will tell you not to bother allocating anything to stocks unless you're willing to allocate *a lot*. That's why advisors routinely recommend portfolios that place 60% to 100% of assets into stocks.

But if you apply that line of thinking to digital assets, you will make one of two big mistakes. First, you might allocate a massive portion of your portfolio to digital assets, just as you do with stocks, bonds, and real estate. But digital assets are still emerging and thus remain very risky; they could easily result in a total loss. So, investing a large portion of the portfolio into digital assets could irreparably harm your personal finances. That'd be a big mistake.

To avoid such an outcome, you'd have to limit yourself to a tiny allocation. But you know that doing so is pointless because small allocations won't materially impact your overall returns. This could cause you to conclude not to bother investing in digital assets at all. Again, big mistake.

Investing a lot is a mistake. But investing nothing is also a mistake. What is the remaining option?

Investing a little.

If that seems to contradict the prior explanation that tiny allocations to a given asset class are pointless, let's recall one other key point we've learned: digital assets are unlike any other asset class ever invented. Therefore, you'd be making an error if you apply standard principles of portfolio modeling to this asset class. Instead, a different approach is warranted. Let me show you what that is.

Ric Edelman's 1% Digital Assets Allocation Strategy

I pioneered this strategy in 2015. Placing a mere 1% of your portfolio into digital assets is counterintuitive, yet that amount is indeed sufficient to meaningfully impact your portfolio without exposing yourself to unacceptable risks.

To help you understand why, let me ask you three questions.

1. What average annual return would you expect from a typically diversified portfolio over many years?

2. In 2017, bitcoin rose 1,500%. The following year, it crashed, losing 84% of its value. Could something like that happen again?

3. Could bitcoin become worthless?

I often pose these questions during my webinars and live events, and most people say they expect a diversified portfolio to grow 7% per year, that another "wave and crash" could certainly occur, and that bitcoin could indeed become worthless. I agree with all these answers.

So, let's apply those answers to three portfolios over a two-year period, as shown in Figure 15.1. The first portfolio is a traditional 60/40 combination of stocks/bonds. The other two have allocations of 59/40/1—meaning we are allocating a mere 1% of each portfolio to bitcoin. Of these two, the first is the "wave and crash" portfolio: the 1% bitcoin portion will gain 1,500% in the first year but lose 84% in the following year. In the other portfolio, bitcoin will suffer a "wipeout" and become worthless immediately.

Figure 15.1 shows you the results. After year one, the traditional portfolio is up 7%. The Wave and Crash Portfolio's return is three times higher, with a gain of 22%. And the Total Loss portfolio? Its gain for the

Ric Edelman's 1% Digital Asset Allocation Strategy			
	Asset Mix	Total Return	
		1 Year	2 Year
Typical Portfolio	60/40	+7%	+14.5%
Digital Asset *Wave + Crash*	59/40/1	+22%	+15.4%
Digital Asset *Total Loss*	59/40/1	+6%	+13.4%

FIGURE 15.1

year is 6%—not much different from the 60/40 portfolio that didn't own any bitcoin.

Clearly, the potential damage of a 59/40/1 portfolio is small. But the potential for outsize gains is huge. This makes a strong case for placing a small allocation into digital assets.

But wait! We're not done, because the Wave and Crash Portfolio hasn't yet crashed. So, let's see the results after year two.

After the second year, the two-year total return of the 60/40 portfolio is 14.5% (it's more than 14% thanks to the power of compounding). But the bitcoin in the Wave and Crash Portfolio has fallen 84%, leaving the total portfolio with a two-year gain of . . . 15.4%. Meanwhile, the Total Loss portfolio's total return is 13.4%.

This illustration makes the point clearly: a mere 1% allocation can materially improve returns without jeopardizing your future financial security. But this is merely an illustration. Does my 1% allocation strategy work in the real world?

Well, let's look at data compiled by Bitwise Asset Management. In its landmark study, "The Case for Crypto in an Institutional Portfolio," Bitwise reveals that for the period January 1, 2014 to June 30, 2021, a 60/40 stock/bond portfolio with a 1% bitcoin allocation would have earned an average of 14% more per year (8.9% versus 7.8%) than a comparable portfolio without bitcoin. And, as Figure 15.2 shows, a

Jan 1, 2014 - June 30, 2021				
	Annual Return	Sharpe Ratio	Standard Deviation	Max Drawdown
60/40 Portfolio	7.8%	+0.61	+10.2%	-21.1%
with 1% Bitcoin	8.9%	+0.72	+10.2%	-21.3%

FIGURE 15.2

1% bitcoin allocation improved the Sharpe ratio without harming the standard deviation, and the max drawdown remained virtually unchanged.

During this period, a 1% allocation would have increased returns and reduced risks in 77% of one-year periods, 97% of two-year periods, and 100% of all three-year periods. The data is compelling.

I'm not alone in suggesting that a 1% portfolio allocation is sufficient for this new asset class. The September 25, 2021, issue of the *Economist* said, "It is wise to hold bitcoin in an investment portfolio. . . . [The] allocation looks sensible as part of a highly diversified portfolio. . . . An optimal portfolio [is] 1–5%."

Also, Yale University researchers published a paper in 2018 that reached the same conclusion. Even if you think bitcoin will outperform other asset classes by 200% a year, you should invest only 6.1% of your portfolio in bitcoin, as Figure 15.3 shows.

Maybe I'm being too cautious by advocating a mere 1% crypto allocation. Bitwise's study, for example, highlights a 2.5% bitcoin allocation. But you might be suspicious about making *any* allocation. After all, bitcoin's price has skyrocketed since its inception. In the seven-and-a-half-year period shown in Figure 15.2, for example, bitcoin gained more than 10,000%. But bitcoin experienced four crashes of 50% or more during that time. So how would you have fared if you had invested at different times?

YALE STUDY 2018	
If you believe the market will outperform by:	You should allocate this much to your portfolio:
30% a year	1.0%
50% a year	1.6%
100% a year	3.1%
200% a year	6.1%
Half as much as in the past	3.1%

FIGURE 15.3

Bitwise's study answers that question, by examining not only the period beginning in 2014, but for every three-year rolling interval since then.

As Bitwise notes, there are 1,642 three-year intervals during that seven-and-a-half year period, each with a different start date—and bitcoin contributed positively to every one of them.

The worst interval added nearly two percentage points to the portfolio's return, while the best added 22 percentage points. The median improvement was 13.3 percentage points. Figure 15.4 displays the results for you.

The Right Allocation for You

When Jean and I were new to crypto, we followed my 1% strategy. As we gained more knowledge and experience, we increased our allocation.

Let your knowledge level (and tolerance for risk) be your guide. And don't fret too much over this decision. Remember, you're debating whether to invest 1%, 2.5%, or maybe even (gulp) 6.1%. This

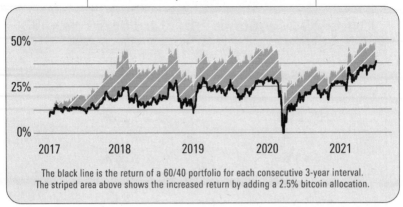

The black line is the return of a 60/40 portfolio for each consecutive 3-year interval.
The striped area above shows the increased return by adding a 2.5% bitcoin allocation.

Source: Bitwise Asset Management

FIGURE 15.4

debate is not worth 50% of your time or brainpower. Nail-biting is not warranted.

Figure 15.5 might help you decide the right allocation for you. It shows the performance of three-year rolling intervals (with quarterly rebalancing, which we'll discuss in chapter 17) from 2014 through June 30, 2021, for portfolios holding bitcoin allocations of 0% to 10%. As you can see, the more you invest, the higher your return and the better the Sharpe ratio—but note that standard deviations and max drawdowns rise as well.

There's a big difference between "percent" and "percentage point." Say a 60/40 portfolio earns 10%. If we were to say that adding bitcoin boosts the return by 22%, the return would be 12.2%. But if we instead said that adding bitcoin boosts the return by 22 percentage points, the return would be 32%.

So, yeah, there's a big difference between "percent" and "percentage point"—and that's why the results of Bitwise's study are a very big deal.

Three-Year Rolling Intervals with Quarterly Rebalancing January 1, 2014 - June 30, 2021				
Portfolio Allocation	Average Return	Sharpe Ratio	Standard Deviation	Maximum Drawdown
60/40	20.1%	0.64	7.6%	11.4%
with 1% Bitcoin	25.5%	0.84	7.7%	11.3%
with 2% Bitcoin	31.1%	1.02	7.8%	11.2%
with 3% Bitcoin	36.9%	1.17	8.1%	11.1%
with 4% Bitcoin	42.8%	1.29	8.5%	11.3%
with 5% Bitcoin	48.9%	1.38	9.0%	12.1%
with 6% Bitcoin	55.2%	1.45	9.5%	13.1%
with 7% Bitcoin	61.6%	1.51	10.1%	14.1%
with 8% Bitcoin	68.3%	1.56	10.7%	15.1%
with 9% Bitcoin	75.1%	1.60	11.4%	16.1%
with 10% Bitcoin	82.1%	1.63	12.1%	17.1%

Source: Bitwise Asset Management

FIGURE 15.5

It appears from Figure 15.5 that a 3% allocation is optimal—but keep in mind that the chart only refers to the S&P 500, Barclays Aggregate Bond Index, and bitcoin. Other digital assets are not factored in—and portfolios with different components would have performed differently. Also, past performance does not guarantee future results.

All that is a long-winded way of saying that you need to decide, ideally with the aid of your financial advisor, the allocation that's right for you.

Chapter 16

Choosing the Right Digital Assets for Your Portfolio

I'm proud of you! We've covered a lot of material so far, and you've made lots of progress. You now understand what blockchain technology is, how it works, and the many coins and tokens that exist—and how all this is about to disrupt global commerce on an unprecedented scale.

You also now know the basis for evaluating the value (!) and price of digital assets—as well as the risks associated with investing in them. Despite those risks, you're still interested in investing some of your money into digital assets. (Welcome to the club!)

This chapter will help you decide which investment opportunities are right for you. As you'll see, the offerings vary greatly—not just in terms of fees and expenses, risks, liquidity, income and growth potential, availability, issuers, and other factors, but even in how you access them.

Mining the Coins

The most basic way to obtain bitcoin is to mine it. We explored that in chapter 5.

If the bitcoins you earn from mining are worth more than what it costs you to mine them (think about the cost of buying, operating, and maintaining all those computers), then you'll be happy to mine all day long. Even though the price of bitcoin could fall, the cost of your efforts likely won't. So, you could make or lose a lot of money. It all depends on your costs, the number of bitcoins you obtain, and their price.

"Alexa, mine me some bitcoin."

Investing in the Miners

Mining is an active business, not a passive investment—and that might discourage you from mining. Still, you might find the idea appealing. So, instead of mining yourself, you could invest in a mining company. Riot Blockchain, for example, is the largest publicly traded bitcoin miner in the United States (Nasdaq ticker: RIOT). The company says it spends about $15,000 to mine a single bitcoin. If bitcoin's price is higher than that, Riot is profitable—and the higher bitcoin's price, the more profit Riot earns.

As of December 31, 2021, Riot owned more than 1,600 bitcoins and was mining nearly six bitcoins per day. It and miners like it could be the only companies in the world that have no products and no customers; Riot's product, essentially, is its stock price, which tends to rise and fall with the price of bitcoin itself.

RIOT Blockchain

Publicly Traded Bitcoin Mining Companies

Argo Blockchain
argoblockchain.com

Argo Blockchain (ARBKF) is engaged in large-scale crypto mining. The shares are listed on the London Stock Exchange and cross-trade in the United States on the OTCQX Best Market.

Bitfarms, Ltd.
bitfarms.com

Bitfarms, Ltd. (ticker: BFARF) is a blockchain infrastructure company that operates one of the largest digital asset mining operations in North America. It is headquartered in Toronto.

EcoChain
ecochainmining.com

EcoChain, a subsidiary of Soluna Holdings, Inc. (SLNH), is a cryptocurrency mining business powered by renewable energy.

Hut 8 Mining Corp.
hut8mining.com

Hut 8 (HUTMF) is a cryptocurrency mining company focused on mining bitcoin.

Marathon Digital Holdings, Inc.
marathondh.com

Marathon Digital (MARA) mines cryptocurrencies with a focus on the blockchain ecosystem and the generation of digital assets in the United States. The company is based in Las Vegas.

Marathon Digital

Riot Blockchain
riotblockchain.com

Riot Blockchain (RIOT) is the largest publicly traded bitcoin miner in the United States, with mining operations in New York and Texas.

RIOT Blockchain

For an up-to-date list, complete with hyperlinks, visit the
DACFP Yellow Pages
at dacfp.com

Buying Coins and Tokens

If you don't want to mine or invest in miners but want to own coins or tokens, you'll have to buy them. To do that, you must go to a marketplace where you'll find owners willing to sell. There are two kinds of marketplaces: exchanges and custodians.

Digital Assets Exchanges

These operate just like a stock exchange. You open an account and deposit money into it (any fiat currency will do—dollar, euro, yen, and so on). Then, you place your order(s) to buy the digital asset(s) you want, using your currency to pay for your purchase(s).

The exchange will attempt to fill each order by pairing it with matching orders. If you submit a *market order*, you'll get the coin's price as of the moment your order is filled. A *limit order* lets you set the worst price you're willing to accept, and your trade will be filled at that price (or better) when the exchange finds a willing counterparty. Your limit order can expire at the end of the day or it can be GTC—*good till canceled.*

Some exchanges cater solely to institutional investors, but most serve retail customers as well. The best ones provide high levels of security to reduce the risk that hackers will gain access to your hot wallet, and they go to great lengths to protect cold wallets as well. Cold wallets are placed on a portable drive disconnected from the internet and taken to an undisclosed, remote location—in some cases, deep inside a mountain—with few of the exchange's staff knowing the whereabouts. That offsite vault is then heavily guarded. On top of that, the exchanges provide insurance to each customer promising to reimburse you if a theft or hack does occur.

Exchanges also do more than just facilitate trading. Services include:

- Data and research to help you analyze the market.
- Margin, options, and futures, enabling you to buy more than you're actually able to buy with the money in your account.

This is called *leverage*, with which you can buy, say, $200 worth of bitcoin with a $100 investment. This means you could make a lot more money if bitcoin rises in price—and you could lose a lot more if the price falls. You'll also incur fees and expenses to do this.

- Digital wallets to help you securely store your digital assets. Every exchange provides hot wallets; many also offer cold wallets. (Return to chapter 5 for more on wallets.)

- Savings accounts: you deposit your digital assets into them, and you earn interest.

- Interest-bearing, FDIC-insured bank accounts for your cash deposits.

- Loans, collateralized by your digital assets.

- Visa or MasterCard credit cards. Instead of getting miles or cash back on purchases, you get bitcoin.

You'll incur costs when using an exchange. These include:

- **Spreads.** You know that one hundred pennies equal one dollar. Say you walk into a bank and hand the teller a dollar bill, and the teller gives you 99 pennies. You've just incurred the cost of a spread. That penny is the bank's fee to provide you the service of exchanging your dollar into pennies. And if you later want to exchange your pennies for a dollar, you'll incur the spread again. No bank actually charges a spread to make change for customers, but you do pay spreads when buying stocks and bonds. You'll pay them when you buy or sell digital assets or trade one for another.

- **Taker fees and maker discounts.** If your market order removes liquidity from the market, the exchanges might charge you a taker fee. Limit orders often add liquidity to the market, so you might receive a maker discount when placing a limit order.

- **Trading fees.** You'll pay this fee with each transaction. It will either be a flat rate or a percentage of the trade's value. The bigger the trade and the more often you trade, the less you'll pay. You can lower this fee by buying your exchange's utility token (if available) in bulk at a volume discount; you'd then use them to pay for your trades.

- **Service fees.** You'll incur costs similar to those charged by banks and brokerage firms. Fees apply to the exchange's credit and debit cards, to transfer and wire money, to make deposits and withdrawals, and more.

- **Custody fees.** We'll talk more about custody in the next section.

Choosing an Exchange

Shop and compare, as you would when buying a dishwasher. Here are the features to look for:

1. **Coins offered.** No exchange offers every digital asset, so make sure yours provides the ones you want.

2. **Liquidity.** Prices move extremely fast in the digital assets world. Therefore, you want to know your orders will be filled fast, especially when volatility is high and levels of trading are likely to be far higher than usual. Ask about the exchange's trading volume; the higher, the better.

3. **Access.** Is the exchange available in your country or state? Can you quickly and easily access your account and its assets? What is the user interface experience? How easy is it to use? How quickly does money move between the exchange and your bank account?

4. **Customer service.** Many exchanges have no human service team whatsoever; they rely solely on chatbots that provide

generic answers to questions. If a problem occurs, how easily and quickly can you get it resolved?

5. **Security.** Does the exchange offer cold wallet storage? Does it use enhanced encryption to protect its data?

6. **Regulation.** Although stock exchanges operate under federal laws and regulations, digital assets exchanges don't. They can operate like comic-book stores, doing business pretty much as they please. Some exchanges, however, choose to conform to regulatory requirements, and have obtained approvals from a federal or state agency. (Changpeng Zhao, CEO of Binance, the world's biggest crypto exchange—it's bigger than the London, New York, and Hong Kong stock exchanges combined—said in October 2021, "We run a very legit business. But if you look at cryptocurrency adoption worldwide, it's probably less than 2% of the population. In order to attract the other 98%, we need to be regulated.") Do not use an exchange that doesn't have and follow proper processes and controls. For example, the exchange should be able to show it has audited SOC 1 and SOC 2 reports; the former confirms the design and implementation of the exchange's financial operations and reporting controls, while the latter confirms the design and implementation of security, availability, and confidentiality controls.

7. **Insurance.** Can the exchange reimburse you if your assets are lost to hacking or other incident? What is the claims-paying ability of the insurer? What does the policy cover, and what are its limits per account and in the aggregate?

8. **Scale.** You want to know that your exchange is a financially strong organization that can continue to serve you efficiently as it grows.

Digital Assets Exchanges

Binance
binance.com

Binance is the world's largest cryptocurrency exchange. Binance.US provides a fast, secure, and reliable platform to buy and sell cryptocurrencies in the United States.

Bitfinex
bitfinex.com

Bitfinex allows users to exchange bitcoin, Ethereum, EOS, Litecoin, Ripple, NEO, and many other digital assets with minimal slippage.

BitFlyer
bitflyer.com

BitFlyer is the largest bitcoin exchange in the world by volume, transacting $250 billion year-to-date.

BittyLicious
bittylicious.com

BittyLicious is a British bank account with online banking fully set up. Payment must come directly from the BittyLicious account holder.

BitOasis
bitoasis.net

BitOasis is a pioneer in the MENA region cryptocurrency ecosystem and aims to offer secure and regulated infrastructure in cryptocurrency trading for retail and institutional clients.

Bitpanda
bitpanda.com

Bitpanda is a user-friendly, trade-everything platform empowered for investing in stocks, cryptocurrencies, and metals.

Bitstamp
bitstamp.net

Bitstamp is a cryptocurrency exchange based in Luxembourg that allows trading between fiat currency, bitcoin, and other cryptocurrencies. It allows USD, EUR, GBP, bitcoin, ALGO, XRP, Ether, litecoin, bitcoin cash, XLM, Link, OMG Network, USD Coin, or PAX deposits and withdrawals.

For an up-to-date list, complete with hyperlinks, visit the
DACFP Yellow Pages
at dacfp.com

Digital Assets Exchanges

Changelly
changelly.com

Changelly gives customers a one-stop-shop experience for purchasing, selling, swapping, and trading digital assets.

Coinbase
coinbase.com

Coinbase is a digital wallet service that allows traders to buy and sell bitcoin and other digital assets. It is publicly traded (ticker: COIN).

CoinCorner
coincorner.com

CoinCorner is an exchange platform for buying bitcoin in the United Kingdom and Europe with a credit card or debit card. Investors can buy and sell bitcoin, and store digital assets.

Coinfloor
coinfloor.org

Coinfloor is an established group of digital asset exchanges for institutional and sophisticated investors and traders.

CoinJar
coinjar.com

CoinJar is an Australian platform that enables the buying and selling of bitcoin and allows merchants to accept bitcoin payments.

Coinmama
coinmama.com

Coinmama is a digital asset exchange that allows individuals and companies to buy and sell bitcoin and other altcoins fast, in 188 countries since 2013.

Coinspot
coinspot.com

Coinspot has constructed an interface with usability in mind, quick-to-access features, and information that you actually want to see.

For an up-to-date list, complete with hyperlinks, visit the
DACFP Yellow Pages
at dacfp.com

Digital Assets Exchanges

eToro
etoro.com

eToro is a social trading and investment network that allows users to trade currencies, commodities, indices, crypto assets, and stocks.

Gemini
gemini.com

Gemini is a licensed digital asset exchange and custodian built for both individuals and institutions. Its crypto products are simple, elegant, and secure, allowing you to buy, sell, and store digital assets.

HitBTC
hitbtc.com

HitBTC is a blockchain platform for buying and selling bitcoin and other digital assets.

Kraken
kraken.com

As one of the largest and oldest bitcoin exchanges in the world, Kraken is consistently named one of the best places to buy and sell crypto online. They've been on the forefront of the blockchain revolution since 2011.

KuCoin
kucoin.com

KuCoin is a global cryptocurrency exchange offering 400+ digital assets, providing crypto services to more than eight million users.

Luno
luno.com

Luno is a platform that makes digital assets such as bitcoin and Ethereum easily accessible to the public.

Mercatox
mercatox.com

Mercatox is an exchange platform for trading cryptocurrency by using bitcoin, Ethereum, and Litecoin. The company also provides a deposit and withdrawal service.

OKEx
okex.com

OKEx is a digital asset exchange that provides advanced financial services to traders globally by using blockchain technology.

For an up-to-date list, complete with hyperlinks, visit the
DACFP Yellow Pages
at dacfp.com

Digital Assets Exchanges

Paxful
paxful.com

Paxful is a people-powered marketplace for money transfers with anyone, anywhere, at any time.

Plus500
plus500.com

Plus500 is a global financial firm providing online CFDs trading services.

Poloniex
poloniex.com

Poloniex is a crypto exchange with advanced trading features.

Revolut
revolut.com

Revolut is a financial services company that specializes in mobile banking, card payments, money remittance, and foreign exchange.

Robinhood
robinhood.com

Robinhood is a stock brokerage firm that allows customers to buy and sell stocks, options, ETFs, and crypto commission-free.

ShapeShift
shapeshift.com

ShapeShift is a crypto platform enabling customers to buy, sell, trade, track, send, receive, and interact with their digital assets.

For an up-to-date list, complete with hyperlinks, visit the
DACFP Yellow Pages
at dacfp.com

Custodians

After you buy a digital asset, you must decide where to house it. That's called custody. You have two choices: you can take custody yourself by simply storing your digital assets on your phone's wallet or on a flash drive, or you can have another party take custody of your assets for you.

Any person or entity can provide custody services for digital assets, so make sure you are (or your financial advisor on your behalf is) working with a *qualified custodian*. That's a legal definition. The custody rule is designed to safeguard investors against the possibility of theft or misappropriation of their funds.

Qualified custodians can be banks, registered broker-dealers, futures commission merchants, and certain foreign entities. They either maintain your assets in a separate account under your name or in an aggregate account under the name of your financial advisor, who's serving as an agent or trustee for all their clients. By working with a qualified custodian, you gain an extra level of confidence that the business is operating as a *fiduciary* (meaning, serving your best interests) and adhering to regulations. Although nonqualified custodians might also be doing so, you can't be as certain.

Only the SEC can approve an organization as a "qualified custodian." But states are trying to do so as well; the first was Wyoming, which declared in 2020 that Two Ocean Trust (a funny name for a firm in Wyoming) could act as a qualified custodian. The SEC quickly issued a statement saying that Wyoming's decision "should not be construed to represent the views of the SEC or any other regulatory agency." So there.

Just because an institution is a qualified custodian doesn't mean it handles digital assets. So, you want a qualified custodian that does.

IRA Custodians

You can buy and sell digital assets or even mine them with your IRA. Federal laws and regulations simply require you to use a custodian for your IRA and Roth IRA accounts.

Custodians for Digital Assets

Anchorage Digital
anchorage.com

Anchorage Digital is the first federally charted digital asset bank in history and is a Qualified Custodian. Anchorage uses its own hardware to safely secure digital assets in an efficient manner with 90% of transactions processing in under 15 minutes. Anchorage also offers customization to fit clients' needs and industry-leading insurance products to protect digital assets.

Bakkt
bakkt.com

The Bakkt Warehouse supports the physical delivery of bitcoin futures, and is also available for institutional custody services for bitcoin storage outside of futures markets. To protect customers, Bakkt rebalances between warm and cold wallets, which are covered by a $125 million insurance policy from a leading global carrier.

BitGo
bitgo.com

BitGo is a regulated trust company under the Division of Banking in South Dakota. Cold storage assets are held in segregated accounts, insured, and secured by BitGo's peer-reviewed multi-signature security.

Brown Brothers Harriman
bbh.com

Brown Brothers Harriman provides professional custody of digital assets to institutional clients.

Copper
copper.co

Copper offers custody through online and offline technology, giving access to more than 150 digital assets. Specializing in multiparty computation, Copper can co-sign transactions remotely without risk of private key exposure, so users can configure their wallets offline and online.

For an up-to-date list, complete with hyperlinks, visit the
DACFP Yellow Pages
at dacfp.com

Custodians for Digital Assets

Fidelity Digital Assets
fidelitydigitalassets.com

Fidelity Digital Assets is one of the world's largest diversified financial services providers. Its custody service uses cold storage and additional multilevel safeguards. The company integrates top-of-the-line trade execution into its custody platform.

Fireblocks
fireblocks.com

Fireblocks' platform allows every business to easily and securely support digital assets.

Gemini
gemini.com

Gemini is a fiduciary and Qualified Custodian, licensed by New York to custody digital assets.

Hex Trust
hextrust.com

Hex Trust's Hex Safe is a bank-grade custody solution for digital assets, providing a state-of-the-art security framework in partnership with IBM, along with seamless integration with core banking systems and comprehensive insurance coverage.

Paxos
paxos.com

Paxos offers investors best-in-class security measures, including multiparty computation signing for warm and hot wallets, and multi-sig signing for cold wallets.

Prime Trust
primetrust.com

Prime Trust is a qualified custodian that offers custody as well as sub-custody to various types of accounts. It focuses on securing digital assets by using specialty API focusing on infrastructure to build and scale in a secure manner.

For an up-to-date list, complete with hyperlinks, visit the
DACFP Yellow Pages
at dacfp.com

Custodians for Digital Assets

Tetra Trust Company
tetratrust.com

Tetra is Canada's first licensed digital asset custodian. Its platform provides enterprise-grade custody of digital assets for institutional investors. The company is backed by Coinsquare, Coinbase Ventures, Mogo, and executives from the financial services industry.

For an up-to-date list, complete with hyperlinks, visit the
DACFP Yellow Pages
at dacfp.com

Yield Farming

You don't earn interest or dividends when you buy digital coins and tokens. Thus, the only way you can profit is by selling what you bought for a higher price than you paid to buy it.

At least, that's the way it was when bitcoin was invented. Today, though, you *can* earn interest on your coins and tokens. How? By lending them to others. It's called *yield farming*—the practice of lending or staking your coins in exchange for earning interest. Dozens of platforms facilitate this process, paying annual yields of 12% or more.

The platforms are often advertised as "savings wallets" or "interest accounts." They promote themselves as safe. Maybe they are. But there's little regulatory oversight (and no FDIC protection).

At one large exchange, 100,000 account holders have lent $2 billion in bitcoin and other digital assets, and they're earning 7.5% at this writing. The loans, the exchange's site says, are to "third parties."

Let's put this into perspective. When you buy a junk bond—defined by the SEC as a "speculative" investment—you're loaning money to a company with less than top-notch financial strength; there's a significant risk that the company might not be able to pay the interest it owes or even return your money to you upon maturity. But you know who

Qualified IRA Custodians That Hold Digital Assets

Alto
altoira.com

Alto is a self-directed IRA platform that enables individuals, advisors, and institutions to access and invest in alternative assets. CryptoIRA lets you buy, sell, and trade 100+ crypto assets in real time through integration with CoinBase Pro. AltoIRA lets you diversify across alternative asset classes, including professionally managed digital asset strategies.

Bitcoin IRA
bitcoinira.com

Bitcoin IRA is a crypto IRA platform that allows customers to purchase bitcoin and other crypto for retirement accounts.

BitIRA
bitira.com

BitIRA has partnered with Equity Trust Company and Preferred Trust Company, two leading custodians of self-directed IRAs, to manage accounts and prepare documentation for an account's administration.

BitTrust IRA
bittrustira.com

BitTrust IRA is a platform to start trading crypto with a low-cost investment.

BlockMint
blockmint.com

BlockMint uses cold storage wallets to make sure your investments aren't exposed to hacking, theft, or electronic errors.

Choice
choiceapp.io

Choice, the first platform to allow self-directed retirement accounts holding bitcoin and Ether, is an independent Qualified Custodian regulated by the South Dakota Division of Banking. Choice maintains strict policies, procedures, controls, and disclosures to meet the highest of custody standards for clients. Choice partners with Fidelity Digital Assets for cold storage solutions and has partnered with Kraken and CoinShares for digital asset trading.

For an up-to-date list, complete with hyperlinks, visit the
DACFP Yellow Pages
at dacfp.com

Qualified IRA Custodians That Hold Digital Assets

Coin IRA
coinira.com

Coin IRA was one of the first companies in the United States to offer investors the ability to add digital assets to retirement plans.

ITrustCapital
itrustcapital.com

iTrustCapital is a digital asset IRA trading platform that lets clients directly buy and trade crypto in real time through retirement accounts. iTrustCapital has partnered with Coinbase Custody to provide custody and storage services.

Madison Trust
madisontrust.com

Madison Trust Company is an investment custodian that offers accounting, audit, IRA representation, and financial and risk management services.

MyDigitalMoney
mydigitalmoney.com

MyDigitalMoney is a self-trading crypto investment platform with unparalleled military-grade security and US-based client service.

For an up-to-date list, complete with hyperlinks, visit the
DACFP Yellow Pages
at dacfp.com

the company is, so you can assess the risk by evaluating the reasons it's seeking to borrow money. You can also review the company's financial statements to gauge the likelihood it will be able to pay the interest and return the principle as promised. You can do all this because you know whom you're lending the money to. But when yield farming with crypto, you have no idea who's borrowing your coins and tokens—or why they're doing so.

And Why? is an important question. If you're earning 7.5%, the borrowers are clearly paying that much—and more, due to the fees they incur to obtain the loan. What are they going to do with your bitcoin that will allow them to generate a profit that exceeds their cost of the loan?

I honestly don't know—because I don't know who they are. Maybe they'll sell your bitcoin on the belief the price is about to fall more than 7.5%. After it does (assuming it does), they'll buy it back and return the coins to you, keeping the profit for themselves. Perhaps they'll exploit pricing differences; various exchanges around the world often have different prices for digital assets at the same time; by buying low at one exchange and simultaneously selling high on another, you can produce large profits (a practice known as *arbitrage*)—*if* those anomalies exist and *if* you can capture them. Possibly they're going to borrow your coins, pay you 7.5%, and lend them to someone else who pays them 8% or more. Other gambits can also be played, I'm sure.

Before you engage in yield farming, consider the risks. And ask yourself why you bought bitcoin in the first place? If you think the price will rise 100%, why are you trying to earn interest? You're taking plenty of risk to get that 100%. How much extra risk are you taking to get extra yield—and is that extra risk worth the yield you're hoping to get?

When I posed these questions to one investor, he emphatically said, *"Yes!"* His reasoning: He expects bitcoin to double in price in 10 years. He expects to earn 7.5% per year by lending his bitcoin. That'd be a gain of 106% over the 10-year period (thanks to compounding). If all goes according to plan, his $100,000 investment would be worth $306,103 in 10 years instead of $200,000 if he didn't engage in lending.

You can boost your returns substantially by yield farming. There's a risk to this. So, decide for yourself.

GET YOUR BONUS CONTENT!

Exclusively for Readers of
The Truth About Crypto

Learn more about generating yield via digital assets. You'll find this bonus content and more—free—at https://www.thetayf.com/TACbonuscontent

---

Digital Assets Lending and Borrowing Platforms

Aave
aave.com

Aave is an open-source and noncustodial protocol that lets you earn interest on deposits and borrow assets.

BlockFi
blockfi.com

BlockFi provides credit services to markets with limited access to simple financial products, pairing market-leading rates with institutional-quality benefits. Gemini Trust Company is the primary custodian.

Celsius Network
celsius.network

Celsius Network is a blockchain-based platform giving curated financial services not available through traditional financial institutions. Celsius specializes in consumer lending, fintech, and financial services. It is headquartered in London.

Colendi
colendi.com

Colendi helps consumers, merchants, and financial institutions with its bank-independent credit scoring, micro credit, and financial services platform.

Compound
compound.finance

Compound is an algorithmic, autonomous interest-rate protocol built for developers, to unlock a universe of open financial applications.

Everex
everex.io

Everex develops a blockchain-powered credit card for consumers and payment processing solutions for online merchants.

Kava
www.kava.io

Kava Labs is focused on making financial services openly accessible to anyone, anywhere in the world. It offers lending, minting, and swaps.

For an up-to-date list, complete with hyperlinks, visit the
DACFP Yellow Pages
at dacfp.com

Digital Assets Lending and Borrowing Platforms

Nexo
nexo.io

Nexo is a crypto interest account and lending platform. The company holds itself out as the world's largest and most trusted lending institution in the digital finance industry.

SALT Lending
saltlending.com

SALT Lending provides crypto-backed loans, enabling consumers, businesses, banks, and governments to collateralize digital assets for a US dollar or stablecoin loan.

Silvergate Bank
silvergate.com

Silvergate Bank provides secure, institutional-grade access to capital through US dollar loans collateralized by bitcoin.

Zerion
zerion.io

Zerion is a DeFi asset management tool that lets users yield farm via their digital wallets and have access to liquidity pools.

For an up-to-date list, complete with hyperlinks, visit the
DACFP Yellow Pages
at dacfp.com

Buying Stocks of Companies That Own Coins and Tokens

Major corporations have billions of dollars in cash reserves. They each face a decision of what to do with all that money. They could buy other companies, invest in research and development, buy back shares of their own stock (which reduces the supply and thus theoretically causes their share price to rise), or distribute the money to shareholders as a dividend. Most companies do a combination of all these.

A growing number are now also buying bitcoin. MassMutual, the sixth-largest life insurance company in the nation, invested $100 million in bitcoin in 2021. Tesla owns 42,000 bitcoins. The biggest buyer is MicroStrategy, a 32-year-old company that's the nation's largest publicly traded provider of business intelligence software. It owns more than 100,000 bitcoins—an investment so large that the company's stock price now tracks the price of bitcoin more than it does the company's actual business.

Publicly Traded Companies That Own Digital Assets

Company	Ticker
MicroStrategy	MSTR
Tesla	TSLA

Micro-Strategy

Publicly Traded Digital Asset Exchanges

Coinbase
coinbase

Coinbase (NASDAQ: COIN) is the largest and best-known digital assets exchange in the United States. Users include retail, accredited, and institutional investors.

Voyager Digital
investvoyager.com

Voyager Digital (OTC: VYGVF, TSX: VOYG) is a crypto-asset broker that supports bitcoin, top DeFi coins, stablecoins, and a variety of altcoins.

For an up-to-date list, complete with hyperlinks, visit the
DACFP Yellow Pages
at dacfp.com

Taking the "Picks & Shovels" Route

You know the story of Levi Strauss: Like thousands of others, he went to San Francisco during the California Gold Rush of the mid-1800s to make his fortune. And he did indeed become wealthy—but not by seeking gold. Instead, he sold clothing to the gold diggers. Strauss's brilliance came to be known as the *picks & shovels* strategy—instead of engaging directly in a venture, provide the adventurers with the tools and infrastructure they need. You'll make money even if they never do.

You can play in the digital assets space the same way. Instead of mining or buying coins and tokens, invest in the companies that are building the infrastructure that makes all that activity happen. Without computers, miners can't mine—so invest in the chip manufacturers. Investors need to track the market, so invest in the companies compiling and selling the data. Buyers need a platform to engage in their activities, so invest in the exchanges and custodians that serve them. And many Fortune 500 companies are developing or deploying blockchain technology to grow their businesses.

Your investments can take the form of:

- **Stocks.** This makes you an owner of a company; you'd buy if you believe the stock price will rise.

- **Bonds.** This makes you a lender to a company; you'll earn interest on the money you lend.

- **Convertible notes.** These pay interest—usually less than bonds, but you can convert your investment into stock, which you'd do if the stock price rises.

- **SAFEs.** These *simple agreements for future equity* are similar to the SAFTs we covered in chapter 9.

Making Bets via Derivatives

As the name implies, a *derivative* is not an asset. It's based on an asset—a way to make a bet about how much money an asset might gain or lose. Derivatives are contracts; you and the counterparty take opposite positions. One of you thinks the price of an asset will rise a certain amount within a certain period, and the other party thinks that won't happen. One of you will be proven correct—and the winner makes money while the loser, well, loses money.

There are many kinds of derivative contracts. The most common are options, futures, forwards, and swaps. They've been around for centuries, serving an important, legitimate purpose in commerce.

Here's one example: A farmer growing corn needs to sell the crop for $10/bushel. Although that's the current price, the farmer won't harvest the crop for four months—by which time the price might fall. So, the farmer sells an options contract to a cereal company; the company needs the crop to make its product and knows it can earn a profit if it pays $10/bushel. Even though both parties realize that the future price might be higher or lower, both are happy to lock in the current price. Thus, derivatives help the world of commerce by de-risking price fluctuations caused by weather and other events.

Over the years, bankers and investors—the folks providing the cereal companies the cash they need to strike their deals with farmers—began to pay attention to these activities. While financiers have no particular interest in corn (they aren't growing any and don't make cereal from it), they realized that they could make a lot of money if they could accurately predict future prices and use those predictions to buy or sell derivatives contracts themselves.

After all, if you sign a contract to buy the farmer's crop for $10/bushel and the price at harvest is $12/bushel, you'll still pay the farmer just $10. Then you resell it for $12. That's a 20% gain in just a few months! Nice!

As you can imagine, it didn't take long for speculators to get into the action. Why let General Mills be the only one that gets to make guesses about future crop prices?

Anyone can now engage in options and futures trading, and you can speculate on the future price of just about anything—crops of all kinds as well as oil, gold, stocks, you name it. And, digital assets. The Chicago Mercantile Exchange and Bakkt both offer fully regulated end-to-end derivatives contracts for digital assets.

These complex products are doubly risky—because the asset itself is already risky—for four reasons:

1. **Leverage.** To place a $10,000 bet that bitcoin will be higher in value in six months, you don't invest $10,000 into a bitcoin futures contract. Instead, you pay as little as $500. Stated another way, your $10,000 could enable you to buy or sell a contract that controls $200,000 of bitcoin. This exaggerates the results—huge profit potential but with the simultaneous risk of losing massive amounts of money, far more than you invested (or perhaps can afford).

2. **Time.** When you buy digital assets—or any other investment—you can hold them forever. But all derivatives come with an expiration date, from one day to one year. This means you must not only be right about what the future price will be, you must be right about *when* that price will be reached. Otherwise, your investment could end up worthless. It's challenging enough to be right, and far more challenging to be right at the right time. The likelihood of being wrong on one or the other (price or time) is high.

3. **Price deviation.** As with OTC securities (later in this chapter), futures contracts often trade at prices different from that of the underlying asset. That's because the contract itself is a security—and that's what you're buying, not the asset on which the contract is based. For example, In October 2021, the CME price for bitcoin futures was 15% higher than the price for bitcoin itself, due to higher demand for the futures contract than for bitcoin. And sometimes, the prices of the contracts

themselves go wacky relative to each other. There are even names for when this happens (*contango* and *backwardation*), which we won't bother delving into here.

4. **Fees and taxes.** Whether you're right or wrong, you'll pay commissions to buy your contract and additional commissions to cancel the contract prior to expiration. And if you manage to profit from your trades, you'll owe a lot of taxes. That's because all this trading is *short-term*, defined by the IRS as occurring in a year or less. That means your profits won't qualify for long-term capital gains rates. Instead, you'll pay taxes at your top marginal Ordinary Income tax rate. For a lot of investors, that's a combined federal and state rate of 40% or more. (More on taxes in chapter 20.)

Approach derivatives with caution.

Bitcoin Futures ETFs

Bitcoin Futures ETFs don't hold bitcoin directly. Instead, they hold bitcoin futures contracts—those derivatives we just explored.

When you buy a futures contract, you're promising to buy a specific quantity of an asset on a specific date for a specific price. The prices for futures contracts don't mimic their underlying assets perfectly, but they are usually pretty close.

We covered the pitfalls of derivative products, so here are the merits of a bitcoin futures ETF:

1. As an ETF, these products are governed by the Securities Act of 1940—the strongest law of the investment world. It's more stringent, with greater consumer protections, than OTC securities.

2. Investors (and their advisors) are very familiar with this vehicle, and you may already own several ETFs. They are inex-

US Bitcoin Futures ETFs

Global X ETFs
globalxetfs.com

The Global X Blockchain & Bitcoin Strategy ETF (ticker: BITS) is an actively managed fund that seeks to capture the long-term growth potential of the blockchain and digital assets theme. The fund takes long positions in US-listed bitcoin futures contracts and companies positioned to benefit from the increased adoption of blockchain technology.

ProShares
proshares.com

ProShares Bitcoin Strategy ETF (BITO) is the first US bitcoin-linked ETF offering investors an opportunity to gain exposure to bitcoin returns in a convenient, liquid, and transparent way. The fund seeks to provide capital appreciation primarily through managed exposure to bitcoin futures contracts.

Valkyrie
valkyrie-funds.com

Valkyrie Bitcoin Strategy ETF (BTF) is an actively managed ETF that invests primarily in bitcoin futures contracts.

VanEck
vaneck.com

VanEck Bitcoin Strategy ETF (XBTF) is an actively managed ETF that seeks capital appreciation by investing in bitcoin futures contracts.

Note: some of these ETFs don't invest solely in bitcoin futures. For example, Global X's Bitcoin Futures ETF also invests in companies or funds that directly own digital assets, or are involved in the blockchain technology ecosystem. Such ETFs are therefore more diversified than those investing solely in bitcoin futures contracts.

For an up-to-date list, complete with hyperlinks, visit the
DACFP Yellow Pages
at dacfp.com

pensive, transparent, and easy to buy and manage along with the rest of your portfolio.

3. Bitcoin futures are likely to have higher levels of correlation to bitcoin than other proxies, such as public companies that buy bitcoin (like MicroStrategy or Tesla).

4. Bitcoin futures ETFs do not use leverage and manage expiration dates. Thus, these ETFs can be considered by both short-term traders and long-term investors.

Buying Coins, Tokens, Picks & Shovels, Companies, and Derivatives Indirectly

Everything we've explored thus far is referred to as *direct investing*. That's because you're buying the actual investments.

But doing so is a hassle. You must search for investment opportunities, analyze and evaluate each one, then buy them. This often entails opening an account with a digital assets exchange or custodian—and that means you must research them, too! And after selecting one, you must open the account, fund it, choose the investments you want to buy, arrange for their storage, and handle all the record-keeping and tax-reporting chores.

Ugh.

But wait a minute. You already have a portfolio. And that portfolio already has stocks in it. Did you go through all that hassle with your stocks? Probably not. Instead, you likely placed your money into some stock funds. That's so much easier!

So why not do the same thing with your digital assets? Increasingly, you can. When you buy funds of digital assets, you avoid the hassle of dealing with exchanges, wallets, and custody.

Let's look at the different kinds of funds that are available. As we do, keep in mind that all funds charge fees, which are often higher than what exchanges and custodians charge. Also, you still face all the risks of investing in this space.

ETFs Investing Exclusively in Companies Engaged in Blockchain and Digital Assets

Amplify ETFs
amplifyetfs.com

Amplify Transformational Data Sharing ETF (BLOK) invests in stocks of companies actively developing or using blockchain technologies.

ARK Invest
ark-funds.com

ARK Innovation ETF (ARKK) gives investors access to "disruptive innovation"—technologically enabled products and services that can change the way the world works. ARKK is actively managed.

Bitwise Investment Management
bitqetf.com

Bitwise Crypto Industry Innovators ETF (BITQ) tracks an index designed with Bitwise's industry expertise to identify the pioneering companies that generate the majority of their revenue from crypto-business activities.

Bitwise

Capital Link ETFs
cli-etfs.com

Capital Link Global Fintech Leaders ETF (KOIN) tracks the ATFI Global NextGen Fintech Index.

First Trust
ftportfolios.com

First Trust Indxx Innovative Transaction & Process ETF (LEGR) seeks investment results that correspond generally to the price and yield of the Indxx Blockchain Index.

Global X ETFs
globalxetfs.com

Global X Blockchain ETF (BKCH) provides exposure to companies involved in the growth of blockchain technology.

Global X

Hashdex ETFs
hashdex.com

Hashdex Nasdaq Crypto Index ETF (HDEX BH) tracks the performance of the Nasdaq Crypto Index.

For an up-to-date list, complete with hyperlinks, visit the
DACFP Yellow Pages
at dacfp.com

ETFs Investing Exclusively in Companies Engaged in Blockchain and Digital Assets

Invesco ETFs
invesco.com

Invesco CoinShares Global Blockchain UCITS ETF (BCHN) tracks the performance of the CoinShares Blockchain Global Equity Index.

Invesco

---

iShares by BlockRock
ishares.com

iShares Exponential Technologies ETF (ticker: XT) tracks a Morningstar index of global companies that displace older technologies and create new markets. The index features global stocks of technology producers and users across nine technology themes. It is composed of 200 stocks, equal-weighted and reconstituted annually.

Simplify ETFs
simplify.us

The Simplify US Equity PLUS GBTC ETF (SPBC) invests 100% of assets into the S&P 500 Stock Index, then leverages 10% and invests those additional funds in the Grayscale Bitcoin Trust (GBTC).

Siren ETFs
sirenetfs.com

Siren Nasdaq NexGen Economy ETF (BLCN) tracks the Reality Shares Nasdaq Blockchain Economy Index of large-cap companies that develop, research, support, innovate, and use blockchain technology. The index selection committee favors pure-play blockchain.

VanEck ETFs
vaneck.com

VanEck Digital Transformation ETF (DAPP) tracks the performance of the MVIS Global Digital Assets Equity Index.

Volt Funds
voltfunds.com

Volt Bitcoin Revolution ETF (BTCR) focuses on companies that have exposure to bitcoin and the infrastructure surrounding it. BTCR is an actively managed fund using the stock-to-flow model to determine concentrations in its bitcoin-related investments.

For an up-to-date list, complete with hyperlinks, visit the
DACFP Yellow Pages
at dacfp.com

You might own digital assets without even knowing it. Fidelity, Vanguard, and BlackRock are the largest holders of Marathon Digital, one of the biggest bitcoin mining operations in North America. ARK Investment Management and Morgan Stanley are the largest owners of the Grayscale Bitcoin Trust. American Funds, a $2.2 trillion mutual fund company, owns 12% of MicroStrategy; BlackRock owns even more.

They're not the only ones giving investors exposure to digital assets. Kinetics, FOMO, Emerald, Appleseed, and other fund companies invest in the Grayscale Bitcoin Trust—so if you own any of those funds, you're indirectly investing in digital assets. You could be an investor in bitcoin without even knowing it.

Exchange-Traded Notes

ETNs are more common outside the United States, and they have important fundamental differences from ETFs.

You know that an ETF buys an actual asset or basket of them. Now, picture this: A financial institution (such as a bank) issues an unsecured debt obligation. The ETN buys that offering, and the bank uses the money to buy the asset. So, the bank owns the asset and the ETN owns the bond issued by the bank, with payment terms of the bond linked to the asset's performance.

ETNs, therefore, are riskier than ETFs. ETNs don't own the underlying asset and instead are only as safe as the creditworthiness of the issuer. The SEC has posted a warning about Exchange-Traded Notes: "You should understand that ETNs are complex and involve many risks for interested investors and can result in the loss of your entire investment."

I'm not a fan of ETNs. I don't buy them, don't own any, and have never recommended them to anyone. But I want you to know they exist, so if a financial advisor pitches one to you, you'll understand that an Exchange-Traded Note is materially different from an Exchange-Traded Fund.

Exchange-Traded Products Investing Exclusively in Companies Engaged in Blockchain and Digital Assets

Single-Asset

Sponsor	Product Name	Ticker
21Shares	Algorand ETP	ALGO
	Avalanche ETP	AVAX
	Binance ETP	ABNB
	Bitcoin ETP	ABTC
	Bitcoin Cash ETP	ABCH
	Cardano ETP	AADA
	Ethereum ETP	AETH
	Polkadot ETP	ADOT
	Polygon ETP	POLY
	Ripple ETP	AXRP
	Short Bitcoin ETP	SBTC
	Solana ETP	ASOL
	Stellar ETP	AXLM
	Tezos	AXTZ

Index-Based and Multiple-Asset

Sponsor	Product Name	Ticker
21Shares	**Bitwise Select 10 ETP** tracks the Bitwise Select 10 Large Cap Crypto Index	KEYS
	Crypto Basket Index ETP tracks an index of the top 5 digital assets ranked by 2050 market capitalization.	HODL
	Crypto Basket 10 ETP tracks an index of the 10 largest digital assets	HODLX
	Crypto Basket Equal Weight ETP tracks an equal-weighted index of the 5 largest digital assets, based on market capitalization	HODLV
	Bitcoin Suisse Index ETP tracks an index composed of bitcoin and ether	ABBA
	Sygnum Platform Winners Index ETP tracks an index of the largest native tokens of original protocols	MOON

For an up-to-date list, complete with hyperlinks, visit the
DACFP Yellow Pages
at dacfp.com

OTC Trusts

Crypto community to SEC: "Will you let us sell a bitcoin ETF to the investing public?"

SEC to crypto community: "No."

Crypto community to SEC: "Oh, yeah? *Watch this.*"

As of this writing, the SEC still says it's too risky for the general investing public to be allowed to invest in an ETF that exclusively buys bitcoin, but the commission has no problem letting sophisticated, experienced, and wealthy investors do it.*

Okay, fine. It's no-go on the bitcoin ETF. But the story doesn't end there.

The crypto community is undaunted and thus has instead launched *bitcoin trusts*—with the SEC's approval. Go figure.

Don't confuse these trusts with the kind of trusts that are associated with estate planning.† Instead, think of these trusts to be kinda like mutual funds.

These trusts begin as *private placements*, which are investment funds available only to *accredited investors*. That's why the SEC is okay with them: accredited investors are deemed to have sufficient net worth and investment experience to warrant the risks associated with the investment. Specifically, you're an accredited investor if you

- earned $200,000 or more ($300,000 if married) in each of the last two years and expect to do so this year; or

- have a net worth of $1 million or more (excluding your primary residence); or

- hold a Series 7, 65, or 82 securities license.

---

* The SEC also has no problem letting people buy 3x inverse ETFs—investments you're meant to hold for a single day that generate three times the gains or losses of the daily movements of the stock market. That's okay, but a bitcoin ETF isn't?!

† Why, then, are they called *trusts* instead of *funds*? I dunno. Doesn't matter. Let's move on.

Here's the timeline. A fund company launches a bitcoin fund for accredited investors. The investors buy shares of the fund just as you would buy mutual funds or ETFs. But these private funds are not liquid; they typically have a 10-year life. (This is one reason the SEC considers them inappropriate for retail investors, who might need liquidity sooner than that.)

But even rich people sometimes want to sell their investments. So, these funds offer a nifty feature: After a *restricted period* (six months or a year), you can transfer your shares to your brokerage account. You can sell your shares in the open marketplace through that account. And in the open marketplace, *anyone*—accredited or not—can buy the shares you're selling.

In the open marketplace, the private fund morphs into what's called an OTC-traded trust, a reference to securities that trade *over the counter*, usually via OTCQX Best Market (OTCmarkets.com). It just means that your brokerage firm will seek a counterparty for your trade by connecting directly with another brokerage firm rather than going through the New York Stock Exchange or Nasdaq.

So, here's a riddle. A rich guy buys $100 worth of the accredited shares in the private fund. Ignoring expenses, that $100 investment buys him $100 worth of bitcoin. Later, the rich guy transfers his shares to his brokerage account, and he then offers to sell the shares via the OTC market. You offer to buy the shares for $100. Assuming the price of bitcoin hasn't changed, and again ignoring expenses, how much bitcoin do you own?

The answer: you could own bitcoin worth a whopping $500 or a teeny $50. How could this happen? Well, let's start at the very beginning, which is, with thanks to Julie Andrews, a very good place to start.

With mutual funds, ETFs, and private funds, the share price is called the *net asset value*; it's simply the total value of the fund's assets divided by the number of shares held by the public. For example, if the fund owns $100 worth of bitcoin and 20 shares are outstanding, the NAV of each share is $5.

Want to cash in your shares of a mutual fund? You don't really "sell" them; you "redeem" them—meaning you give them back to the fund company, which essentially erases them from its books and gives you whatever they're worth at that moment.

Using our above example, if an investor redeems three shares, only 17 of the original 20 will now exist, and the fund's total assets will be $85. And, thus, all the outstanding shares will still be $5 each.

But when an accredited investor sells their shares OTC, the price of the shares is *not* the NAV. Instead, the price is *whatever the seller and buyer agree on*. The trust is not involved in the transaction; therefore, there is no creation or elimination of shares—nothing is redeemed. The shares are simply moving from one party to another. And those parties might agree on a price that's different from the NAV.

Indeed, if investors are buying more shares than they are selling, the price can rise above the NAV. This is called *trading at a premium to NAV* or, in shorthand, a *premium*. If there are more sales of shares than purchases, the share price can fall below the NAV. That's called *trading at a discount to NAV* or, in shorthand, a *discount*.

What's fascinating is that the price of the shares often does move independently from the price of bitcoin. Sometimes, the OTC shares rise while bitcoin is falling and vice versa.

If this sounds familiar, that's because you know about *closed-end mutual funds*, which operate similarly. But where those securities tend to trade close to NAV (discounts of less than 5% are common), shares of bitcoin OTC trusts have been known to swing from 500% premiums to 20% discounts.

Yep, investors have been willing to pay $600 to buy $100 worth of bitcoin (huh?) while others have paid just $80 to buy $100 worth (cool!).

A Gambit

This premium/discount feature creates a fascinating opportunity for shrewd (aka aggressive) accredited investors. If that's you, consider this strategy: You buy shares of the trust at NAV via the private placement. Then, after the restricted period ends, you transfer the shares to a brokerage account. If the shares are trading at a premium, you sell them OTC for a profit—a profit that's independent of the price of bitcoin itself!

Say bitcoin is trading for $100 and you buy accredited shares at NAV. Say that a year later, bitcoin is trading 50% higher. Ordinary bitcoin investors have a 50% gain. But if the trust's share price is trading at a 75% premium, your gain would be 162.5%.

There's even a way for non-accredited investors to engage in this gambit. If the shares are trading at a discount, you buy them in the OTC market—essentially buying a dollar's worth of bitcoin for less than a dollar. If the discount shrinks or becomes a premium, you enjoy a profit that's independent of the price movement of bitcoin itself.

Of course, the gambit adds risk. Accredited investors buying shares at NAV via the private placement must wait for the restricted period to end; during that time, the OTC trading price could become a discount. And that discount might grow instead of shrink, resulting in losses instead of gains. This has happened before and is an important risk to consider.

Why would anyone knowingly buy a product whose price might vary significantly from NAV? Lots of reasons, including:

1. In the absence of a bitcoin ETF, these trusts are the most convenient and transparent way to buy bitcoin within a brokerage account. The securities can seamlessly be added to a diversified portfolio. That, in turn, allows for easy dollar cost averaging, rebalancing, record keeping, and tax reporting—which we'll cover in chapter 20.

2. If you're working with a financial advisor, using these trusts makes it easy for your advisor to assist you with all the above. As with the rest of your portfolio, your advisor can help you avoid costly mistakes.

3. The premium/discount feature offers an opportunity to enhance the profit potential.

Publicly Traded OTC Trusts Investing in Blockchain and Digital Assets
(also available to accredited investors at NAV, directly from fund company)

Single-Asset

Sponsor	Product Name	Ticker
Grayscale	Bitcoin Trust	GBTC
	Bitcoin Cash Trust	BCHG
	Ethereum Trust	ETHE
	Ethereum Classic Trust	ETCG
	Horizen Trust	HZEN
	Litecoin Trust	LTCN
	Stellar Lumens Trust	GXLM
	Zcash Trust	ZCSH
Osprey	Osprey Bitcoin Trust	OBTC

Osprey

Index-Based and Multiple-Asset

Sponsor	Product Name	Ticker
Bitwise	Bitwise 10 Crypto Index Fund	BITW
	holds the 10 biggest digital assets	
	(by market capitalization)	
Grayscale	Digital Large Cap Fund	GDLC
	holds large-cap digital assets	
	comprising 70% of the digital	
	asset market	

For an up-to-date list, complete with hyperlinks, visit the
DACFP Yellow Pages
at dacfp.com

4. When discounts have occurred, there have been large purchases of trust shares, which in theory should reduce the discount.

5. Many sponsors of OTC trusts say they will convert the trusts into ETFs as soon as the SEC permits them to do so. Should that occur, shares trading at a discount would be expected to rise to NAV. (The opposite is also true: any shares trading at a premium would fall to NAV.)

Blockchain and Digital Assets Funds for Accredited Investors

Single-Asset

Sponsor	Product Name
Bitwise bitwiseinvestments.com	Aave Fund Bitcoin Fund Compound Fund Ethereum Fund Polygon Fund Uniswap Fund
BlockFi blockfitrust.com	Bitcoin Trust Ethereum Trust Litecoin Trust
First Trust SkyBridge skybridgebitcoin.com	Bitcoin Fund Ethereum Fund
FS NYDIG fsnydig.com	Select Bitcoin Fund
Galaxy galaxyfundmanagement.com	Bitcoin Fund Ethereum Fund
Grayscale grayscale.com	Basic Attention Trust Chainlink Trust Decentraland Trust Filecoin Trust Livepeer Trust
IDX idxdigitalassets.com	Risk-Managed Bitcoin Trust Risk-Managed Ethereum Trust
Osprey ospreyfunds.io	Algorand Trust Solana Trust Polkadot Trust Polygon Trust
Pantera panteracapital.com	Bitcoin Fund

For an up-to-date list, complete with hyperlinks, visit the
DACFP Yellow Pages
at dacfp.com

Blockchain and Digital Assets Funds for Accredited Investors

Index-Based and Multiple-Asset

Sponsor	Product Name
Bitwise bitwiseinvestments.com	**DeFi Crypto Index Fund** holds the largest DeFi digital assets, based on the Bitwise Decentralized Finance Crypto Index **10 ex Bitcoin Crypto Index Fund** holds the 10 largest crypto assets, excluding bitcoin **10 Crypto Index Fund** holds the 10 digital assets, based on the Bitwise 10 Large Cap Crypto Index **10 Index Offshore Fund** similar to the 10 Crypto Index Fund, this fund is available to non-US investors
Galaxy galaxyfundmanagement.com	**Crypto Index Fund** tracks an index of the largest digital assets **DeFi Index Fund** tracks an index of the largest DeFi digital assets
Grayscale grayscale.com	**DeFi Fund** holds the digital assets comprising the CoinDesk DeFi Index
Invictus Capital invictuscapital.com	**Bitcoin Alpha** invests in bitcoin and delivers yield via options and lending **Crypto20** tracks an index of the top 20 digital assets, using staking to generate additional return **Crypto10 Hedged** active shifts between the top 10 digital assets and cash depending on market activity **Margin Lending** aims to generate interest income without risk of loss **DeFi Index** 70% of assets track a semi-passive index; 30% is actively managed

For an up-to-date list, complete with hyperlinks, visit the
DACFP Yellow Pages
at dacfp.com

Blockchain and Digital Assets Funds for Accredited Investors

Morgan Creek
morgancreekcap.com

Risk-Managed Bitcoin Fund
seeks to reduce volatility via
quantitative risk management techniques

Digital
invests in blockchain technologies,
artificial intelligence, and digital assets

Pantera
panteracapital.com

Blockchain Fund
invests in venture equity, early-stage
and liquid tokens
Early-Stage Token Fund
invests in teams building new protocols,
following an early-stage, venture-style model
Liquid Token Fund
invests in 15-20 tokens, using a quantitative
strategy to trade hourly

SarsonFunds
sarsonfunds.com

Crypto and Income Strategy
generates monthly income via
options trading and staking
Cryptocurrency ESG Strategy
invests in digital assts that meet
Environmental, Social, or Governance standards
Large Coin Strategy
invests in the 10 largest digital assets
Small Coin Strategy
invests in 20-40 small-cap digital assets,
including ICOs
Smart Crypto 15 Equal Weight Index
invests equally in the 15 largest digital assets
Stablecoin Index
invests in a basket of stablecons
that track the US dollar

For an up-to-date list, complete with hyperlinks, visit the
DACFP Yellow Pages
at dacfp.com

These OTC securities hold tens of billions of dollars in digital assets. They are among the most popular ways for investors to gain exposure to this new asset class. As you consider these securities, either via the open market or private placement, be sure you understand the premium/discount feature.

The sponsors of OTC trusts offer more than just bitcoin. Most of their trusts are still available only to accredited investors, but some trade OTC and are available to everyone.

Separately Managed Accounts

These are popular with many financial advisors, for reasons that will become apparent in a moment.

When you buy an ETF, you and all the other shareholders jointly own a pro rata share of the ETF's assets. But in a *separately managed account* all the assets in the account are directly owned by the investor. SMAs are therefore a hybrid between owning investments directly and owning them indirectly via a fund. Think of an SMA as an ETF where you're the only investor who owns it.

Because the SMA is yours and yours alone, your portfolio can be customized specifically for you. This lets you exclude assets you don't want (which you can't do with an ETF) and engage in tax optimization strategies. Because of this, many advisors use SMAs. They can provide their clients with more specific portfolio management than can be obtained by buying ETFs and mutual funds.

Traditionally, SMAs have been used to build stock portfolios. But some SMA providers now engage in digital assets—which is why we're talking about them here.

SMAs charge fees, just like all funds.

Digital Assets SMA Providers

Arbor Digital
arbordigital.io

Arbor Digital offers its first-of-its-kind SMA designed specifically for digital assets, giving RIAs and their clients access to qualified custodians to ensure compliance and security.

BITRIA
bitria.io

BITRIA SMA Network provides the "easy on-ramp" to digital asset investing for advisors looking for simplicity when owning digital assets. SMA partners have expertise in digital assets and manage all aspects of the clients' journey, from onboarding through portfolio management.

DAiM
daim.io

DAiM manages institutional investments in separately managed accounts according to a custom plan for a fixed fee.

Eaglebrook Advisors
eaglebrookadvisors.com

Eaglebrook is a tech-driven investment manager specializing in digital assets. Its SMA platform provides seamless onboarding, tax optimization, and custom investment strategies tailored specifically for advisors. Assets are secured in an offline, institutional-grade custody account at Gemini Trust Company.

Honeycomb Digital
honeycombdigital.io

Honeycomb Digital offers an SMA platform for professional wealth managers.

Kingsly Capital Management
kingslycapital.com

Kingsly Capital manages and sub-advises digital asset portfolios for individuals, institutions, family offices, and RIAs. The firm is one of the first SEC-registered investment advisors to specialize exclusively in digital assets, DeFi, NFTs, and other blockchain assets.

For an up-to-date list, complete with hyperlinks, visit the
DACFP Yellow Pages
at dacfp.com

Digital Assets SMA Providers

Leavenworth Capital
leavenworthcapital.com

Leavenworth is a quantitative investment firm that manages cryptoasset strategies for individuals, institutions, RIAs, and financial advisors. The firm uses proprietary analytical and trading models to generate alpha.

PM Squared Financial
pmsquaredfinancial.com

PM Squared's investments span the full range of blockchain possibilities. Its solution leverages blockchain technology with experience from the traditional securities world.

Rubicon Crypto
rubicon.finance

Rubicon bridges the gap between the digital and traditional investment worlds. It offers familiar, commonsense investment solutions that bring asset allocation and disciplined professional management to the emerging digital asset space.

Willow Crypto
willowcrypto.com

Willow Crypto specializes in digital asset management. It creates professionally managed portfolios to provide core exposure to the most promising digital assets and tactical allocations to emerging and evolving trends.

For an up-to-date list, complete with hyperlinks, visit the
DACFP Yellow Pages
at dacfp.com

Turnkey Asset Management Programs

Turnkey asset management programs (TAMPs) are all-in-one back-office systems that help financial advisors manage client assets, offering investment research, asset allocation, account administration, billing, and reporting.

In my former life as a financial advisor, my colleagues and I built EMAP—the Edelman Managed Asset Program. At the time, it was one of the largest TAMPs in the industry, and it was available only to clients of our firm. So, it's safe to say I'm a fan of these investment solutions.

By the way, SMAs, which we just covered, are a type of TAMP.

Venture Capital, Hedge Funds, and Funds of Funds

If there's a problem with ETFs, SMAs, and TAMPs, it's that they traditionally invest only in the stocks of publicly traded companies. This wasn't an issue 50 years ago; back then, young companies often went public, giving retail investors the opportunity to buy shares early. That's generally not the case today; companies tend to stay private much longer, going public only after they're hugely successful.

When Microsoft went public in 1986, for example, it raised a mere $61 million. But when Facebook went public in 2012, it was already worth $102 billion.

What does this mean? Just this: if you limit your investments to public stocks—buying them directly or via mutual funds, ETFs, SMAs, and TAMPs—you can no longer buy the Microsofts of tomorrow. Instead, you're stuck with owning the Facebooks of today, missing out on the massive growth they enjoy before going public.

Indeed, some of the largest new tech companies are still private, as shown in Figure 16.1.

These are *unicorns*—tech companies less than 10 years old that are each worth more than $1 billion. CB Insights lists more than 800 of them from all over the world.

Digital Assets TAMP Providers

BITRIA
bitria.io

The BITRIA Digital Turnkey Asset Management Platform brings professional-grade portfolio management capabilities to digital asset investing, empowering advisors, and asset managers with distributed access and control of firm accounts, client accounts, and model strategies. It will onboard client funds, adopt templated or custom portfolio allocations, rebalance positions, and much more.

BlockFi
blockfi.com

BlockFi bridges the gap between digital asset markets and traditional financial institutions and their need for backward compatibility to the world of traditional securities: executing, margining, shorting, and reporting.

BlockFi

Fidelity Digital Assets
fidelitydigitalassets.com

Fidelity Digital Assets provides financial intermediaries with a platform to securely participate in the digital asset space. Fidelity Digital Assets provides professional custody services as well as execution solutions.

Flourish
flourish.com

Flourish gives advisors a way to offer simple, secure, and compliant access to this emerging asset class. It offers a highly regulated, qualified custodian, an easy-to-use experience, and all the tools advisors need to get started.

SFOX
sfox.com

SFOX is the leading independent crypto prime dealer, unifying global liquidity and best-price execution from a single account.

For an up-to-date list, complete with hyperlinks, visit the
DACFP Yellow Pages
at dacfp.com

Company	2021 Value
Stripe	$95 billion
SpaceX	$74 billion
Instacart	$39 billion
Databricks	$28 billion
Epic Games	$17 billion
Chime	$15 billion

FIGURE 16.1

There's nothing you can do about this situation if you're a retail investor. However, if you're an accredited investor, you have an opportunity. You can invest in *venture capital funds*. As the name implies, capital provided by investors is used to buy equity in young companies. VC funds are created by both small VC firms and the nation's largest brokerage firms, such as Goldman Sachs and JPMorgan, for wealthy clients, pension funds, endowments, sovereign funds (money belonging to a government), and institutional clients (such as insurance companies). More than half a trillion dollars has been placed into VC funds, according to the National Venture Capital Association.

Although lots of mutual funds and ETFs are alike—every S&P 500 Stock Index Fund is pretty much the same except for fees—every VC fund is unique. That's because each invests in a different set of early-stage companies. So, while it might not matter much which S&P 500 fund you buy, it matters greatly which VC fund you choose.

That's because, in the VC world, it's all about *deal flow*. The manager of the VC fund must know about these young companies and persuade their founders to let the fund invest in them. Connections are key—and it explains why many VC funds are staffed in regions where start-ups thrive, such as Silicon Valley, Boston, and New York. The more companies you can evaluate, the greater your odds of finding the next Facebook.

Each VC firm issues several VC funds—one at a time. They raise a certain amount of capital from investors, find companies to invest in, then launch a new fund and repeat the process. So, each VC fund is available only for a limited time and to a small number of investors. And no two VC funds are identical. Like wine, VCs have vintages—the 1999 funds that bought dot-com stocks before the crash did poorly, while the 2009 funds that invested after the credit crisis did well.

The risks to investing in VC are extreme:

- No liquidity for 5 to 10 years.

- No dividends or interest paid during this time.

- Large investment minimums—from $50,000 to $10 million.

- Complex tax reporting. VC funds don't issue one-page IRS Form 1099 like mutual funds and ETFs. Instead, they issue IRS Form K-1. This complicated document can run dozens of pages and demands that you hire a professional tax preparer to complete your tax return. Your preparer's fee will rise—and you'll most likely have to file an extension, because K-1s are rarely mailed to investors by the April 15 tax deadline. Plan on filing your return each October.

- High fees. The average ETF investor pays 0.45% per year, according to Morningstar. VC funds, though, typically feature a "two and twenty" fee schedule: they charge 2% per year *plus* an incentive fee, equal to 20% of the profits over the life of the fund.

Despite the negatives, VCs have generated the best returns over the past decade, according to PitchBook, as shown in Figure 16.2.

Asset Class	10-Year Average Annual Return
Venture Capital	13.9%
S&P 500	13.9%
Private Equity	13.2%
Real Estate	12.3%
Private Capital	12.0%
MSCI World Index	9.7%
Private Debt	8.3%
Global High Yield Corporate Bonds	6.4%
Real Assets	5.3%

FIGURE 16.2

Of course, past performance does not guarantee future results. And VCs themselves know, but may not tell you, that they expect to lose money on most of their investments. For every 10 companies they invest in, they might hope to break even on two or three and hit a home run on one—earning enough to cover the losses they'll incur on the other six to eight while still producing double-digital annual returns, net of fees.

Hedge funds are similar to VC funds. As an added feature, they strive to *hedge*, or reduce, their risk via strategies that include more than simply buying equity stakes in a variety of companies. They also invest in derivatives, engage in *short selling* (a bet that the value of a company will fall, not rise), and *leverage* (borrowing money to invest more capital than is provided by investors, which can increase returns but losses as well).

Unlike VC funds, which accept money upon launch and then remain closed until they self-terminate in 5 to 10 years, hedge funds are *open-end funds*, like mutual funds. In other words, investors can almost always acquire or redeem shares. I say "almost" because hedge funds sometimes close those windows—either refusing to accept new money or limiting the ability of current investors to sell. As you might imagine, those "gates" tend to open and close when the markets are performing particularly well (they won't accept new money) or poorly (you can't sell).

Because deal flow is so important to VC and hedge funds, the challenge for investors is choosing the right fund. That's why an additional breed of funds has emerged: *funds of funds.**

Instead of investing in a single VC or hedge fund, you could invest in several. But each has its own minimum investment requirement, often $500,000 or more. Thus, investing in 10 of them would require you to pony up $5 million. Instead, you could place your $500,000 into a single fund of funds. It will invest in those 10 funds for you—giving you broader diversification without your having to invest 10 times more money.

The biggest downside is that you'll incur two sets of fees: those of the underlying VC or hedge fund plus those of the wrapper, the fund of funds itself.

---

* That's not a typo, even though Word's spellchecker persists in telling me it is.

VC Funds Investing in Blockchain and Digital Assets

10T
10tfund.com

10T is a mid- to late-stage growth equity fund that invests in private companies operating in the digital asset ecosystem.

a16z by Andreessen Horowitz
a16z.com

a16z by Andreessen Horowitz has sizable AUM across several funds, including a16z crypto and Crypto Fund III. Investments span across nonspeculative use case companies and protocols at various stages, and are in the form of equity, convertible notes, coins, and security tokens.

Abstract Ventures
abstractvc.com

Abstract Ventures is a sector-agnostic venture investor in Pre-seed, Seed, and Series A start-up companies.

AlphaBlock
alphablock.com

AlphaBlock Investments is a venture capital firm that invests in innovative blockchain technology firms.

Arrington XRP Capital
arringtonxrpcapital.com

Arrington XRP Capital focuses on blockchain-based capital markets. Founded in 2017 in Seattle, it invests in early-stage ventures, Seed, Series A, initial coin offerings, and corporate rounds.

Atomic Fund
atomic.fund

Atomic's platform offers a range of products focusing on trading tools, a dashboard for monitoring, market data, and cold storage wallets, thereby enabling users to invest in cryptocurrencies without hassle.

AU21 Capital
au21.capital

Founded in 2017, AU21 Capital is a venture capital firm based in San Francisco. The firm seeks to invest in companies operating in the blockchain and artificial intelligence sectors.

For an up-to-date list, complete with hyperlinks, visit the
DACFP Yellow Pages
at dacfp.com

VC Funds Investing in Blockchain and Digital Assets

Binance Labs
labs.binance.com

Binance Labs identifies, invests, and empowers viable blockchain entrepreneurs, start-ups, and communities, providing financing to industry projects that help grow the larger blockchain ecosystem.

BitFury Capital
bitfury.com

BitFury Capital invests in entrepreneurs building the next generation of blockchain and crypto solutions. It provides seed and later-stage funding to businesses that show potential for long-term success in blockchain technology, digital assets, artificial intelligence, and renewable energy.

Bloccelerate
bloccelerate.vc

Bloccelerate invests in projects that promote sophisticated implementation of blockchain technology by companies and enterprises.

Blockchain Capital
blockchain.capital

Blockchain Capital is a blockchain-focused VC fund group that has funded several unicorns to date, including Anchorage, Coinbase, Ripple, and Kraken. It was the first-ever tokenized fund, issuing shares via the world's first security token. Diversification is risk-adjusted across growth stage and geography. The fund provides operational support, including governance and staking protocol design.

Blockchange Ventures
blockchange.vc

Blockchange Ventures invests in early-stage blockchain companies, protocols, and applications.

BlockTower Capital
blocktower.com

BlockTower applies trading, investing, and portfolio management to the digital asset class.

For an up-to-date list, complete with hyperlinks, visit the
DACFP Yellow Pages
at dacfp.com

VC Funds Investing in Blockchain and Digital Assets

Block Ventures
blockventures.com

Block Ventures is a permanent venture capital company that thinks differently about investing and scaling deep tech companies by supporting and growing the next generation of early-stage technology businesses across Europe.

BlockWealth Capital
blockwealthcapital.com

BlockWealth Capital is focused exclusively on ventures, tokens, and projects related to blockchain tech, digital currency, and crypto assets.

Castle Island Ventures
castleisland.vc

Castle Island Ventures is an early-stage venture capital firm exclusively focused on public blockchains.

CMT Digital Ventures
cmt.digital

CMT Digital is a venture capital firm engaging in the digital asset and blockchain technology industry.

Coinbase Ventures
coinbase.com

Coinbase Ventures is an investment arm of Coinbase that invests in early-stage cryptocurrency and blockchain start-ups.

CoinFund
coinfund.io

CoinFund invests in venture and liquid opportunities within the blockchain sector with a focus on digital assets, decentralization technologies, and key enabling infrastructure.

Collaborative Fund
collaborativefund.com

Collaborative Fund focuses on supporting and investing in the shared future. Funds center on two macro themes: the growth of the creative class, and the concept of the collaborative economy.

ConsenSys Ventures
consensys.net

ConsenSys Ventures is a venture capital arm of ConsenSys, a blockchain venture production studio.

For an up-to-date list, complete with hyperlinks, visit the
DACFP Yellow Pages
at dacfp.com

VC Funds Investing in Blockchain and Digital Assets

Defiance Capital
defiance.capital

Defiance Capital is a DeFi-focused crypto asset fund that combines fundamental research with an activist investment approach.

Delphi Labs
delphidigital.io

Delphi Labs is an outsourced investment team, generating insights for many of the top funds through bespoke research solutions.

Delphi Ventures
delphiventures.com

Delphi Ventures is a global team of analysts, specializing in specific sectors of the digital asset industry.

Digital Currency Group
dcg.co

Digital Currency Group is a New York venture capital company focusing on the digital asset market.

Distributed Global
distributedglobal.com

Distributed Global is an investment firm focused on the blockchain and digital asset ecosystem.

Divergence Ventures
div.vc

Divergence Ventures is a venture capital firm based in San Francisco. The firm seeks to make investments in the digital asset sector.

Dragonfly Capital
dcp.capital

Dragonfly Capital Partners brings together leading participants in the decentralized economy to invest in and support the most promising opportunities in the crypto-asset class.

Draper Goren Holm
drapergorenholm.com

Draper Goren Holm is a fintech venture studio incubating and accelerating early-stage blockchain start-ups.

Electric Capital
electriccapital.com

Electric Capital is an early-stage venture firm focused on crypto, blockchain, and fintech marketplaces.

For an up-to-date list, complete with hyperlinks, visit the
DACFP Yellow Pages
at dacfp.com

VC Funds Investing in Blockchain and Digital Assets

Eos Fund
eosventurepartners.com

Eos is focused exclusively on InsurTech. Eos was founded in 2016 to bridge the "digital chasm" between InsurTech start-ups and traditional insurance companies.

Fabric Ventures
fabric.vc

Fabric Ventures is a venture capital firm that invests in scalable decentralized networks.

FinShi Capital
finshi.capital

FinShi Capital is a venture fund formed on blockchain technology, founded in alliance with Capinvest 21 and Asia LP.

Framework Ventures
framework.ventures

Framework Ventures is a venture capital firm that invests in founders that enable blockchain technologies.

Future Perfect Ventures
futureperfectventures.com

Future Perfect Ventures is an early-stage VC firm focused on decentralized technologies including blockchain, crypto, IoT, and AI.

Galaxy Interactive Fund
galaxyinteractive.io

Galaxy Interactive is a leading sector-focused VC investing in interactive entertainment, at the intersection of content, social, finance, and technology.

#hashed
hashed.com

Hashed is a global, early-stage venture fund focused on backing founders who are pioneering the future of blockchain and digital assets.

HyperChain Capital
hyperchain.capital

HyperChain is a digital assets management company focused on blockchain-based projects and decentralized protocols.

For an up-to-date list, complete with hyperlinks, visit the
DACFP Yellow Pages
at dacfp.com

VC Funds Investing in Blockchain and Digital Assets

Hyperion VC
hyperionvc.com

Hyperion is an early-stage blockchain VC helping start-ups disrupt incumbents globally.

IDG Capital LPs
idgcapital.com

IDG Capital funds early- to growth-stage companies in the technology sector.

Kenetic Capital
kenetic.capital

Kenetic is focused on digital assets and blockchain-related companies.

KR1 Fund
kr1.io

KR1 is a publicly listed investment company focused on the blockchain ecosystem, investing in early-stage projects, and blockchain-based digital assets.

Medici Ventures
mediciventures.com

Medici Ventures manages Overstock.com's investments in firms building solutions and leveraging and servicing blockchain technologies.

Moonrock Capital
moonrockcapital.io

Moonrock Capital is a blockchain advisory and investment partnership based in London and Hamburg.

NGC Ventures
ngc.fund

NGC Ventures is an investor of blockchain and distributed ledger technologies.

North Island Ventures
northisland.ventures

North Island Ventures is a digital-assets-focused venture capital fund.

For an up-to-date list, complete with hyperlinks, visit the
DACFP Yellow Pages
at dacfp.com

VC Funds Investing in Blockchain and Digital Assets

Pantera Capital
panteracapital.com

Through its venture funds, Pantera offers investors actively managed, multistage exposure to companies building blockchain products and services. Pantera launched the world's first blockchain-exclusive venture fund in 2013 and has since raised two subsequent venture funds.

Paradigm
pdvpl.com

Paradigm Ventures was founded to challenge traditional approaches for analyzing, investing in, and developing technology focused ventures.

PayPal Ventures
pypl.com

PayPal Ventures is a corporate VC, investing in financial services, commerce enablement, and data and infrastructure companies.

PNYX Ventures
pnyx.ventures

PNYX Ventures is a digital asset management firm specializing in blockchain capital markets.

Polychain Capital
polychain.capital

Polychain Capital is a digital assets hedge fund and venture capital firm based in San Francisco. The firm makes early-stage investments in blockchain companies, invests in ICOs, and trades digital assets.

PostModern Partners
postmodernpartners.com

PostModern Partners is a leading investment manager open to accredited investors only. It oversees an aggressive cross-market investment fund that focuses on high-risk, high-return blockchain investment opportunities.

Rarestone Capital
rarestone.capital

Founded in 2020, Rarestone Capital is a venture capital firm based in London. The firm invests in blockchains and digital assets.

For an up-to-date list, complete with hyperlinks, visit the
DACFP Yellow Pages
at dacfp.com

VC Funds Investing in Blockchain and Digital Assets

Spark Digital Capital
sparkdigitalcapital.com

Spark invests in the future of blockchain and tech.

SPiCE VC
spicevc.com

SPiCE provides investors with wide exposure to the massive growth of the blockchain and tokenization ecosystem.

Union Square Ventures
usv.com

Union Square funds start-ups in the internet and mobile industries and has been a major investor in blockchain start-ups.

Valar Ventures
valar.com

Valar Ventures invests in high-margin, fast-growing technology companies that are pursuing huge market opportunities.

Volt Capital
volt.capital

Volt Capital is a research- and community-driven crypto fund.

Woodstock Fund
woodstockfund.com

Woodstock is an emerging technology investment fund that invests in early- and growth-stage blockchain start-ups and companies.

For an up-to-date list, complete with hyperlinks, visit the
DACFP Yellow Pages
at dacfp.com

Hedge Funds Investing in Blockchain and Digital Assets

BlockTower
blocktower.com

BlockTower is a crypto and blockchain investment firm, applying professional trading, investing, and portfolio management to the digital asset class.

Ikigai Asset Management
ikigai.fund

Ikigai is a long/short multistrategy hedge fund investing in digital assets. The firm seeks to generate superior risk-adjusted returns through venture-stage pre-ICO investments and liquid hedge fund strategies.

Multicoin Capital
multicoin.capital

Multicoin is a thesis-driven investment firm that invests in digital assets and blockchain companies reshaping trillion-dollar markets. It manages a hedge fund and a venture fund, investing across both public and private markets.

Pythagoras Investments
pythagoras.investments

Pythagoras manages a crypto arbitrage trading fund and a crypto trend-following fund. Pythagoras has $100 million in AUM, a seven-year track record, and 10 full-time quant traders and programmers trained at Harvard and Columbia.

For an up-to-date list, complete with hyperlinks, visit the
DACFP Yellow Pages
at dacfp.com

Funds of Funds Investing in Blockchain and Digital Assets

Accolade Partners
accoladepartners.com

Accolade specializes in a concentrated portfolio of hard-to-access funds across the venture capital and growth equity landscape.

Blockchain Coinvestors
blockchaincoinvestors.com

Blockchain Coinvestors is an open-ended liquid fund. It manages a bundle of blockchain funds as well as equity investments. It was the first blockchain fund-of-funds.

Galaxy Vision Hill
galaxyfundmanagement.com

Galaxy Vision Hill Venture FOF II invests in long-term disruptive trends brought by blockchain technology, including DeFi, Web 3.0, NFTs/Digital Goods, and other novel crypto-related services and infrastructure.

Hutt Capital
huttcapital.com

Hutt partners with venture firms to provide diversified exposure to globally promising blockchain and digital asset start-ups through secondary and direct investments. It strives to offer long-term global exposure to blockchain innovation with reduced risk and volatility.

Protocol Ventures
protocolventures.com

Protocol has strong relationships with top hedge fund managers in highly liquid digital assets, SAFTs, and blockchain/crypto-related equity. The fund aligns with fund managers who have a deep technical understanding of blockchain technology, asymmetric knowledge and vision of the industry, a network of respected leaders worldwide, a value-add approach to the ecosystem, and a clear and differentiated investment thesis.

For an up-to-date list, complete with hyperlinks, visit the
DACFP Yellow Pages
at dacfp.com

Chapter 17
How to Manage Your Portfolio's Digital Assets

Buy-and-Hold vs. Market Timing

Congratulations! You're making great progress. You now know which investments (or which kinds) you want to own, and how to buy them. You also know how much of your portfolio you want to allocate to digital assets.

Here's the next question for your consideration: When you buy digital assets, should you hold them for years or for much shorter periods, owning them only when prices are rising, and selling before they decline?

That notion of buying-and-selling is called *market timing*. In other asset classes, history has shown us that market timing doesn't work.* But is that also true for digital assets?

For example, we know that you need to place large portions of your money into other asset classes when allocating to them in order to meaningfully impact your return, but we now also know that this isn't necessary when investing in digital assets. So could it be that we need to treat market timing differently for digital assets as well?

Let's answer that question by looking at bitcoin's price history, from July 17, 2010 (regarded as the first date establishing a price for bitcoin), through December 31, 2020, as shown in Figure 17.1.

The data in this chart suggest that the longer you held bitcoin, the more profit you'd have enjoyed. But let's look at a more recent interval, 2015 to 2020, as shown in Figure 17.2.

---

* For more on this, read any of my books—it's a constant theme.

228

Bitcoin Price History 7/17/10 - 12/31/20					
	Start	End	Start Price	End Price	Gain
1-yr	10/31/20	10/31/21	$13,737	$61,319	347%
5-yr	10/31/16	10/31/21	$727	$61,319	8,335%
10-yr	10/31/11	10/31/21	$3.11	$61,319	1,971,572%
Inception	7/17/10	10/31/21	$0.07	$61,319	87,598,471%

Source: 99bitcoins.com

FIGURE 17.1

Annual Bitcoin Returns 2015-2020		
	Gain	10 Best Days
2015	34%	96%
2016	124%	80%
2017	1,369%	163%
2018	-73%	108%
2019	92%	123%
2020	303%	108%

Source: YahooFinance, DACFP

FIGURE 17.2

As you can see in Figure 17.2, bitcoin suffers high levels of volatility—gains as high as 1,369% (in 2017) and losses as deep as 73% (in 2018). When you look more closely, though, at each year's 10 best days, you see something different. In 2015, for example, bitcoin rose 34%, but it gained 96% during that year's 10 best days.

And in 2016, bitcoin posted an annual gain of 124%—with an 80% increase in just 10 days. Figure 17.2 shows you that each year performed similarly.

Let me summarize it for you:

- Since the inception of bitcoin, if you missed the one day that bitcoin rose the most, you would have missed 35% of all the gains bitcoin has ever produced.
- If you missed the best week, you'd have missed 50% of the gains throughout the entire history of bitcoin.
- If you missed the best month, you'd have missed 72% of the gains.
- And if you missed the best two months, you would have missed 92% of the total gains.

If that motivates you to engage in market timing, ask yourself this: What would happen if, instead of capturing the 10 best days, you accidentally captured the 10 worst?

Here's the answer:

- In 2015, even though bitcoin rose 34%, you would have lost all your money.
- In 2016, bitcoin rose 124%, but you would have lost 81%.
- In 2017, bitcoin rose nearly 1,400% but you'd have lost your entire investment.
- In 2018, you'd again have lost all your money.
- Ditto 2019, even though bitcoin almost doubled.
- And you got wiped out in 2020, a year in which bitcoin tripled.

In other words, market timing in digital assets is no different from market timing in the stock market. All the warnings about market timing you get from financial advisors are applicable in this asset class.

Before you start to argue with me, by claiming that bitcoin's unusual and excessive volatility makes it ideal for market timing, consider this: in 2020, 30% of the stocks in the S&P 500 were more volatile than bitcoin. Are you market timing with stocks? If not, then don't do it with bitcoin.

Reducing Risk via Dollar Cost Averaging

Does volatility scare you? If so, here's a strategy that turns volatility to your advantage.

It's called dollar cost averaging (DCA). Instead of investing your money all at once, you invest slowly over time. Here's how to do it:

First, decide how much money you're going to invest in digital assets. Then, decide the time frame for making those investments. Say you decide to invest $10,000 over one year. You'd thus invest $833 per month. (The interval doesn't matter, nor does the amount. What does matter is that you are consistent in your deployment.)

To help you understand the benefits of dollar cost averaging, let me pose this riddle: You have $100, and you buy an investment worth $10. Thus, you get 10 shares. Next month, you invest another $100, but the investment is now worth just $5. Thus, you get 20 shares. What's the average price of all your shares?

Is your answer $7.50? If so, this is how you derived it:

($10 + $5) / 2 = $7.50.

But that answer is wrong.

The correct answer is $6.67. You invested a total of $200 and you own a total of 30 shares. Here's the formula you should have used:

$200 / 30 = $6.67.

Confused? That's because you used the *arithmetic mean*, which you learned in third grade. I used the *harmonic mean*, which we learned about in fourth grade.

Both averages are legitimate. They simply provide us different information. The harmonic mean reveals the *average cost*, while the arithmetic mean reveals the *average price*. Since harmonic means are always lower than arithmetic means, the average cost is always lower than the average price! Dollar cost averaging therefore always produces a profit!*

Cool, huh! You know the best time to buy is when prices are low, and DCA makes that happen for us automatically. You get more shares when prices are lower, and you get fewer shares when prices are higher. Thus, you accumulate shares in a cost-efficient manner.

To work best, DCA needs to be applied to assets that fluctuate in value. Savings accounts always have a stable $1 price, so DCA offers no particular benefit. The stock market is volatile, though, and that's why DCA is a common strategy for stock investments. And you can apply it to digital assets just as effectively.

To illustrate the impact of dollar cost averaging, let's return to December 31, 2017, when bitcoin's price was $13,379. Say you invested $10,000 in a lump sum, buying 0.75 bitcoins. Fourteen months later, on January 31, 2019, bitcoin's price had fallen 74%. Your $10,000 investment was worth only $2,592.

But bitcoin's price then began rising; by October 31, 2020, it reached $13,737, and you've recovered your losses. That's not terribly exciting, because after three years, you've only broken even.

The story would be very different if you had DCA'd. If you'd invested that $10,000 over a 12-month period ($833 per month) instead of in a lump sum, here's what would have happened:

- Instead of being down 74% at the January 2019 low, your loss would have been a third smaller than the lump-sum investor's loss.

---

* Unless the asset becomes worthless, in which case nothing will save you.

- Instead of having to wait until October 31, 2020, to break even, you'd have recovered your loss six months sooner.

- Most important, you'd have accumulated nearly twice as many bitcoins as the lump-sum investor. By owning so many more coins, your investment by December 2020 would have quadrupled in value to nearly $40,000, while the lump-sum investor's account would have been worth only about $21,000.

	Loss as of Jan 2019 low	Recovered Loss in	Value at Dec 2020
$10,000 Lump Sum in Dec 2017	74%	Dec 2020	$21,000
$833 / month Dec 2017 - Jan 2019	46%	May 2019	$40,000

FIGURE 17.3

Of course, dollar cost averaging will also reduce your gains if the asset's price steadily rises. But digital assets have a history of extreme volatility, and that argues for investing via DCA if you want to reduce your risk.

Reducing Risk by Rebalancing

All the data and charts we've seen assume that you add a small amount of bitcoin (our proxy here for the broader digital assets ecosystem) to your portfolio. And we've been assuming you've deployed a set-it-and-forget-it approach.

That's not ideal. A far better way to manage your money is to engage in *periodic portfolio rebalancing*. This is crucial because, if left alone, the portfolio you've created will drift from deliberate to reckless.

The reason is that each investment you own performs independently from each other. Some investments will rise while others fall—

and eventually your portfolio won't resemble the asset allocation model you created.

For a simple illustration, consider placing your money equally into cash and stocks, a 50/50 portfolio. Over time, it's highly likely that the stocks will grow faster than your cash. An unattended portfolio would drift from 50/50 to 60/40, 70/30, 80/20, and eventually to 90/10.

To solve the problem of drift, you must periodically rebalance. You do this by selling enough stocks to bring that allocation back to 50% and adding that money to cash, raising it back to 50%. This will return your portfolio to its original proportions.

This might seem counterintuitive because rebalancing requires you to sell the investments that made the most money, and to buy the investments that made the least (or perhaps even lost money). But the idea is actually brilliant, because when you rebalance, you always sell assets at relatively higher prices while buying others that have relatively lower prices.

Selling high and buying low. Or, as it's more commonly phrased, *Buy low, sell high.*

Consider the period of December 16, 2017, through March 3, 2020, when bitcoin fell 67%. A 59/40/1 portfolio that was rebalanced had higher returns and lower risks than a 60/40 portfolio that wasn't rebalanced. *Even when its price is falling, you're better off with bitcoin than without it.*

Indeed, history shows that adding bitcoin to a portfolio improves the Sharpe ratio 69% of the time, and when you add bitcoin *and* rebalance the portfolio, you improve the Sharpe ratio 100% of the time.

You can rebalance monthly, quarterly, annually, or based on percentage movements within the portfolio. Which is best? You might as well ask who the best painter of the Renaissance was—it's subjective. All I can tell you is that the data show that every rebalancing strategy lowers volatility.

PART FOUR

Regulation, Taxation, and Compliance

Chapter 18
How Digital Assets Are Regulated

Patent medicines became popular in the 1700s and 1800s. In truth, they weren't really medicine, and nothing was really patented—the name itself was part of the scam.

And scams they were. Slick salesmen touted them as remedies for dozens of ailments, including kidney problems, baldness, venereal disease, tuberculosis, cancer, cholera, epilepsy, scarlet fever, paralysis, "female complaints," and more. The products were bogus—placebos at best, but often dangerous (heroin and cocaine were common ingredients).

To protect the public, Congress passed dozens of laws, starting with the Pure Food and Drug Act of 1906, and created many federal agencies, including the FDA, National Institutes of Health, Department of Agriculture, and the Centers for Disease Control and Prevention, among others. Although scams persist—you routinely see ads for "nutritional supplements" that claim to boost energy, increase sexual potency, cure baldness, and whatnot—it's safe to say we're all happier to be living under today's system than the one in place in 1850.

Ditto with automobiles. It couldn't have taken long after the first car left the factory for the first car accident to occur. The federal and state governments soon realized the need for laws and regulations governing how cars should be built and how we should operate them, and we've enjoyed astonishing improvement: in 1913, according to the National Safety Council, 33 people died for every 10,000 vehicles on the road; by 2019, there were fewer than 2 deaths per 10,000 vehicles, a 96% improvement.

From a regulatory perspective, the digital assets field is like the 1800s and early 1900s for medicines and cars. Digital assets are so new that legislators and regulators haven't been able to catch up, but they're working hard to do so.

Policymakers must resolve four major issues:

- **Jurisdiction.** Digital assets don't exist in a set place, making it difficult to know who has jurisdiction over products and transactions.

- **Terminology.** It's difficult to write laws and regulations about digital assets if we can't even agree on what words to use.

- **Anonymity.** It's often difficult to determine who is behind or engaging in digital transactions because most blockchains or their transactions are anonymous. Others are pseudonymous, meaning the transactions are connected to a traceable account but not to the account's owner. How do you regulate transactions when you can't identify the parties involved?

- **Dispute resolution.** Arguments are inevitable. Even if you know who the parties are (perhaps by self-identification), how can you enforce a verdict if the parties are in different jurisdictions?

Policymakers have three choices: they can be encouraging, permissive, or strict. *Encouraging countries* let blockchain and blockchain-related companies flourish. They've created laws and regulations to provide clarity over how transactions are treated and what rules must be followed. These nations include Bermuda, Hong Kong, Japan, Malta, Singapore, and Switzerland.

Permissive countries aren't interfering with trading and transactions in digital assets, but their rules aren't yet clear. Essentially, these governments are permitting operations while the government figures it all out. Most countries are in this category.

Strict countries have either banned certain digital assets transactions or exchanges or taken a hostile approach to citizens who use digital assets. These nations include Algeria, Bolivia, Morocco, Pakistan, and China.

The United States is among the permissive countries. As the world's leading capitalist nation, it understands the importance of innovation—and realizes that banning the industry would merely push innovation overseas, benefiting other nations.

But crafting laws and regulations is challenging in the United States because of our governmental system. In the executive branch alone, the Treasury Department has a multitude of agencies asserting jurisdiction: the Office of the Comptroller of the Currency, the Office of Foreign Assets Control, the IRS, and FinCEN (the Financial Crimes Enforcement Network). That doesn't include the independent agencies: the Federal Reserve Board, Securities and Exchange Commission, and Commodity Futures Trading Commission. And let's not forget Congress, which decides which agency gets jurisdiction (and funding). And since someone is sure to complain about whatever decisions are made, the courts will eventually weigh in as well.

And that's only the USA. It's a big world, with 197 countries recognized by the United Nations. Work is being done by the Financial Action Task Force, a policymaking body for global financial regulation. All the member states (which includes the United States) typically agree to adhere to FATF's rules.* In October 2021, it released guidance for digital asset regulation, including a rule requiring digital asset exchanges to take greater steps to combat money laundering. That builds on FATF's "travel rule" (in place since 1995), which requires institutions to collect information about all cross-border transactions of $1,000 or more. The rule now also applies to digital assets exchanges, requiring them to capture your name, account number, address, identity of your financial institution, the amount of the

---

* Assisting governments worldwide with these issues is the Global Blockchain Convergence, a group of about 200 experts from across the globe. I've been part of this group since 2019.

transaction and its execution date, and the identity of the recipient's financial institution.

We haven't even mentioned the 50 states yet—each of which has a structure similar to the federal government's. So, multiply everything by 51.

New York, for example, requires companies that want to offer digital assets products and services to obtain a BitLicense—considered onerous by the crypto community (causing some to declare that they'll operate in all states except New York). Wyoming, Texas, and Miami (distinct from the rest of Florida) have taken a different approach. They have all passed the most crypto-friendly laws in the country. Their laws provide great clarity regarding what is and is not permitted—making it easy for companies to operate in a manner they know is compliant.

Wyoming also created a *FinTech sandbox* for digital assets companies. Regulators realize that the community is innovating and thus isn't always sure about what it's doing or what will work. Instead of having to follow prescribed rules, Wyoming merely requires companies to keep the government informed about their activities—so it can work alongside entrepreneurs, developing regulations as the products themselves are developed. That welcoming embrace has turned Wyoming into a hub for the digital assets community, as significant as Silicon Valley was for computers 30 years ago.

Texas is also providing regulatory and legal clarity; the state is now among the few favored by bitcoin miners. And Miami's goal is nothing less than to become "the crypto capital of the world," according to Mayor Francis Suarez. Entrepreneurs even launched the digital token

FTX

MiamiCoin, giving part of the proceeds to the city. Cryptocurrency exchange FTX secured the naming rights for the city's NBA arena, while stock-trading platform eToro and crypto wallet Blockchain.com have established offices in Miami.

Miami is well positioned to succeed. The city is a major international financial hub; many immigrants from Latin America, Central America, and the Caribbean live there. They've experienced hyperinflation or wealth confiscation and are inclined to use bitcoin to send money to friends and family in their native land. Miami is also one of the most unbanked cities in the United States, with 20% of its households lacking bank accounts. (Some 400 bitcoin ATMs are in South Miami alone.)

But Miami isn't alone in courting crypto to the community. New York City Mayor Eric Adams is openly competing with Miami in what he calls a "friendly competition." He wants New York City to have its own digital coin, and has declared, "We're going to become the center of bitcoin." To prove his point, he took his first three paychecks in bitcoin—outdoing Miami Mayor Francis Suarez, who received one paycheck in bitcoin.

Adams and Suarez both better look over their shoulders, because El Salvador is building a "bitcoin city" funded by billion-dollar government bonds backed by bitcoin. The entire city purportedly will be powered by geothermal energy, produced by a nearby volcano. Residents will pay no real estate, property, or income taxes—just a value-added tax common in Europe.

The race is on to embrace crypto.

All this is happening because most governments have concluded that digital assets can't be stopped. All they can do is try to regulate and govern them and, if they're smart, capitalize on them.

Government officials strive to balance security and privacy. The government doesn't have a right to know what you do with your money unless you want to use it to harm others or the nation itself. Efforts to strike a middle ground for digital assets involve four areas of regulation: money and banking (the movement of digital assets between accounts or people), securities, nonsecurities, and taxation. Let's examine each.

How Crypto Is Regulated Around the World

Let's take a brief look at how digital assets are viewed by governments in regions around the globe.

Asia

South Korea has established clear regulations and thus has one of the largest crypto markets in the world. Likewise for Japan, where digital asset companies and transactions flourish. But both countries have experienced large frauds and failures, so they are expanding regulations and oversight to protect their citizens. Singapore is also highly supportive and is encouraging digital assets businesses to locate there. Its rules mostly relate to money laundering and FATF compliance.

India is a different story. The government there has sought to ban digital assets—with the Indian legislature proposing a 10-year prison term for engaging in certain digital assets transactions. Those and other efforts were overturned by the Indian Supreme Court. At this writing, the situation remains uncertain.

Then there's China. China has long been a leader in digital assets (most bitcoin has been mined there), and its government is at the forefront of CBDC development. But China is a Communist regime, and the government despises anything that threatens its control. Yet its economy operates with strong capitalist leanings, and that has created a major philosophical struggle within its borders.

China doesn't know whether to fear the threat that digital assets impose on its control or love the economic benefits that this new asset class brings. Increasingly, the political side of the government has been winning that debate. In 2009, just six months after bitcoin was invented, China banned it. In 2013, China banned banks from handling bitcoin transactions. In 2017, it banned ICOs. In 2019, the country threatened to ban bitcoin mining—and finally did in 2021. That same year, China also banned all bitcoin activity.

China's loss has been the USA's gain. When the Chinese government banned bitcoin mining, lots of Chinese miners moved their operations to New York and Texas. Today, the United States is the world leader in bitcoin mining, mostly at China's expense.

And as Figure 18.1 shows, China's bans have not had any long-term impact on bitcoin's price.

Middle East

The Saudi Arabian government is working hard to encourage digital assets businesses to relocate there. A Canadian bitcoin ETF gained permission to trade on Nasdaq Dubai in 2021, illustrating that nation's

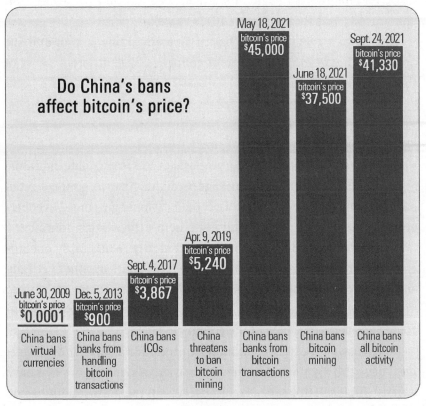

FIGURE 18.1

stance on the topic, while Israel's central bank released a study saying a CBDC could improve the economy—and chose Ethereum for a trial. The United Arab Emirates is also regarded as crypto-friendly, as are Iran and Lebanon, two countries suffering from crushing inflation. (Five percent of all bitcoin mining is done in Iran.)

Turkey also suffers from inflation, but the Turkish government prohibits the use of digital assets for payment. Despite that, crypto usage there increased elevenfold in 2021, and 18% of Turks now own digital assets, according to ING Bank.

Bahrain's central bank approved Rain, a digital assets trading platform that serves both local residents and those in Saudi Arabia, UAE, Kuwait, and Oman. The Saudi and UAE central banks are collaborating on a blockchain project called Aber, which would be a dual-issued CBDC for cross-border payments. Israel, Lebanon, and Turkey have all announced plans for their own CBDCs as well.

But Qatar's regulatory authority is maintaining a wait-and-see posture—illustrating how different countries have different views of this emerging asset class.

Europe

The European Union published a proposal in 2020 to regulate digital assets, part of a comprehensive package on digital finance, strategy, retail payment, and digital resilience. If adopted, it would give the EU a coherent, consistent strategy for digital assets across the western continent.

The United Kingdom is moving more slowly. While fairly encouraging so far, the British are acting more like Americans: not yet fully embracing digital assets, but expected ultimately to do so.

Ukraine is more definitive. At this writing, it plans to declare bitcoin to be a legal currency of the country.

And Russian President Vladimir Putin said in 2021 that digital assets "have the right to exist and can be used as a means of payment." Deputy Finance Minister Alexei Moiseev said the government has no plans to ban the asset class.

Africa

South Africa has officially embraced digital assets, with regulators predicting an increase in activity. That sets South Africa apart from most other African nations, whose central banks are prohibiting the use of digital assets. Millions of citizens in Zimbabwe, Kenya, and Ghana are trading digital assets anyway, despite bans in those countries.

But Nigeria took the opposite approach and created encouraging policies for digital assets companies.

North America

Canada is one of the most progressive nations in the world, having approved several bitcoin ETFs, among other permissions. Mexico is favorable as well and encourages the use of digital assets. Cuba's central bank now recognizes bitcoin—a vital step in helping its citizens receive money from relatives in other countries. (Western Union closed its 400+ locations there in 2020.)

Central America

In 2021, El Salvador became the first country to adopt bitcoin as legal tender, buying 550 bitcoins to support its efforts. There was so much initial demand for the government's digital wallet—70% of its citizens lack bank accounts—that the government briefly had to stop opening new accounts. Officials say Salvadorans using bitcoin will save $400 million a year in commissions for remittances.

Inflation protection is a major reason for bitcoin's popularity. El Salvador has one of the highest inflation rates in the world, and being paid in bitcoin protects buyers and sellers from its ravages.

At this writing, Panama is planning to follow El Salvador's lead and establish bitcoin as official currency.

Canadian ETFs Investing in Blockchain and Digital Assets

Single-Asset

Sponsor	Product Name	Ticker
3iQ Digital Asset Management 3iq.ca	Bitcoin Fund	BTCQ for Canadian investors BTCQ.U for US investors
	Ether Fund	ETHQ for Canadian investors ETHQ.U for US investors
CI Galaxy cifinancial.com	Bitcoin ETF	BTCX.U for US investors
	Ethereum ETF	ETHX.U for US investors
Purpose Investments purposeinvestments.com	Bitcoin ETF	
	Carbon Offset Non-FX Hgd	BTCC.J
	FX Hedged	BTCC
	Non-Fx Hedged	BTCC.B
	For US Investors	BTCC.U
	Ether ETF	
	Carbon Offset Non-FX Hgd	ETHH.J
	FX Hedged	ETHH
	Non-FxHedged	ETHH.N
	For US Investors	ETHH.U
Evolve ETFs evolveetfs.com	Bitcoin ETF	EBIT EBIT.U for US investors
	Cryptocurrencies ETF	ETC ETC.U for US investors
	Ether ETF	ETHR ETHR.U for US investors

Galaxy Digital

Multi-Asset

Sponsor	Product Name	Ticker
Evolve ETFs evolveetfs.com	Cryptocurrencies ETF Invest in both bitcoin and ether	ETC ETC.U for US investors
Fidelity ETFs fidelity.ca	Advantage Bitcoin ETF	FBTC FBTC.U for US investors

For an up-to-date list, complete with hyperlinks, visit the
DACFP Yellow Pages
at dacfp.com

South America

Venezuela also struggles with inflation (its 2021 rate exceeded 1,600%) and has thus seen its citizens move massive amounts of money into bitcoin. Faced with such competition, Venezuela has adopted severe restrictions, which many ignore.

Bolivia has also banned digital assets and exchanges, while Ecuador permits only its own digital asset, the SDE token. Argentina, Brazil, and Chile tend to allow digital assets, acknowledging broad usage is already in place. And, at this writing, Paraguay is preparing to establish bitcoin as official currency, following El Salvador, demonstrating the divergent views that exist on this subject.

Chapter 19

Are Digital Assets Securities?

Time for another riddle! This one is multiple choice. According to US regulators, bitcoin is:

1. a currency

2. a security

3. a commodity

4. property

Yes, it's another trick question. The answer is—all the above.

So much for regulatory clarity.

There are many answers because there are many government regulators answering the question. This matters because how an agency answers the question determines whether it has jurisdiction, and if it does, which of its regulations apply.

Let's start with the SEC. The SEC says bitcoin is not a security. The SEC is certain about this. Why? Because bitcoin fails the *Howey Test*.

Before I explain what that is, it'll be helpful for you to understand why the Howey Test came to be. The story starts with the Crash of 1929 and the ensuing Great Depression. To prevent that from occurring again, Congress passed a variety of laws, including the Securities Act of 1933 and the Securities Exchange Act of 1934. These laws require those creating and selling securities to follow strict rules—rules that weren't in place in the 1920s.

Creating and selling a security? Fine, but what's a security? A security, according to these new laws, is an *investment contract*. Fine, but what's an investment contract?

There was considerable disagreement over this, and the argument went all the way to the Supreme Court. In 1946, the court ruled, in the landmark case *SEC v. Howey*, that a transaction is an investment contract (and thus a security) if:

1. It is an investment of money.

2. There is an expectation of profits from the investment.

3. The investment of money is in a common enterprise.

4. Any profit comes from the efforts of a promoter or third party.

This came to be known as the Howey Test. If the four criteria describe what you are doing, then you are dealing with a security.

The SEC applied the Howey Test to bitcoin and concluded that bitcoin is not a security. Ditto for Ethereum. But other digital assets are or can be securities, the SEC says. And if you buy a fund that is a security and the security buys bitcoin, then you are dealing with a security even though the underlying asset is not a security.

FIGURE 19.1

Remember the remake of the film *The Fly*? Jeff Goldblum played Seth Brundle, the scientist trying to build the equivalent of *Star Trek*'s transporter. He tested it on himself, not realizing that a fly was in the chamber with him. When he tried to figure out what went wrong, Brundle asked his computer what emerged from the test. The computer's reply: "Not Brundle."

Not terribly helpful.

And neither is the SEC. Ask the agency, "What is bitcoin?" And it will reply, "Bitcoin is not a security." Okay, then what is it?

The Federal Reserve has weighed in and says bitcoin is not currency. That's important, for reasons we'll get to when we discuss everyone's favorite topic (taxes). But it still doesn't tell us what it is.

The Commodity Futures Trading Commission says bitcoin is not a commodity, although other digital assets are. It depends on the tests that agency uses, such as how contracts are delivered. There's not complete clarity yet, and the CFTC has created the Digital Asset Task Force to figure it out.

So, we still don't know what bitcoin is. We only know what it is not.

The CFTC, SEC, and Treasury Department are working together to develop regulations for digital assets. But one agency within the Treasury Department isn't playing well with the others. It's developing its own policies without regard to what the others are doing. That agency?

The Internal Revenue Service. So, it gets its own chapter, next.

Chapter 20
How Digital Assets Are Taxed

⚠ WARNING

This Content is Essential but Boring!

Read It – But Not Aloud at Dinner Parties!

Preface

What's the worst part of personal finance? Nope, it's not paying taxes (although that's bad enough). The worst part is not knowing what taxes you have to pay. Talk about frustrating!

And that's often the case with digital assets. Some aspects of this asset class are so new that Congress hasn't yet updated the Internal Revenue Code, and the IRS hasn't revised or issued regulations. While there is clarity in a lot of areas—more than most people realize—there's still much murkiness. I'll explain it all to you as best I can. I'll also provide you with footnotes containing relevant citations. You won't be interested in them, but your tax and financial advisors will be—so share this book with them.*

---

* Better yet, make them buy their own copy.

Tax laws and regulations change frequently, so be sure to check with your tax adviser before acting on any of the information you read here.

Let's Use the Right Words

What is a child? The United Nations says that's someone under age 18. US immigration law, though, says a child is anyone under age 21, while the Children's Online Privacy Protection Act of 1998 says children are those under the age of 13. And the Department of Health and Human Services says parents can include children on their health insurance policies provided the "child" is under age 26.

If we can't agree on how to define a "child," is it any wonder that we can't agree on how to refer to this new asset class?

For purposes of this chapter, we're going to use the terms as defined by the IRS. They are:

- **Digital asset.** Generally, this is the binary representation of anything having an economic value that can be owned.

- **Crypto asset.** This is any digital asset that uses cryptography to secure transaction records on a ledger, such as on a blockchain, to control the creation of additional such assets and to verify the transfer of their ownership.

- **Virtual currency.** This is a digital representation of a medium of exchange, a unit of account, or a store of value other than the US dollar or other government currency.*

- **Convertible virtual currency.** This is virtual currency that has an equivalent value in or is a substitute for real currency. Convertible virtual currency is considered property,† and therefore general tax principles applicable to property apply to transactions involving convertible virtual currency.‡ Importantly, the IRS says bitcoin is an example of convertible virtual currency. (Ha! We finally begin to know what bitcoin is!)

- **Cryptocurrency.** This is virtual currency that uses cryptography to secure transactions digitally recorded on a distributed ledger, such as blockchain.§ Bitcoin, Ether, and Litecoin are all forms of cryptocurrency.¶ (Ha! More clarity!)

Introduction

Tax collectors love people with money—because they get to take some of it. Digital assets have generated massive amounts of wealth since bitcoin's introduction in 2009, so like a longhorn to a salt lick, tax authorities all over the world are drooling over this new asset class and the people engaging in it.

The IRS first addressed digital assets in 2014. Notice 2014-21** says digital assets are property; thus, long-standing tax principles involving

---

* Notice 2014-21. Rev. Rul. 2019-24, https://www.irs.gov/pub/irs-wd/202124008.pdf.

† Notice 2014-21.

‡ Notice 2014-21. Rev. Rul. 2019-24, https://www.irs.gov/pub/irs-wd/202124008.pdf.

§ IRS's Frequently Asked Questions on Virtual Currency Transactions, FAQ #3,https://www.irs.gov/individuals/international-taxpayers/frequently-asked-questions-on-virtual-currency-transactions.

¶ Rev. Rul. 2019-24 at 2 (as stated in https://www.irs.gov/pub/irs-wd/202124008.pdf).

** Notice 2014-21, 2014-16 I.R.B. 938,https://www.irs.gov/pub/irs-drop/n-14-21.pdf.

property apply to this new asset class.* Believing that lots of taxpayers were ignoring this notice, the IRS served a summons on Coinbase in 2016, demanding the company give the IRS records of all its customers. Coinbase refused to comply, but after the IRS narrowed the scope of its summons, the District Court for the Northern District of California ruled in favor of the IRS. Coinbase gave the IRS the data it wanted.

In 2019, concerned that a lot of people engaging in digital assets weren't paying taxes on their transactions,[†] the IRS issued more guidance, including Revenue Ruling 2019-24[‡] and answers to Frequently Asked Questions.[§]

"It's funny how two intelligent people can have such opposite interpretations of the tax code!"

---

* See also IRS's Frequently Asked Questions on Virtual Currency Transactions, FAQ #2, https://www.irs.gov/individuals/international-taxpayers/frequently-asked-questions-on -virtual-currency-transactions.

† IR-2019-167, https://content.govdelivery.com/accounts/USIRS/bulletins/2651117?reqfrom =share.

‡ https://www.irs.gov/pub/irs-drop/rr-19-24.pdf.

§ IRS's Frequently Asked Questions on Virtual Currency Transactions, https://www.irs .gov/individuals/international-taxpayers/frequently-asked-questions-on-virtual-cur rency-transactions.

But that velvet glove covered a hammer: the IRS also announced it would be enforcing compliance with audits and criminal investigations. As part of those efforts, the IRS began requiring taxpayers to answer this question on tax returns (Form 1040):

At any time during 2019, did you receive, sell, send, exchange, or otherwise acquire any financial interest in any virtual currency?

The question was buried on a subschedule, but in 2020, the IRS moved it to the top of page 1, where it can't be missed!

The IRS upped its enforcement efforts in 2021 with Operation Hidden Treasure: specially trained IRS agents are now on the hunt for unreported crypto-related income.

Is all this too much Big Brother for you? Well, let's remember that you have an obligation to the government to pay all taxes due. But you have an equally important obligation to yourself and your family not to pay any more taxes than required or any sooner than necessary.

You're not a tax cheat. You're willing to pay what you owe. But how do you determine whether you owe taxes, or the amount you owe?

That's a smart question. Here's a stupid answer: you don't owe any tax until you experience a taxable event.

Well, duh. So, what's a taxable event?

A *taxable event* is any event that results in a tax liability. Events include sales, exchanges, conversions, trades, payments, donations, receipts, and the earning of income. You must report all taxable events somewhere on your tax return—and you must do this even if the amount is immaterial. It doesn't matter if the other party (or an intermediary) doesn't send you a tax-related document such as a Form 1099 or W-2. The IRS holds *you* responsible for reporting all income and transactions, whether you receive a tax form from someone or not. There's nothing special or magical about digital assets that exempts them from taxation.

To help you understand all the issues you need to consider, let's explore the life cycle of digital assets ownership. There are three stages: acquisition, holding, and disposition.

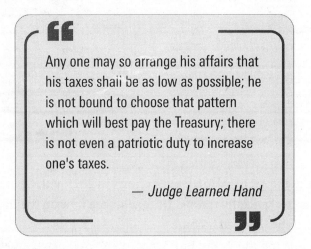

> Any one may so arrange his affairs that his taxes shall be as low as possible; he is not bound to choose that pattern which will best pay the Treasury; there is not even a patriotic duty to increase one's taxes.
>
> — *Judge Learned Hand*

Acquiring Digital Assets

Notice I didn't say *buying*. That's because there are multiple ways one can *acquire* a digital asset. You can even come into possession of a digital asset without taking any action; instead, you might merely "receive" it. Let's look at all the ways you can acquire digital assets.

Purchasing

You can purchase digital assets via a

1. centralized exchange. For example, you pay cash to buy bitcoin.

2. decentralized exchange. For example, you own bitcoin and you use it to buy Ether.

3. non-cryptocurrency platform. For example, you have an account at Robinhood, PayPal, or Venmo.

4. ATM in exchange for cash.

5. bank. (Nah, you can't do that yet, but one day . . .)

In each of these cases, your *tax basis* is the asset's *fair market value* (FMV), in US dollars, at the time of purchase. Your basis is the amount you spend to acquire a digital asset, including fees, commissions, and other expenses. Your *adjusted tax basis* is your cost basis plus certain allowable expenditures.

Receiving Digital Assets as Payment for Wages or Services

Your employer might pay you in bitcoin instead of dollars. That's how Sean Culkin gets his pay—all $920,000 of it. While a tight end for the Kansas City Chiefs, he became the first NFL player to be paid entirely in bitcoin. Offensive tackle Russell Okung gets half of his $13 million salary in bitcoin, the other half in dollars. Los Angeles Rams wide receiver Odell Beckham Jr., a three-time NFL Pro Bowl player, is receiving his entire $4.25 million salary in bitcoin. Green Bay Packers quarterback Aaron Rodgers, a three-time NFL MVP, is also taking part of his salary in bitcoin.

From a tax perspective, what these guys are doing doesn't matter because wages are wages, regardless of the form of payment.*

Tax law is clear on this point: if you receive digital assets as wages, the FMV of that asset, measured in US dollars, is taxable income to you when you receive it, and the amount you receive is subject to taxation as ordinary income based on your tax bracket.[†]

If the digital asset you receive doesn't have a published value, then the FMV is equal to the FMV of the services when the transaction occurs.[‡] For example, an NFL player with a $1 million contract might choose to receive NFTs instead of dollars. The NFTs might not have a

"If it's all the same to you, I'd like my allowance in bitcoins."

---

* IRS's Frequently Asked Questions on Virtual Currency Transactions, FAQs #9 and #11, https://www.irs.gov/individuals/international-taxpayers/frequently-asked-questions-on-virtual-currency-transactions.

† IRS's Frequently Asked Questions on Virtual Currency Transactions, FAQ #13, https://www.irs.gov/individuals/international-taxpayers/frequently-asked-questions-on-virtual-currency-transactions.

‡ IRS's Frequently Asked Questions on Virtual Currency Transactions, FAQ #28, https://www.irs.gov/individuals/international-taxpayers/frequently-asked-questions-on-virtual-currency-transactions.

published value. In that case, the player must use the $1 million price set by his contract.

Ditto for contractors. Your house painter might ask to be paid in digital assets instead of cash. It's handled the same way as above.

Receiving Digital Assets in Exchange for Property

If you transfer Property A to someone and receive Digital Asset B in exchange, your tax basis in Digital Asset B is equal to the FMV of the Digital Asset B you received, in US dollars, as of when you receive the digital assets.[*]

If Property A was a capital asset, you have a capital gain or loss on the disposition of it. If Property A was not a capital asset, then you have an ordinary gain or loss.[†] In both cases, the gain or loss is the difference between the FMV of Digital Asset B when received (generally, the date it's recorded on the distributed ledger) and your adjusted tax basis in Property A, which you transferred.[‡]

If there's no published value of the digital assets, then the FMV is equal to that of the property you exchanged for the digital assets as of the date of the transaction. [§]

---

[*] IRS's Frequently Asked Questions on Virtual Currency Transactions, FAQ #21, https://www.irs.gov/individuals/international-taxpayers/frequently-asked-questions-on-virtual-currency-transactions.

[†] IRS's Frequently Asked Questions on Virtual Currency Transactions, FAQ #19, https://www.irs.gov/individuals/international-taxpayers/frequently-asked-questions-on-virtual-currency-transactions.

[‡] IRS's Frequently Asked Questions on Virtual Currency Transactions, FAQ #20, https://www.irs.gov/individuals/international-taxpayers/frequently-asked-questions-on-virtual-currency-transactions.

[§] IRS's Frequently Asked Questions on Virtual Currency Transactions, FAQ #28, https://www.irs.gov/individuals/international-taxpayers/frequently-asked-questions-on-virtual-currency-transactions.

Receiving Digital Assets as Payment for Money Owed to You

Say Sally owes you $1,000 and she sends you digital assets worth $1,000. You both treat the transaction the same as if cash were used.[*]

Receiving Digital Assets as a Rebate When Using a Debit or Credit Card

For years, credit card companies have offered rebates and rewards to incentivize you to use their cards. Rewards include airline miles and cash—and now, digital assets. There are tax implications (of course!), so let's look at the details.

Use of Credit Cards

Whether you use a personal or business credit card, the IRS has long held that a rebate is treated as an adjustment to the purchase price. Thus, rebates do not count as income—but when crypto is involved, tax basis is created.

Say you charge $5,000 in purchases to your credit card, and your credit card company deposits $50 worth of bitcoin into your crypto account. The IRS treats the transactions as though you spent $4,950 on purchases and $50 to buy bitcoin. You'll have no taxable income on the bitcoin you received, but when you sell it, you'll have a $50 tax basis. (That's good—because the higher your basis, the less you owe in taxes.)

Credit Card Use by Individuals When Purchases Are Reimbursed

It's common for people to use their personal credit cards for business expenses (such as travel) and then be reimbursed by their employers. If you get a rebate from the credit card company for charges that are reimbursed, the FMV of the reward you receive is reportable income—

---

[*] IRS's Frequently Asked Questions on Virtual Currency Transactions, FAQ #20, https://www.irs.gov/individuals/international-taxpayers/frequently-asked-questions-on-virtual-currency-transactions.

even if you don't receive a Form 1099 or other tax document—and the amount is then considered to be your tax basis.

If You Get a Crypto Rebate or Reward for Buying Cash Equivalents with Your Credit Card

If you use a credit card to buy "cash equivalents," such as money orders and reloadable debit cards, the Tax Court has ruled that any rebate or reward you get is taxable income.*

If the Bonus You Earn for Opening an Account Is Paid in Digital Assets

You might receive digital assets simply for opening a credit card account. If you do, the FMV is generally considered to be taxable income. If the value exceeds $600, the credit card company should send the IRS and you Form 1099-MISC. (Whether you get one or not, you're still required to report these amounts as income on your tax return.) As in the above cases, your tax basis will be the amount of reportable income.

If You Receive Digital Assets for Referring a Friend or Other Promotions

If making a purchase is not required to receive the reward, then the FMV is generally considered to be taxable income. If the value exceeds $600, the credit card company should send the IRS and you Form 1099-MISC. (Whether you get one or not, you're still required to report these amounts as income on your tax return.) As in the above cases, your tax basis will be the amount of reportable income.

Learn to Earn

Some digital assets exchanges post educational content on their websites. To entice you to view it, they deposit into your account a token

---

* *Anikeev and Ankeev v. Commissioner of Internal Revenue*, T.C. Memo, 2021-23, https://assets.kpmg/content/dam/kpmg/us/pdf/2021/02/tc-memo-2021-23.pdf.

of modest value ($5 value). When you earn these tokens, you've earned taxable income. Your tax basis is the FMV of the asset, in US dollars, as of the time you receive the token.

Because the amount is usually tiny, some exchanges don't issue Form 1099-MISC. Nevertheless, you're required to report the income on your tax return.

Gifts Received

If you receive digital assets as a gift, you retain the donor's tax basis. You will have a capital gain or loss when you sell or dispose of it (unless you donate it to charity). If you do not have any documentation to substantiate the donor's basis, then your basis is zero—which means you'll pay the maximum possible tax. In other words, get and retain the donor's basis!*

Inheritance

If you receive digital assets as an inheritance, the executor of the estate determines your cost basis as of the date of death or six months later, whichever FMV is higher. You will have a capital gain or loss when you sell or dispose of it (unless you donate it to charity).

Unusual Ways to Acquire Digital Assets

Everything we've covered so far is probably familiar to you since the rules I've described pertain to all assets, not just digital ones. But you might acquire or receive digital assets in less common ways. These include:

Earning Digital Assets

In general, the value of any item that you receive in exchange for providing goods or services is always taxable unless there is a specific ex-

---

* IRS's Frequently Asked Questions on Virtual Currency Transactions, FAQ #32, https://www.irs.gov/individuals/international-taxpayers/frequently-asked-questions-on-virtual-currency-transactions.

ception or exclusion in the tax law. The income is the FMV at the time you received it. The income you report when receiving digital assets then becomes your tax basis for the asset, and you use this data to determine your capital gain or loss when you dispose of it.

However, how you earn the digital assets will dictate how, when, and where you report your earnings. For example, mining incurs tax implications that vary based on how you participate (using your own mining equipment, joining a mining pool (groups of people working together over a network, such as the one provided by Norton antivirus software [chapter 6]), or cloud mining (where your contribution to a mining pool is the computing power you buy from cloud services).

As a miner, you are generally considered to have earned income, taxed as ordinary income, based on the FMV of the tokens you receive on the day you receive them. But how and where you report this on your tax return depends on whether you mine as a hobby or as a business.

If it's a hobby, you use Form 1040, Schedule 1. If your mining operation is part of a trade or business, you report the income on Schedule C. (The IRS says miners are self-employed. That means you could be responsible for self-employment taxes on mining income. More on self-employment income later.)

Staking

At this writing, the IRS has not provided much clarity regarding the taxation of staking and earning staking rewards. Therefore, the cautious approach is to consider income generated by staking to be ordinary income as of the time of receipt and then have the token become a capital asset as of the day after you receive it—so that any subsequent appreciation would be treated as capital gains when you dispose of it.*

If you'd rather take a less draconian (and less expensive) position, you can ask your tax advisor about treating staking the way rentable

---

* IRS's Frequently Asked Questions on Virtual Currency Transactions, FAQ #29, https://www.irs.gov/individuals/international-taxpayers/frequently-asked-questions-on-virtual-currency-transactions.

property is treated. Under that theory, staking rewards could be regarded as rental income (using Form 1040, Schedule E); doing so offers the potential for lower tax liabilities.

Transfers from One of Your Wallets to Another of Your Wallets

Investors often have multiple wallets and accounts at a variety of exchanges and custodians, and it's easy to move tokens and coins between them. There's no tax implication if you move a dollar from your savings account to your checking account, but could such movement of digital asses from one wallet or account to another be deemed a taxable event?

You wouldn't think so. But if you move crypto from one exchange to another, the "from" exchange might treat the transfer "to" the other exchange as a disposition—and thus send you Form 1099. The IRS is aware that such mistakes could occur and has published reassuring guidance that you don't have a taxable event even if you receive such a 1099.* You might have some paperwork to do—to explain to the IRS that the 1099 you received was in error—but at least you don't have to pay taxes because of the mistake.

Transferring Digital Assets to Another Person or Entity

If you transfer a coin or token from one digital wallet, address, or account to one that's owned by someone else, the IRS will regard your transfer as either a sale of assets or a gift, subject to the relevant rules as we've covered in this book.

There's probably no intermediary, meaning no one to issue Form 1099. Regardless, both parties are responsible for complying with the tax law.

Transferring Digital Assets Ownership to a Co-owner

If you transfer a coin or token from one digital wallet, address, or account that you own to one that's jointly owned by you and another person, there could be a number of tax consequences.

---

* IRS's Frequently Asked Questions on Virtual Currency Transactions, FAQ #38, https://www.irs.gov/individuals/international-taxpayers/frequently-asked-questions-on-virtual-currency-transactions.

There may or may not be immediate tax implications for transferring digital assets from your ownership. It depends to whom you're transferring. (A spouse? A person who is not your spouse? A minor?* An entity you own or control? A trust, and if so, what kind of trust— revocable, irrevocable, charitable?) There are so many variables that it would require a whole different book to explain all the considerations and strategies.† So, please consult a financial planner, tax advisor, or estate attorney for advice pertaining to your situation.

Transferring Digital Assets to Your IRA

You cannot transfer digital assets into an IRA; all IRA contributions must be made in US dollars. Once the cash is placed into the IRA, you can use the money to purchase digital assets. Just make sure you're using a qualified custodian that permits the purchase of the assets you want.

Once you have digital assets in your IRA, you can transfer them to a different custodian anytime, with no tax consequence. If you want to keep your digital assets, you should execute an *in-kind transfer*, so your coins or tokens move as is to the new custodian. The new custodian will facilitate the transfer for you in what is known as a *trustee-to-trustee transfer*. No tax reporting is required.

Airdrops

Airdrops are generally taxable as ordinary income as of the date you receive them—provided you can trade or remove them. If you can't (because the issuer doesn't allow that yet), declare it as income on the date you are able to transfer, sell, exchange, or otherwise dispose of it. You'll then have a cost basis equal to the amount you reported as income.‡

---

* That's *or*, not *er*. I'm referring to a child, not a bitcoin miner.

† Oh, I wrote that book. It's called *The Truth About Money*: $19.95 at your favorite bookseller.

‡ IRS's Frequently Asked Questions on Virtual Currency Transactions, FAQ #25, https://www.irs.gov/individuals/international-taxpayers/frequently-asked-questions-on-virtual-currency-transactions.

Digital Assets Estate Attorneys

Anthony S. Park, PLLC
anthonyspark.com

Park represents clients worldwide as their professional executor, trustee, or probate lawyer. The team is skilled at working with courts, taxes, banks, and all other bureaucracies associated with the probate process.

Brady Cobin Law Group, PLLC
ncestateplanning.com

Brady Cobin helps clients ensure proper access to and distribution of their digital assets.

Dilendorf Law Firm
dilendorf.com

Dilendorf offers cutting-edge strategic, transactional, and regulatory solutions to a wide range of participants in the blockchain and fintech space—token issuers, crypto exchanges, traditional and crypto investment funds, as well as businesses and managers looking to integrate blockchain technology into their existing business and investment models.

E.A. Goodman Law
eagoodmanlaw.com

Goodman is a premier elder law and estate planning firm serving clients in New Jersey. Its services range from planning small estates to complex planning for high-net worth individuals. Its attorneys also design succession planning strategies for clients who operate closely held businesses and professional practices.

Estate & Probate Legal Group
estateandprobatelegal group.com

The Estate & Probate Legal Group focuses on probate and trust administration and litigation practice.

Frost Law
askfrost.com

Frost Law assists with tax controversy, business, litigation, estate planning, and bankruptcy.

Gordon Fischer Law Firm
gordonfischerlawfirm .com

Gordan Fischer Law Firm helps people plan their legacies and nonprofit organizations manage their philanthropic efforts.

For an up-to-date list, complete with hyperlinks, visit the
DACFP Yellow Pages
at dacfp.com

Digital Assets Estate Attorneys

Guttman Law
guttmanlaw.com

Guttman Law assists with all forms of digital asset planning, helping its clients prepare for what will happen to online accounts, password-protected files, digitally stored media, and more.

Harrison Estate Law
harrisonestatelaw.com

Harrison Estate Law offers years of experience preparing everything from basic wills and trusts to complex estate plans.

Hart David Carson, LLP
hartdavidcarson.com

Hart David Carson is a Chicago law firm that works with businesses and individuals.

John Mangan, P.A.
palmcitylawyer.com

Mangan works with clients to form estate plans.

McCord & Hemphill
ourbendlawyer.com

McCord & Hemphill helps you plan for your digital assets just as you do for physical belongings, real estate, and financial accounts.

Murphy & Berglund, PLLC
murphyberglund.com

Murphy & Berglund protects every branch of the family tree. They strive to build relationships with clients to last a lifetime. Their focus is providing clients with precise legal advice and guiding them through life's transitions.

Paul Black Elder Law & Estate Planning
georgia-estatelaw.com

Paul Black is an estate planning lawyer who provides legal services to people throughout the Atlanta area.

Poole Shaffery
pooleshaffery.com

Poole Shaffery assists in the formulation and implementation of an estate plan that carries out each client's intentions.

For an up-to-date list, complete with hyperlinks, visit the
DACFP Yellow Pages
at dacfp.com

Digital Assets Estate Attorneys

Proskauer proskauer.com	Proskauer has a network of 725+ lawyers serving clients from offices located in the leading financial and business centers of the Americas, Europe, and Asia.
Singh & Singh singhandsingh.com	Singh & Singh is an Indian law firm with years of experience providing services in intellectual property law, media and telecommunications laws, arbitration, competition law, law of taxation, and drug regulatory laws.
White and Bright, LLP whiteandbright.com	White and Bright provides transactional and litigation services to businesses and individuals throughout Southern California.

For an up-to-date list, complete with hyperlinks, visit the
DACFP Yellow Pages
at dacfp.com

Forks

Recall the difference between soft forks and hard forks (chapter 5). Because in a soft fork you don't receive anything new, soft forks do not result in any reportable income.*

But if you receive crypto from hard forks, that new crypto is taxable as ordinary income (provided you have control over it, meaning you can transfer, sell, exchange, or otherwise dispose of it).† The FMV is what someone would pay for it on the date you received it.

---

* IRS's Frequently Asked Questions on Virtual Currency Transactions, FAQ #30, https://www.irs.gov/individuals/international-taxpayers/frequently-asked-questions-on-virtual-currency-transactions.

† IRS's Frequently Asked Questions on Virtual Currency Transactions, FAQ #24, https://www.irs.gov/individuals/international-taxpayers/frequently-asked-questions-on-virtual-currency-transactions.

"Other folks have to pay taxes, too, Mr. Herndon, so would you please spare us the dramatics!"

In chapter 5, I mentioned that hard forks are similar to corporate spin-offs. That's true—except for the tax implications. The tax rules pertaining to stock spin-offs do not apply to crypto hard forks. There's a good lesson here: don't assume that rules you're familiar with in other aspects of the tax code are helpful in this category. I've said it before, and I'll say it again: digital assets are unlike any other asset, and therefore you cannot apply rules you use for other assets to this asset class.

Holding Digital Assets

You now have a digital asset. You haven't moved it or disposed of it. It's just sitting there . . . wherever that is—a wallet, an account, whatever.

No tax consequence yet, right?

Not necessarily. Forks and airdrops could create taxes for you even though you didn't seek or initiate them. Staking your digital assets could generate tax liabilities, too, as we've seen. Ditto for lending and borrowing digital assets.

Borrowing

Borrowing money (and repaying the loan) is never a taxable event. However, you will incur a taxable event if you fail to repay the loan. For example, if you borrow $100,000 and default, you will be deemed to have $100,000 in taxable income.

Collateral

Say you have money in digital assets, but you need cash. You don't want to sell your digital assets because doing so will trigger a tax liability. So, you deposit your digital assets with a lender as collateral, and the lender loans you fiat currency. When the loan matures, you repay the lender with the same fiat currency plus interest, and the lender returns your digital assets to you.

If you fail to repay the loan, the lender will sell (and keep) your collateral. Whatever the lender gets from the sale will leave you (not the lender) with a capital gain or loss.

Most lenders require cash as collateral, but some will accept a digital asset that's different from the one you're borrowing. (For example, you post bitcoin as collateral so you can borrow Ether.) When repaying the loan, you return the same number of the same digital asset you borrowed. When you do, the lender returns your collateral.

Tax Treatment of Loans

At this writing, there is no IRS or Treasury Department guidance regarding loans involving digital assets—either for the borrower or the lender. Therefore, we're forced to use tax principles that apply to loans in general.

The IRS says a loan is an obligation to pay money, not an obligation to deliver property. But at the same time, the IRS says "convertible virtual currency" is regarded as property. That's why this conversation is murky. It's generally held that most digital assets are fungible (other than, obviously, non-fungible tokens), but some tax practitioners aren't so sure that the IRS would agree. If they're right, and ordinary digital assets such as a given bitcoin is "similar to but different from" other individual bitcoins, then borrowers (when repaying loans) and lenders (when returning collateral) would be returning similar-but-not-exactly-the-same property. And if that's true, these tax practitioners wonder, would the IRS characterize the loan as a taxable sale? After all, if you provide a car as collateral for a loan but the lender returns to you a different but similar car, the IRS will view that transaction as a sale.

I don't support this theory or share the above concern. But given the lack of clarity from the IRS, I suppose we must acknowledge that the possibility exists.

It gets even murkier. Consider these questions:

- Which party bears the risk of economic loss if the price of the digital asset falls? Which party benefits if the price rises? And what are the ensuing tax implications?
- If there's an airdrop or fork during the term of the loan, which party gets the new units?

In the absence of authoritative tax guidance, you should:

1. Talk with your tax advisor about the appropriate way to treat the interest you pay or receive on loans involving digital assets. How you treat it will be determined, in part, by how the borrowed property is used (personal versus investment use).

2. Properly document that the intent of both parties is for the transaction to be treated as a loan.

3. Structure the loan in a manner consistent with standard lending practices.

Finally, as with any asset posted as collateral for a loan, be aware of the consequences if the asset drops in price. The lender may issue a *margin call*, demanding that you post additional collateral; if you fail to do so (often required within 24 hours), the lender can sell your collateral to cover its loss. This liquidation can create a realized capital gain (or loss) for you—meaning you might not only lose your collateral, but you'll also have a tax bill to pay as well. Yikes!

Ownership of Certain Trusts

We looked at private placements and their subsequent OTC trusts in chapter 16. Those vehicles don't pay taxes themselves; instead, they pass any tax liabilities to you, the investor.

That means you must pay your pro rata share of any tax liability generated by the trust. If the trust sells assets to raise cash so it can pay expenses, it's as though you sold a portion of your investment. This means you'll have a gain or loss—even though you took no action. Worse, those expenses are regarded as investment management expenses, which you cannot deduct on your tax return.

Disposing of Digital Assets

Whenever you dispose of a digital asset and receive something in return—whether by selling it, trading it, or using it to purchase goods or services—you trigger a taxable event.

That means, for an asset held for investment purposes, you incur a capital gain or loss on the transaction just as if you had disposed of any other investment.

- If your holding period is one year or less, you will have a *short-term* capital gain or loss.
- If your holding period is more than one year, you will have a *long-term* capital gain or loss.

The holding period begins the day after you acquire the asset and ends the day you sell or exchange it. You report net gains and losses on Form 8949 and summarize them on Form 1040, Schedule D.*

The takeaway is that you should keep detailed records for each digital asset, including the dates of all purchases and dispositions, tax basis, and FMV at the time of sale.† A solution for this comes soon, so keep reading.

The most common way for people to dispose of their digital assets is to sell them, receiving US dollars in exchange. But there are other disposal methods, too. Let's look at them.

Converting One Digital Asset into Another

This is treated as a sale. For example, you trade bitcoin for Ether. That's really two transactions: the sale of bitcoin and the purchase of ether. You must calculate the FMV of each at the time of the trade.

Using Digital Assets as Payment for Goods and Services

AMC movie theaters let you buy movie tickets and popcorn with bitcoin, Ether, Litecoin, and Bitcoin Cash. Fun!

Except that doing so creates a tax issue. Using digital assets as payment is the same as selling it. Thus, you've created a capital transaction to see that movie, leaving you with a capital gain or loss.‡ Your gain or

---

* IRC Section 1001, 26 CFR 1.61-6.

† IRS's Frequently Asked Questions on Virtual Currency Transactions, FAQ #26, https://www.irs.gov/individuals/international-taxpayers/frequently-asked-questions-on-virtual-currency-transactions.

‡ IRS's Frequently Asked Questions on Virtual Currency Transactions, FAQs #14 and 16, https://www.irs.gov/individuals/international-taxpayers/frequently-asked-questions-on-virtual-currency-transactions.

loss is the difference between the FMV of the property or services you received and your adjusted basis in the digital asset you exchanged.*

All this occurs because the Federal Reserve and IRS both say that digital assets are not currency. With currency, you can swap dollars for products and services anytime, without such events being deemed capital transactions. (Now you know why it's such a big deal whether a digital asset is declared to be a currency. Right now, you're envious of Salvadorans.)

Gifts

The gift tax rules that apply to all assets also apply to digital assets. If you give digital assets to someone, you incur no tax liability. (Note: the IRS imposes limits as to how much you can give away tax-free, both annually and over your lifetime.) The person receiving your digital assets doesn't incur any tax liability at the time of the gift, either. However, when they sell the asset, the tax basis they use to calculate their taxable gain or loss will be your tax basis. This is known as carryover basis.

For example, you buy one bitcoin, paying $50,000. That amount is your tax basis. You give the bitcoin to your sister; at the time, bitcoin is worth $58,000. Your sister later sells it for $60,000. Her taxable gain is $10,000, not just $2,000, because she must use the tax basis carried over from your original purchase.

Donations

The charitable gift rules that apply to property also apply to digital assets. You can deduct your donations to IRC Section 501(c)(3) nonprofit organizations.

- If you held the asset you're donating for more than one year, you get to deduct its FMV as of the date the charity receives it.

---

* IRS's Frequently Asked Questions on Virtual Currency Transactions, FAQs #15 and 17, https://www.irs.gov/individuals/international-taxpayers/frequently-asked-questions -on-virtual-currency-transactions.

- If you held the asset you're donating for a year or less, your deduction is the lesser of your tax basis or its FMV. *

It's easy to give cash to a charity; they'll all accept it. Most will also accept securities, such as stocks, bonds, mutual funds, and ETFs. Some will even take cars, boats, and real estate. But few accept digital assets because they're not used to doing so and don't know how to create and manage wallets.

If you want to donate appreciated digital assets to charity, you can do this in two ways. First, sell the asset and donate the proceeds to charity. Say you bought bitcoin for $10,000 and sold it for $50,000, donating all the proceeds to charity. You must report on your tax return the $40,000 capital gain and the $50,000 donation. This could create unintended side effects. For example, declaring the income could cause you to pay more in Medicare premiums, could impact student loan or financial aid eligibility, or subject you to other income tax rules and phaseouts from having a higher taxable income.

A better strategy is to donate the bitcoin to a Donor Advised Fund. These look and act like mutual funds but are actually charities, so when you donate your digital assets to them, you'll get the full tax deduction without having to sell the assets first. The DAF will sell the digital assets and invest the proceeds into stocks and bonds, just like any mutual fund.

Fidelity Charitable, the country's largest grantmaker, received nearly $275 million in crypto donations in 2021, quadrupling the previous record set in 2017. Owners of digital assets have proven to be more generous than other Americans, Fidelity says: while 33% of all donors give $1,000 or more per year, 45% of crypto holders do so.

---

* IRS's Frequently Asked Questions on Virtual Currency Transactions, FAQ #35, https://www.irs.gov/individuals/international-taxpayers/frequently-asked-questions-on-virtual-currency-transactions.

Donor Advised Funds That Accept Digital Assets

Endaoment
endaoment.org

Endaoment is a tax-exempt community foundation and public charity offering Donor Advised Funds built on the Ethereum blockchain, facilitating donations to almost any US nonprofit organization.

Fidelity Charitable
fidelitycharitable.org

Fidelity Charitable's Giving Account is an easy and efficient way for donors to obtain tax benefits while supporting their favorite charities. Fidelity Charitable's fees are among the lowest of any DAF sponsor.

Fidelity

National Philanthropic Trust
nptrust.org

National Philanthropic Trust is the largest national independent provider of DAFs.

Schwab Charitable
schwabcharitable.org

Serving a wide range of philanthropic investors, Schwab Charitable has accounts ranging from $5,000 to more than $500 million. Schwab Charitable makes charitable giving tax-smart, simple, and efficient for clients and their investment advisors.

Schwab

For an up-to-date list, complete with hyperlinks, visit the
DACFP Yellow Pages
at dacfp.com

Then, whenever you wish, you instruct the DAF to send the money to the charities you designate, as many as you wish. You can make requests immediately or delay doing so for years, and you can send part of the money or all the money. You have almost complete flexibility, and the DAF will handle everything for you.

Be aware that the donations of $5,000 or more require an appraisal. This IRS rule applies to all donations other than cash and securities. (Another reason it's a big deal that the SEC and IRS both say digital assets aren't securities.) So, expect to spend several hundred dollars on an appraisal—and that cost isn't tax-deductible.

Digital Asset Appraisers

Charitable Solutions, LLC charitablesolutionsllc.com	Charitable Solutions is a planned giving risk management consulting firm focused on non-cash asset receipt and disposition, charitable gift annuity risk management, gift annuity reinsurance brokerage services, and appraisals for life insurance and digital assets.
MPI Management Planning Inc. mpival.com	MPI is a business valuation, litigation support, forensic accounting, and M&A advisory firm providing valuations for tax, financial reporting, litigation, and other business applications, as well as corporate advisory services for business owners and their representatives.
PwC pwc.com	PwC has a "one-stop-shop" offering, with such crypto services as transaction advisory, valuation, and due diligence.
Redwood Valuation redwoodvaluation.com	Redwood is a leading provider of token valuations, and works with top law firms and cutting-edge companies to ensure that token issuances are fully compliant.
Teknos Associates teknosassociates.com	Teknos provides global valuation and advisory services, and has extensive experience in the blockchain and digital asset field.
Valtech valtech-valuation.com	Valtech's professional team has valuation expertise across many industries.

For an up-to-date list, complete with hyperlinks, visit the
DACFP Yellow Pages
at dacfp.com

FIFO, LIFO, and HIFO

Did you buy bitcoin once and never more? Nah. If you buy digital coins, tokens, or shares of mutual funds or ETFs related to them, you likely do so often, especially if you engage in dollar cost averaging (chapter 17). Each investment constitutes a *trade lot*, and each trade lot has its own date and cost per coin, token, or share.

So, when you decide to sell some, you'll have a decision to make: Which ones do you sell? You get to choose—but only if you can identify which unit(s) are involved in the transaction and you can substantiate your basis in them.[*]

There's a benefit to choosing the trade lots. By doing so, you get to choose the lot that has the highest basis, and therefore the lowest gain and thus lowest tax. That's called *HIFO*, for *highest in, first out*.

If you don't specify a particular trade lot, you're deemed to have disposed of them in chronological order, beginning with the oldest trade lot—otherwise known as *FIFO*, for *first in, first out*.[†] Odds are that the lots you've owned the longest have the greatest gains—and thus you incur the biggest taxes when you dispose of them.

An alternative is *LIFO*, or *last in, first out*. As these are your newest lots, they likely have the least gains. But you may also have owned these lots for less than a year, so watch out for the risk of incurring short-term gains instead of long-term gains.

As you can see, you need to devote substantial attention to how and when you sell. To make life easier, you should consider using a tax tracker service. These firms manage all your record-keeping and tax-reporting chores for you, including trading, mining, staking, and interest. Some services even prepopulate the IRS forms for you. Tax trackers can be helpful to your financial and tax advisors, as well.

---

[*] IRS's Frequently Asked Questions on Virtual Currency Transactions, FAQ #39, https://www.irs.gov/individuals/international-taxpayers/frequently-asked-questions-on-virtual-currency-transactions.

[†] IRS's Frequently Asked Questions on Virtual Currency Transactions, FAQ #41, https://www.irs.gov/individuals/international-taxpayers/frequently-asked-questions-on-virtual-currency-transactions.

Digital Assets Portfolio Tracking Services

Altrady
altrady.com

Altrady is a complete crypto trading platform made by traders for traders. It integrates some of the most popular exchanges into one easy-to-use interface.

BitUniverse
bituniverse.org

BitUniverse offers a platform to trade 6000+ digital assets. Its trading bot lets programmers design their own trading strategies.

CoinGecko
coingecko.com

CoinGecko is the world's leading cryptocurrency data aggregator. Since 2014, it has been the trusted source of information for millions of digital asset investors.

CoinMarketCap
coinmarketcap.com

CoinMarketCap allows users to keep track of profits, losses, and portfolio valuation with its easy-to-use platform. Users can sync data between their desktop and mobile apps and keep track of digital assets in multiple locations. CoinMarketCap provides real-time price data on thousands of coins and tokens from the largest exchanges. It was founded in 2013 and is headquartered in Delaware.

Coin Market Manager
coinmarketman.com

Coin Market Manager is an industry portfolio tracker built to help traders with risk management and responsible trading to help increase profitability.

CoinStats
coinstats.app

CoinStats provides 1 million monthly active users with the ability to view and manage their crypto holdings in real time from more than 300 exchange and wallet providers, all in one place.

CoinTracker
cointracker.io

CoinTracker is a bitcoin tax software and crypto portfolio manager. It allows users to connect Coinbase, Binance, and all other exchanges and wallets.

For an up-to-date list, complete with hyperlinks, visit the
DACFP Yellow Pages
at dacfp.com

Digital Assets Portfolio Tracking Services

Delta
delta.app

Delta offers a free mobile version, plus a Pro plan for a fee. Delta supports multiple wallets and more than 300 exchanges including Coinbase, Binance, Bithumb, Bitstamp, Bit-Z, Gemini, HitBTC, and Kraken. Delta supports over 7,000 coins and offers customizations, including multiple fiat conversions. Delta is owned by eToro.

FTX
ftx.com

FTX is a popular and free mobile-only portfolio tracker, founded in 2014. The app incorporates portfolio management, news, and digital asset trading. Its dashboard supports tracking of 10,000+ digital assets. The app provides its free Signal customizable news app to 6+ million users. Users can earn interest on digital assets as they trade, plus random coin bonus rewards for the most active traders.

Kubera
kubera.com

Kubera is a wealth management platform that lets users track their digital assets, equity, and bank accounts in a spreadsheet format.

Messari
messari.io

Messari provides investors, regulators, and the public with digital asset portfolio tracking, analytics, and commentary to help drive informed investment decision-making.

TradeBlock
tradeblock.com

TradeBlock is the world's leading provider of institutional trading tools for digital assets.

For an up-to-date list, complete with hyperlinks, visit the
DACFP Yellow Pages
at dacfp.com

Tax Planning and Tax Consulting/Advisory Services for Digital Assets

Azran Financial
azranfinancial.com

Azran Financial provides digital asset accounting, auditing, tax planning and compliance, due diligence, and consulting. The firm has deep expertise with SAFTs and security tokens. Azran prepares federal and state income tax returns and provides coordination with international tax reporting.

Bitcoin Tax Solutions
bitcointaxsolutions.com

Cross Law Group provides tax services to crypto investors in the United States and abroad.

Cohen & Co
cohencpa.com

Cohen & Co is a leading global digital asset audit and tax practice. The firm prepares US federal and state tax returns for investors and provides consulting support to businesses in the digital assets ecosystem, including stablecoin attest services, SOC reports for custodians, CFO operational and risk assessments, and tax compliance for advisors, digital asset funds and exchanges.

Colby Cross
colbycrosscpa.com

Colby Cross serves individuals and small business owners by managing their finances and their US tax obligations.

Crypto Tax Advisors
crypto-taxadvisors.com

Crypto Tax Advisors provides a range of accounting and tax services for individuals and businesses, focusing on cryptocurrency taxation.

The Wolf Group
thewolfgroup.com

The Wolf Group advises digital asset miners, investors, dealers, and traders on opportunities to reduce taxes, simplify information gathering, and reporting and structure operations for tax efficiency.

For an up-to-date list, complete with hyperlinks, visit the
DACFP Yellow Pages
at dacfp.com

Tax Record Keeping and Reporting Services for Digital Assets

Accointing
accointing.com

Accointing is a crypto and bitcoin tax platform that allows you to track your digital assets portfolio.

BearTax
bear.tax

BearTax helps you fetch trades from everywhere, identify transfers across exchanges, and auto-generate tax documents.

CoinTracker
cointracker.io

CoinTracker is a unified interface for digital assets. It lets crypto holders connect their wallets and exchanges, see their portfolios, wallets and transactions in one place, and generate their digital asset tax returns with the click of a button.

CoinTracking
cointracking.info

CoinTracking is cryptocurrency tax software that allows users to track crypto transactions and track portfolios.

CryptoTrader.tax
cryptotrader.tax

CryptoTrader.tax is tax-reporting software for the growing marketplace.

Ledgibile
ledgible.io

Ledgible Crypto TaxPro helps investment advisors retain clients and attract new clients by easily handling tax planning and advisory services around digital assets. It works directly with advisors' clients to collect, correct, and report data. Ledgible features exchange and wallet integrations and tax software integrations that import directly into 1040 tax preparation systems.

Lukka
lukka.tech

Lukka offers a suite of tax-related services to individuals and professionals. Essentials by Lukka allows customers to connect their accounts and see their trades and balances in one place.

For an up-to-date list, complete with hyperlinks, visit the
DACFP Yellow Pages
at dacfp.com

Tax Record Keeping and Reporting Services for Digital Assets

ProfitStance
profitstance.com

ProfitStance is a premier tax and accounting platform for digital asset investors.

TaxBit
taxbit.com

Taxbit provides digital asset tax software for consumers and enterprises.

TokenTax
tokentax.co

TokenTax is a crypto tax software platform and full-service crypto tax accounting firm.

ZenLedger
zenledger.io

ZenLedger provides clients with user-friendly tax and accounting software for crypto investments, trading, and fund operations. ZenLedger helps digital asset traders connect their wallets and exchanges in one platform to quickly generate their tax forms.

For an up-to-date list, complete with hyperlinks, visit the
DACFP Yellow Pages
at dacfp.com

Like-Kind Exchanges

IRC Section 1031 lets you sell an investment without paying capital gains if you use the money to buy a similar investment. (The gain is deferred until you sell the replacement.) Hey, bitcoin and Ether are similar, right? They're both digital assets! So, can you sell one to buy the other and defer the capital gains?

Nice try, but no. In passing the Tax Cuts and Jobs Act of 2018, Congress made it clear that Section 1031 (also called Starker exchanges) applies only to real property (meaning real estate). All other property is excluded from using the provision, including digital assets.

The Wash-Sale Rule

If you sell an investment asset for a loss, you can claim a tax deduction. If you do, you cannot buy the same asset for at least 30 days before or after the sale. If you violate this rule, the sale is considered a "wash sale" and you can't take the deduction until after you sell the new holding.

The wash-sale rule closes a loophole that allowed people to artificially lower their taxes. Here's how the game worked: You buy a stock for $10. It falls to $8. You still want to own the stock and believe in its long-term prospects, so you sell it and then immediately buy it back. You still own the stock, but by selling it, you get to report a $2 loss on your tax return.

By forcing you to wait 30 days to rebuy the stock, during which time the stock's price might rise, the wash-sale rule discourages you from selling. Loophole closed.

So, the bad news is that you can't immediately buy what you just sold (at least, not if you want to capture a tax deduction on the loss). But here's the good news: the wash-sale rule applies only to securities, per IRC Section 1091. Bitcoin, Ether, and many other digital assets are not securities, so the wash-sale rule doesn't apply to them, right?

As I write this, right. But as I write this, President Biden is trying to get Congress to pass the Build Back Better Act. That bill has a clause that would subject all transactions to the wash-sale rule, not just securities. Meaning, if the bill is signed into law as it's currently drafted, all digital assets will be subject to the wash-sale rule. Follow the bill's saga through Congress to see how it ends, ask your tax advisor, or stay tuned to my podcast at thetayf.com for the latest.

Taxation of NFTs

At this writing, the IRS hasn't yet issued any guidance on NFTs. But by looking at how NFTs work, we can make some basic assumptions about their tax aspects.

- **Creation.** It's unlikely there would be any tax consequences for creating an NFT. A painter, after all, doesn't realize any gain or loss merely for creating a painting.

- **Original sale by the creator.** If you create an NFT and sell it, you'll have ordinary income. This income is also subject to self-employment tax.* Also, if you receive royalties when people view the NFT, those royalties are taxable income.

- **Buyer's tax consequences.** If you use digital assets to buy an NFT, you'll incur a capital gain or loss on the disposition of your digital assets, as we've seen.

- **Subsequent sale.** If you buy an NFT and later sell it for a profit, you owe taxes at the capital gains rate or the collectibles tax rate. (People in the business of buying and selling collectibles and art are subject to other rules.)

What's a Collectible?

IRC Section 408(m) defines collectibles as

- works of art
- rugs or antiques
- metals or gems (with exceptions)
- stamps or coins (with exceptions)
- alcoholic beverages (although it's been said that you only collect these temporarily)†
- anything else the IRS decides is a collectible.‡ Except maybe for NFTs: proposed Treasury regulations say the IRS has the

---

* At this writing, the SE tax is 15.3%. Add another 0.9 % if your self-employment income is above $250,000 (for married-filing-jointly taxpayers) or $200,000 (for single taxpayers).

† I crack myself up sometimes.

‡ 26 US Code ß408—Individual retirement accounts | US Code | US Law | LII / Legal Information Institute (cornell.edu).

authority to deem as collectibles any tangible property not specifically listed in the code—but the word *tangible* doesn't apply to an NFT. Did Treasury officials deliberately exclude NFTs, or did they simply fail to consider them when writing the regulation?

Although the IRS hasn't provided guidance about NFTs, works of art are clearly collectibles. Therefore, it's reasonable to assume that NFTs of art are collectibles.

But what about the NBA's digital trading cards via Top Shot (chapter 9)? Although trading cards are not specifically listed by the IRS, they have historically been taxed as collectibles—suggesting that the IRS would consider Top Shot's cards, CryptoKitties, and the like to also be collectibles.

The distinction is important because the tax rate on collectibles is higher than long-term capital gains rates. Collectibles held longer than a year are taxed at 28%. Those held for a shorter period pay the short-term capital gains rate.

If you're an art dealer and NFTs are essentially part of your inventory, ordinary income tax rates apply. And if you buy an NFT for personal purposes and not "for investment," you cannot deduct any losses.

If You Own a Business and Pay for Services with Digital Assets

If you pay someone $600 or more in a calendar year with digital assets, you must report those payments to the IRS and the payee as if you had paid them in US dollars, as stated in IRS Notice 2014-21.

Chapter 21
Operations and Compliance

If you're a financial advisor or executive in the financial services industry, you need to be familiar with the compliance and reporting obligations associated with digital assets if you want to include this asset class in client portfolios.

If you're a financial professional, you're already familiar with custody, Assets Under Management versus Assets Under Advisement, KYC/AML, fiduciary responsibilities, and related issues. So, we'll skip all that here.

Instead, I'll offer you just three key points, starting with the most important:

1. **Always act as a fiduciary.**
   Yeah, I know I just said in the prior paragraph that I wasn't going to cover it, but this one is so important that it must always be highlighted. So

   If you're an advisor, and you don't always act as a fiduciary, do me and everyone else a favor and leave this industry immediately!

here goes. You must always conform to the fiduciary standard, serving each client's best interests—whether or not digital assets are involved.

2. **Treat digital assets as securities.** Remember that some digital assets are considered by the SEC to be securities while other digital assets are not. If you're ever in doubt about whether a particular asset is a security, either don't use it until you are sure, or treat it as though it is a security. That way, from a regulatory perspective, you are operating in the safest manner possible.

3. **Be aware of the latest statements issued by the SEC.** On February 26, 2021, for example, the SEC's Division of Examinations released a risk alert, "The Division of Examinations' Continued Focus on Digital Asset Securities." This alert focused on "unique risks" inherent in digital assets with guidance for SEC-registered advisors and firms. It's essential that you stay current with the latest regulatory releases. See the next few pages for news services that can help you stay current.

Disclosures

How much money do you manage? This number is a big deal for advisors and their firms; for many, it offers bragging rights to help you attract and retain clients. After all, investors want to invest with those they believe will make them a lot of money, and an assumption they often make is that a firm with *lots* of money must be good at it.

This is why the SEC makes sure you really are managing the money you claim to be managing. So, every year, you file your ADV with the SEC, making copies available to your clients and the public, revealing this number (and lots more).

When calculating AUM, the SEC requires you to differentiate between securities and nonsecurities; you're to include in the AUM calcu-

News Services for Blockchain and Digital Assets

Bankless
banklesshq.com

Bankless is a newsletter delivered three times per week to help you hold, lend, borrow, earn, spend, invest, and stake your money in this new crypto economy.

Bitcoinist
bitcoinist.com

Bitcoinist provides breaking news, guides, and price analysis about decentralized digital money and blockchain technology.

Bitcoin Magazine
bitcoinmagazine.com

Bitcoin Magazine is the oldest publication on digital assets and blockchain, having pioneered the space in 2012. It provides thought leadership built around stringent editorial and journalistic standards.

Bitcoin News
bitcoin.com

Bitcoin News is a digital news platform covering such subjects as ICOs, DApps, and blockchain along with market updates of crypto coins.

Blockworks
blockworks.co

Blockworks is a financial media brand that delivers breaking news and premium insights about digital assets to millions of investors.

CoinCentral
coincentral.com

CoinCentral is an all-inclusive newsletter, podcast, and educational site for digital asset enthusiasts.

CoinDesk
coindesk.com

CoinDesk is a media platform that explores how digital assets are contributing to the evolution of the global financial system. Founded in 2013, CoinDesk reaches millions interested in digital assets and blockchain technology through its website, social media, newsletters, podcasts, video, research, and live events.

For an up-to-date list, complete with hyperlinks, visit the
DACFP Yellow Pages
at dacfp.com

News Services for Blockchain and Digital Assets

Coinstats
coinstats.app

Coinstats is a leading crypto portfolio tracker that offers 24-hour crypto reports as well as the latest crypto news.

Cointelegraph
cointelegraph.com

Founded in 2013, Cointelegraph is a leading independent digital media resource covering a wide range of news on blockchain technology, digital assets, and emerging fintech trends. Each day its team of journalists, experts, and contributors delivers up-to-date news from both the decentralized and centralized worlds.

Crypto Daily
cryptodaily.io

Crypto Daily focuses on the latest news from the Binance Smart Chain, Solana, Polygon, and Ethereum ecosystems.

DappReview
dapp.review

Dapp Review helps users find more interesting Dapps, and helps developers promote their Dapps and acquire more customers.

Delphi Insights
delphidigital.io

For advanced users, Delphi's Insights membership includes content including markets coverage (DeFi, Layer 1s, NFTs, etc.), macro analysis, and a digest focused on key sectors like DAO governance and yield strategies.

Delphi Pro is a sophisticated membership tier housing a database of deep-dive, bottom-up research reports. Delphi also offers exclusive access to a members-only community chat that includes constant dialogue with some of the brightest minds in the industry.

For an up-to-date list, complete with hyperlinks, visit the
DACFP Yellow Pages
at dacfp.com

News Services for Blockchain and Digital Assets

Digital Asset Research Newsletter
digitalassetresearch.com

DAR provides multiple newsletters, ranging from daily stories to the latest digital asset regulations for institutional clients, with qualitative and quantitative analysis on digital asset markets.

NewsBTC
newsbtc.com

NewsBTC is a crypto news service that covers bitcoin news, technical analysis, and forecasts for digital assets.

Quantum Economics Newsletter
quantumeconomics.io

The newsletter gives investors information on digital assets, taking into account market conditions and on-chain analysis to evaluate the next move for digital assets.

Securities.io
securities.io

Securities.io provides daily news, interviews, and a monthly recap on security tokens, tokenized funds and real estate, regulation, and crowdfunding.

The Bitcoin Forecast by Willy Woo
willywoo.substack.com

The Bitcoin Forecast is a paid newsletter written by technologist Willy Woo. Willy focuses on the on-chain structure of the bitcoin blockchain.

The Block
theblockcrypto.com

The Block is a leading research, analysis, and news brand in the digital asset space. The Block's team is spread across seven times zones, covering the global crypto and blockchain space 24/7.

The Daily Gwei
thedailygwei.libsyn.com

The Daily Gwei keeps you up-to-date with everything happening on Ethereum.

For an up-to-date list, complete with hyperlinks, visit the
DACFP Yellow Pages
at dacfp.com

News Services for Blockchain and Digital Assets

The Defiant thedefiant.io	The Defiant is a content platform for DeFi. It curates, digests, and analyzes all the major developments in DeFi.
The Pomp Letter pomp.substack.com	The Pomp Letter is highly popular for its daily analysis of the business, finance, and technology industries.
Unchained Newsletter unchainedpodcast.com	The Unchained Newsletter is Laura Shin's daily take on the latest digital asset news. Laura was senior editor at *Forbes* and the first reporter to report on digital assets full-time.

For an up-to-date list, complete with hyperlinks, visit the
DACFP Yellow Pages
at dacfp.com

lation only those accounts or portfolios where at least 50% of the total value consists of securities (including cash and cash equivalents).

So, what do you do if 75% of an account's holdings are digital assets, such as bitcoin, that are not securities? In that case, you must exclude the entire account or portfolio from your AUM calculation.

Also, note that merely having discretion over digital assets in a client's account does not automatically qualify the value as AUM. To count, you must be able to document that you are monitoring and evaluating the client's digital assets positions separately from periodic review meetings or financial planning conversations with the client. Therefore, you must stay current with developments in blockchain and digital assets so you can demonstrate to the SEC when they visit (always a fun time) that you're conducting continuous and regular monitoring and allocation services.

You might still be able to count the assets as AUM even without discretionary authority, but only, in essence, if the firm has the client's Power of Attorney to implement the recommendations or some avenue to complete transactions; it's not AUM if the client decides on their own whether to implement. (That February 2021 risk alert lists "calculation of AUM" as a compliance issue for advisors.)

Valuations

Digital assets trade globally 24-7 across many exchanges, and each posts different prices. This makes valuation far more challenging than for stocks or mutual funds. Valuations are important for many reasons. Among them, they determine your AUM, which you use to determine the fee you're charging your client. So, if you're using an incorrect valuation, you'll be reporting inaccurate account values to your client, which could not only impair the advice you're providing but could potentially cause you to overbill your clients.

Your custodian should be hiring or subscribing to a valuation service that provides the daily closing prices of digital assets; you'll generally rely on that information. However, valuation is a developing area in this field, so your firm must stay current on these developments to ensure you're engaging in best practices. If you don't rely on the custodian's reported pricing, you need to find another way to properly determine valuations. That means finding an independent, reliable party—a difficult process for any firm.

SMAs

SMAs can be counted under AUM, but only if you retain discretion to hire and fire the manager or reallocate assets to another manager. This is true even if you recommended the SMA to the client, are paid an asset-based fee, and the client's account is discretionary because the SMA requires discretion.

ADV, Part 1, Item 5.G.7

This is where you disclose the types of advisory services you provide. "Selection of other advisors" is one choice; your firm should check this box if it recommends SMAs or investments through private funds.

ADV, Part 1, Item 8A

This section addresses any potential conflicts of interest in client transactions. You should answer yes if you personally invest in digital assets while also recommending those same assets to clients (unless those assets are limited to mutual funds).

ADV, Part 1, Item 8C

You need to decide if you have discretionary authority over digital assets transactions in client accounts when responding to this item. Item 8C refers only to discretion over securities, not nonsecurities (so keep the Howey Test in mind).

ADV, Part 1, Schedule D, Section 5K

This is a big table that segments your AUM by asset class. At this writing, digital assets are not shown as an itemized feature, but this might change.

ADV, Part 2A

As you know, clients don't get to see Part 1. But they do receive Part 2 (which is why this is called the disclosure brochure), so references to digital assets are particularly important here. If you're recommending digital assets for the first time, you must update this section to acknowledge that you've made material changes to your ADV.

ADV, Part 2, Item 4

As this describes the firm's advisory business, it might need to be updated based on the AUM calculations shown in Part 1. You're permitted to describe AUM differently in Part 2, but you need to maintain documentation describing the method you use and why your responses in each part, although different, are not misleading. You may also need to update the types of advisory services you offer if you're providing digital assets advice as a separate service.

ADV, Part 2, Item 5

This is perhaps of greatest client interest because it describes how you're compensated for the advice you provide on digital assets, as well as other fees and expenses the client may incur. Any fees and expenses specific to digital assets that haven't been disclosed elsewhere should be described here.

ADV, Part 3, Item 8

Here is your disclosure of your methods of analysis, investment strategies, and risks of loss—which have changed if you're now recommending digital assets. If any security involves significant or unusual risks (and let's admit it, digital assets *do* involve significant or unusual risks), then you need to explain them in detail here.

Key considerations when deciding if you need to change and add risk factors to Part 3, Item 8, include:

- price volatility
- the speculative nature of digital assets
- the fact that digital assets are not generally backed by hard assets or cash flows
- supply and demand drivers of pricing

- technological network risks, also called compromised risk or access risk
- risk of unauthorized transactions and theft
- safekeeping of digital assets and storage risks
- business continuity plans
- loss of private keys
- illiquidity
- uncertain regulatory environment
- assets held in an omnibus account or fund are subject to creditor claims, and the custodian may have the benefit of actual ownership
- digital assets accounts and values are not protected by FDIC or SIPC
- fees and expenses associated with digital assets investing are generally noncomparable

Custody

Custody means holding client funds or securities (both directly and indirectly) or having the authority to obtain possession of them. If you have custody of client funds or securities, you must safeguard those funds. The custody rule is designed to protect investors against the risk of theft or misappropriation by investment advisors. Therefore, you must disclose information about custody on both Parts 1 and 2 of Form ADV.

Are digital assets subject to custody rules? Regulatory clarity is lacking at this writing. The answer will certainly depend on the facts and regulations—both of which change over time. So, consider

- Congress's intent when passing the Investment Advisers Act of 1940;
- the SEC's broad charter of protecting investors and their assets; and

- that digital assets and traditional securities are both exposed to the same issues.

If the firm does not have authority to obtain possession of the digital assets, either directly or by liquidating them and allocating the proceeds, then securities attorneys generally agree that custody does not exist.

The technical requirements for transacting and custodying digital assets securities are different from those for traditional securities. For example, traditional securities transactions typically involve intermediaries, such as infrastructure providers and counterparties, but the digital assets securities market has no comparable intermediaries.

Although the SEC has issued some guidance, saying that custody rules apply only if the digital asset is characterized as a fund or security, keep in mind that even if a digital asset is not deemed a security, you still need to demonstrate that the digital asset does not fall under the category of "client funds" to avoid application of the custody rule.

Qualified Custodians

The law pertaining to custody for digital assets remains under development, but one requirement is that you must only use qualified custodians to hold clients' assets. In November 2020, the SEC published a statement acknowledging that "determining who qualifies as a qualified custodian is complicated, and facts and circumstances based." Some companies have abandoned efforts to win "qualified custodian" status by the SEC and instead seek approval at the state level by becoming a state-chartered trust company, which also lets them offer custody services with regulatory oversight (albeit by the state and not the SEC).

The selection of a qualified custodian is a fundamental duty of a fiduciary. Consider these questions for the custodian:

1. How long have you been in business?

2. How many engineers or software developers do you employ?
   a. What is their experience with digital assets?

3. Are you already deemed to be a qualified custodian?

4. Which assets do you custody and which do you not?

5. Do you accept both qualified and nonqualified accounts?

6. What licenses and certifications do you hold?
   a. How long have you had them?
   b. Have there been any lapses in those licenses and certifications?

7. Describe your level of financial stability.
   a. Are you willing to submit evidence?
   b. Are you audited by an independent third party?
   c. Will you provide those audit results to me?

8. Have you conducted a security audit?
   a. Will you share the results of that audit with me?

9. Do you provide proof-of-existence audits on demand to verify the availability of assets?

10. How long have you been offering digital assets?

11. In what country are your digital assets stored?
    a. If outside the United States, how have you evaluated the risk of government seizure?

12. Are digital assets in segregated wallets or omnibus accounts?
    a. Why are they maintained in that manner?

13. Are the digital assets you custody held in hot or cold wallets?
    a. If cold, describe the cold storage protocol.

14. Do you use a multi-signature protocol?
    a. If so, describe your approach and rationale.

15. How do you handle forks and airdrops?

16. How do you generate keys?
   a. How do you secure those keys?
   b. Are private keys ever exposed to humans?

17. How do you authenticate users and approvers?

18. How do you protect against collusion and coercion?

19. Are nightly data feeds of positions, NAV, and pricing data fed into your portfolio accounting applications?
   a. Which ones?

20. Describe your insurance coverage.
   a. Who is the carrier?
   b. Does the policy protect only the custodian, or also my clients and me?
   c. What are the policy limits per claim, per account, and per client?
   d. What does the policy cover?

21. Are you a subsidiary of a larger company?
   a. If so, is your parent company liable for your errors and omissions or is it shielded from your liabilities?

22. Can you handle bulk or aggregated trades to facilitate rebalancing all accounts?

23. Do you offer best execution?
   a. How quickly are trades typically filled?

24. How do you facilitate the debiting of my advisory fee from client accounts and send payment of my fee to me?

25. What is your fee schedule?

The custodian's answers to the above could cause you to update your ADV.

Privacy and Confidentiality

No advisor should ever accept any information about any client's private key or seed phrases. If you do, you could be deemed as having access to your client's asset, even if the key is also held by the custodian.

Aside from the security risks, taking custody of this information would make it difficult for you or your firm to show whether the transaction was done by the firm, by the client, or by some other party—regardless of whether a qualified custodian is involved.

Code of Ethics

Do you want to personally invest in digital assets? Before you do, read your firm's Code of Ethics. It describes your obligations—which could include getting the firm's approval prior to purchasing any digital assets that are securities. Your firm might also require preapproval for any purchase so it can prevent and monitor front-running, parking, and other issues.

Your firm's Code of Ethics also stipulates your obligation to submit to the firm a quarterly report disclosing your personal holdings of any and all securities. This includes any digital assets that are considered securities. The Code of Ethics may also require that you report on your nonsecurities holdings as well. That would require you to disclose the name and location of the assets, including the custodian, exchange, hardware and wallet you use, in addition to the date and location of purchases, purchase price, and quantity bought. Ditto for any sales. But never provide any information about your private keys or seed phrases—even if you're asked to. (And never ask any employees to provide theirs.)

If you invest via an institutional third party, it will likely produce a summary of activity that you can download and provide to your Compliance Department. That download will probably satisfy your reporting obligation. (If it doesn't, your Compliance Officer will let you know!)

It's your responsibility to know what your firm requires and to comply with its rules. And if you are responsible for making those determinations for your firm, make sure you give proper guidance to your employees and any access persons (such as board members or auditors) so they know what they must and must not do.

Conflicts of Interest

Your Code of Ethics explains how you must avoid conflicts of interest with your client—and disclose them when avoidance is not possible.

For digital assets, specific considerations include whether you or the firm take positions in the same digital assets that are also recommended to clients. If so, disclose the conflicts this presents in Form ADV and how you address those conflicts.

Some of the questions to address include:

- If you're buying for yourself and your client digital assets that have low trading volumes, whose trades will be executed first—your trades or the clients' trades? (In other words, how will the firm avoid front-running?)
- Will the firm require that its advisors and other personnel obtain preapproval before buying or selling digital assets for personal accounts?
- Will the firm restrict trading in limited offerings of digital assets, such as private placements?
- What disclosures, if any, will be made to clients at the time of trading?

KYC

Although investment advisors do not have a Know Your Customer Rule per se, advisors do have a fiduciary obligation to act in the best interest of each client—and that means having an understanding of which investments are suitable for each client. That, in turn, means knowing your client's investment needs, goals, objectives, risk tolerance, and other details, such as any restrictions requested by the client. Add it all up and you essentially have a KYC obligation.

The extent of your KYC requirement depends on your relationship with the client. For example, an asset manager who manages a limited portion of a client's assets may not know anything about the client; this is routine for mutual fund managers, for example. If that describes your relationship with your client, this must be disclosed to the client and reflected in the agreement that the client signs during onboarding.

An important part of being a fiduciary is the due diligence you do on the investments you recommend. It's not good enough to say that you provided a digital assets security to your clients because they asked for it or because "everyone else" is buying it. Keep in mind that the SEC's February 2021 Risk Alert listed portfolio management as a compliance risk—meaning that the SEC is paying attention to the digital assets that advisors are recommending to clients. And that includes the securities classification of digital assets, due diligence on those assets, risk mitigation, and the fulfillment of your fiduciary duty to your clients.

It's also not enough to perform KYC actions when initiating a client relationship. Instead, your requirements are ongoing. You and your firm should periodically request updates from each client about their life and financial circumstances so you can make changes as needed to prior recommendations. Even if your client doesn't respond to your request for updates (which is common), you and your firm should use common sense and make changes that you know are needed. For example, clients who have been with you for twenty years are probably not in the same situation as when they met you; proceed accordingly. And if you don't feel you can act effectively in such a vacuum of information, talk with your Compliance Department about terminating the relationship.

AML

Investment advisors are not subject to the USA PATRIOT Act's requirements regarding Anti–Money Laundering rules. However, your firm may have an AML program in place for other reasons—as a voluntary best-practices decision or perhaps because a third party requires it.

Your firm's AML program, if any, should consider the specific risks associated with digital assets. The biggest risk to investment advisors is most likely the anonymity that is commonplace with digital assets exchanges. (It's challenging to guard against money laundering if you don't know with whom you and your clients are dealing.)

Even though investment advisors are not required to have an AML program, all US citizens are subject to the USA PATRIOT Act. That means you or your firm could be violating the act if a client is allowed to launder money or finance terrorist operations.

Even if the activity is deemed legal, you're exposed to tremendous reputational risk. So, make sure your firm ensures that a third party reviews every client's action for potential money laundering and terrorist financing.

Best Execution

Your duty here is deeply embedded in the fiduciary duty. All advisors must execute securities transactions in such a manner that the client's total cost or proceeds for each transaction are the most favorable under the circumstances. The determinative factor is not the lowest possible commission, but whether the transaction represents the best qualitative execution.

Thus, best execution doesn't mean "best" in an objective way. Instead, and to the consternation of firms, it depends on the facts and circumstances. And those facts and circumstances will be different for digital assets.

For example, try honoring your best execution duty when different digital assets exchanges offer different prices simultaneously. Since prices change on all exchanges constantly, how can you possibly know which exchange is offering the best price? It's unknowable, so when making your choice, consider instead such criteria as speed, safety, transparency, platform quality, research, support services, exchange reputation, and pricing track record.

Compliance Policies and Practices

A comprehensive review of the firm's entire compliance program is warranted if your firm decides to add digital assets to its recommended portfolios. Here are a few areas to review:

- Supervisory responsibilities
- Monitoring of SMAs
- Custody
- Trade allocations
- Valuation of investments for billing and reporting
- Best execution
- Securities orders
- Transactions reviews
- Agency cross and principal transactions
- Cybersecurity

If stolen, digital assets are generally harder to retrieve than other assets, so the firm should review the SEC's views on this issue. Also, track the industry's best practices, which are often ahead of the SEC's alerts, actions, and guidance.

RFIT Program

Your firm should review and strengthen its Red Flags Identity Theft Program, so you and the firm can determine if a client's request to sell or transfer digital assets is really coming from the client—and not a hacker posing as the client.

Marketing

Your firm should review its marketing plan pertaining to digital assets, as these investments could require different disclosures from the standard template you use with other marketing activities. Before using any marketing materials with the public, get approval from your firm's Advertising or Compliance Department.

ADV, Part 3

Also called Form CRS, the Client Relationship Summary is a one- or two-page document summarizing your firm's services, investment authority, fees, costs, conflicts, and other essential facts. You must update Form CRS within 30 days of material changes in your client relationship, and you must communicate those changes to each client within 60 days of that. (Remember that you must provide clients with an amended version that highlights the changes as well as a new revised version.)

Confidentiality

Your fiduciary responsibility requires you to maintain confidentiality about your clients and their transactions. That's routine—but blockchain brings the need for a fresh focus. Deploying blockchain technology in your practice means you have something new to consider regarding confidentiality. For example, you must prevent wallet tracing—something that was never an issue before. You must also ensure that only personnel with a need-to-know have access to the blockchain used by the firm. This is particularly important because of the potential to access, convert, or transfer digital assets improperly.

Dual Registrants

We've been referring to the SEC so far, so let's focus on FINRA. Thousands of financial advisors are registered with both the SEC and FINRA. If that describes you, you must follow the rules issued by both regulators.

Your brokerage firm may require you, as a Registered Representative, to obtain its permission before you buy digital assets for yourself or for clients. You must also promptly notify your firm's Risk Monitoring Analyst if you or any associated persons or affiliates engage or intend to engage in activities related to digital assets. These activities include

- buying or selling digital assets or a fund that invests in them;
- buying or selling futures or options tied to digital assets;
- participating in an ICO;
- taking custody of digital assets;
- accepting digital assets from customers;
- mining;
- displaying quotations of digital assets; and
- using blockchain technology.

Don't assume that your ADV disclosures satisfy FINRA. FINRA has its own rules, so be sure you satisfy them as well.

Protecting You and Your Firm—and Thus Your Clients—When Dealing with Digital Assets Insurance Policies

First, the vast majority of digital assets and the accounts in which they reside are not insured by FDIC or SIPC. This lack of coverage must be part of your analysis in deciding whether and how to recommend digital assets to clients.

To obtain coverage for yourself and your firm, contact your insurance provider to see if your existing Professional-Liability or Errors & Omissions policies cover activities involving digital assets. Ask if you and your firm need additional policies, riders, or coverage for providing advice about digital assets and/or having discretionary authority over digital assets investments—and be sure to obtain this coverage before adding digital assets to your practice since many policies do not cover prior acts.

Registered Representatives who obtain E&O through their broker/dealer (B/D) may not be covered for fee-based activities, even if the RIA activities were approved or even supervised by the B/D.

In addition, look at your policy's cyber coverage. You want to be protected for issues such as a data breach, transfer fraud, media liability, and human error.

Fidelity Bonds

Although they're called bonds, fidelity bonds are a form of insurance, designed to protect you and your clients from financial loss due to theft or crime—such as wrongful acts committed by employees or contractors.

Although you won't custody a client's private keys, for example, someone associated with your firm could come into contact with information about those keys or transfer that data via insecure means (either accidentally or maliciously), with bad results. A fidelity bond can help protect you.

You should also consider extended coverage if you provide tax and accounting services related to digital assets.

Many insurers don't provide coverage in this area yet, while others limit the coverage they'll provide. Coverage opportunities will likely increase as the digital assets market matures; in the meantime, if you and your firm are not able to obtain the coverage you want today, you'll have to make a business decision about whether and how to handle digital assets.

Digital Assets Insurance Providers

BitGo
bitgo.com

BitGo provides investors with institutional custody, trading, and insurance. It offers a variety of secure insurance solutions for custodians as well as businesses. BitGo Business Wallet clients can purchase Key Recovery Service insurance and additional insurance for self-custody keys through third-party company Digital Asset Services.

Coincover
www.coincover.com

Coincover guarantees digital funds are not lost or stolen. Its technology combines insurance with security features to ensure digital asset investments are secure for investors as well as businesses.

HCP National
hcpnational.com

HCP National helps businesses secure high-quality insurance coverage for their digital assets, via general business insurance, Directors & Officers, and Errors & Omissions, crime insurance, custody insurance, and DeFi insurance policies.

Marsh
marsh.com

Marsh's Blockchain and Digital Asset Risk Transfer insurance solutions serve companies in the blockchain technology, cryptocurrency, and digital asset arena.

For an up-to-date list, complete with hyperlinks, visit the
DACFP Yellow Pages
at dacfp.com

How to Implement Digital Assets into Your Practice

Although digital assets are becoming increasingly accepted within the financial community, many advisors still simply tell clients, "It's not something we do."

Because clients are increasingly demanding that digital assets be included in their portfolios, and other advisors—your competitors—

are increasingly meeting that need, you may feel that you have no choice but to engage. After all, you risk losing clients and AUM if you don't. In fact, a 2021 survey by NYDIG found that 92% of clients expect their financial advisors to be able to give them advice about bitcoin, and 62% would switch advisors if theirs couldn't help them. So, you sit on the sidelines at your own risk.

When I say risk, I don't just mean you expose yourself to the risk that you might lose clients. You might also suffer the wrath of regulators. Keep in mind that you are a fiduciary—and that means you have a legal obligation to do what's best for your client. How can you say you're meeting that standard if you don't even consider digital assets?

When SEC examiners visit, you will need to be able to explain why you *aren't* investing in digital assets. You'll need to show them evidence that you engaged in due diligence and that your research and analysis led you to conclude that *not* including this new asset class in *any* client portfolios was correct.

If all you can say is "I think bitcoin is nothing more than a tulip bulb or Beanie Babies," with no data to support that contention, well, good luck with your exam.

So, let me help you design a practice management approach that allows you to truly determine, without bias or preconceived notions, whether digital assets belong in client portfolios.

Firm Philosophy: What Is Your Future Plan?

Let's start with philosophy. Your current answer could be any of the following:

- We've explored this asset class and concluded it's not right for our clients. We continue to observe developments and we may change our mind in the future.
- We are not currently recommending digital assets to our clients, but we are monitoring the issues and continuing to

learn more, and we might decide to engage at some time in the future.

- We are actively seeking managers so we can provide this asset class to our clients.

- We are providing it to clients, but only to those who express an interest in it.

- We provide exposure for some clients but not others, based on each client's situation.

- We routinely provide exposure to this asset class for all clients, with exceptions.

Any of these positions serves well to establish your firm's view. It sets the tone for you and everyone else in the firm and removes any frustration or drama whenever clients ask the question—which usually occurs after they've talked to someone or come across something in the news.

Having that philosophy in place—with the evidence to support it—will also help if the SEC ever asks you about it.

Firm Policies

The philosophy you and your firm select will determine which policies you must adopt—such as those on trade execution, investment decisions, due diligence, and so on.

You'll also need to update your internal compliance procedures, such as those on Outside Business Activities and employee attestations. What information are you seeking, how often do you want it, and how are you collecting it?

Firms should begin by sampling employees. Find out who are interested in the subject, who own digital assets, and what their plans are. By doing this, the firm's leadership is letting everyone know that the firm is paying attention. The firm is also learning whom it can turn to for help—because those engaging in this space are likely to be more knowledgeable than the firm's Legal and Compliance staff.

As part of this, you'll have to resolve your viewpoint on digital assets versus digital assets that are securities. Bitcoin and Ether, for example, are not securities, according to the SEC, but XRP is. So, will you demand everyone in the firm disclose their holdings of bitcoin? You don't ask employees if they own baseball cards or rare stamps—they aren't securities, after all—so why would you ask about bitcoin? And since those who own bitcoin likely realize this, how will you handle objections to your inquiry?

Client Communication and Documentation

Be sure you document all your client conversations involving digital assets—even when the conversation involves nonsecurities such as bitcoin. And handle all digital assets trades with the same processes as you would any other trade.

Be particularly clear with clients—ideally in your client agreement and Investment Policy Statement (if you issue one), but also in current conversations and emails—about your policy regarding trading hours. The New York Stock Exchange is open Mondays through Fridays 9:30 a.m. to 4:00 p.m. EST, except for federal holidays. So, if a client sends you an email at 8:00 p.m. on a Saturday to trade shares of IBM, you (and they) know they must wait until the market opens for that trade to be processed. But digital assets trade 24/7/365—and we know how volatile prices can be. So, if you get an email for a trade on Saturday night but you don't execute it until you're back in the office on Tuesday morning, have you failed to meet your client's expectations? Or worse, exposed yourself to liability? Your client agreement, IPS, and ongoing communications can help you avoid disputes or harm to your reputation.

Blockchain Research and Analytics Firms

AnChain
anchain.ai

AnChain provides smart contract intelligence to protect financial institutions and government agencies from bad actors within the digital asset space.

Amberdata
amberdata.io

Amberdata is a blockchain and crypto asset market data provider.

Binance Research
binance.com

Binance Research provides institutional-grade analysis, in-depth insights, and unbiased information to all participants in the digital asset industry.

Blockchain Research Institute
blockchainresearch institute.org

The Blockchain Research Institute is an independent global think tank dedicated to exploring and sharing knowledge about the strategic implications of blockchain on business, government, and society.

BTCS
btcs.com

BTCS is a blockchain infrastructure and research company focused on providing on-chain analytics.

ByteTree
bytetree.com

ByteTree offes real-time data on blockchain networks, and is a leading provider of institutional-grade crypto-asset data. Its investor terminal tracks more than 80 metrics for digital assets in real time.

CertiK
certik.org

CertiK is the leading security-focused ranking platform to analyze and monitor blockchain protocols and DeFi projects.

For an up-to-date list, complete with hyperlinks, visit the
DACFP Yellow Pages
at dacfp.com

Blockchain Research and Analytics Firms

Chainalysis
chainalysis.com

Chainalysis creates transparency for a global economy built on blockchains, enabling banks, businesses, and governments to have a common understanding of how individuals and institutions use blockchains. Chainalysis provides software and research to government agencies, exchanges, financial institutions, and insurance and cybersecurity companies in 60+ countries. Its platform powers investigation, compliance, and risk management tools used to solve cybercriminal cases.

Chainbeat
chainbeat.io

Chainbeat helps investors understand real usage and retention of DeFi applications, providing an overall understanding of DeFi's adoption.

Ciphertrace
ciphertrace.com

Ciphertrace enables the blockchain economy by protecting digital asset companies and financial institutions from security and compliance risks.

CoinMetrics
coinmetrics.io

CoinMetrics is the leading provider of crypto financial intelligence, offering network data, market data, indexes, and network risk solutions to the most prestigious institutions touching digital assets.

Crystal Blockchain
crystalblockchain.com

Crystal Blockchain provides crypto transaction analysis and monitoring for exchange, bank, and compliance requirements.

Delphi Digital
delphidigital.io

Delphi Digital has built a strong reputation across each of its primary verticals (Research, Labs, Ventures) and is widely considered the premier research firm dedicated to the crypto and digital asset market. Delphi's client base includes many of the industry's most prominent funds, financial institutions, and investors.

Delphi Digital

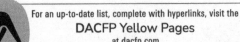

For an up-to-date list, complete with hyperlinks, visit the
DACFP Yellow Pages
at dacfp.com

Blockchain Research and Analytics Firms

Digital Asset Research
digitalassetresearch.com

Digital Asset Research provides comprehensive digital asset market data to institutional participants.

DMG
dmgblockchain.com

DMG (ticker: DMGGF) is a publicly traded, vertically integrated blockchain, and digital asset company that manages, operates, and develops end-to-end digital solutions to monetize the blockchain ecosystem.

Elementus
elementus.io

Elementus is the first universal blockchain search engine and institutional-grade crypto forensic solution.

Elliptic
elliptic.co

Elliptic provides blockchain analytics, training, and certification for crypto businesses, financial institutions, and regulators. It offers services and software to detect and prevent financial crime. The company analyzes 100+ digital asset data points to provide actionable insights that clients rely on to mitigate risk and maintain regulatory compliance. Ciphertrace enables the blockchain economy by protecting digital asset companies and financial institutions from security and compliance risks.

Flipside
flipsidecrypto.com

Flipside works directly with leading crypto projects to reward on-demand analytics through structured bounty programs.

Glassnode
glassnode.com

Glassnode is a blockchain data and intelligence provider generating innovative on-chain metrics and tools for digital asset stakeholders. Glassnode delivers insights into blockchains and digital assets by focusing on the data from the blockchains themselves.

IntoTheBlock
intotheblock.com

IntoTheBlock is a science company applying cutting-edge research in AI to deliver actionable intelligence for the crypto market.

For an up-to-date list, complete with hyperlinks, visit the
DACFP Yellow Pages
at dacfp.com

Blockchain Research and Analytics Firms

Lukka
lukka.tech

Lukka provides data and software solutions to manage digital assets on infrastructure built for the future of commerce.

Mosaic
mosaic.io

Mosaic is a blockchain research platform that enables greater transparency and institutional analysis in cryptofinance.

Nansen
nansen.ai

Nansen is a blockchain analytics platform that enriches on-chain data with millions of wallet labels.

NYDIG
nydig.com

NYDIG delivers bitcoin products and insights across industries, from banking and insurance to fintech and nonprofits.

Omniex
omniex.io

Omniex is a financial services technology company providing a suite of solutions for the access, trading, and management of crypto and digital assets.

QLUE
qlue.io

QLUE is an investigative solution developed in partnership with senior law enforcement investigators and anti-money-laundering specialists that incorporates advanced proprietary search algorithms to detect suspicious activity that criminals attempt to conceal using digital assets.

ScoreChain
scorechain.com

ScoreChain Analytics tracks digital assets and helps you create a structured and coherent AML strategy for identifying, assessing, and managing risk.

For an up-to-date list, complete with hyperlinks, visit the
DACFP Yellow Pages
at dacfp.com

Blockchain Research and Analytics Firms

Sherlock (Fidelity Digital Assets)
fidelitydigitalassets.com

Sherlock is a digital assets and analytics solution that helps institutional investors evaluate the market. It is offered by Fidelity Digital Assets.

SIMETRI
cryptobriefing.com

SIMETRI is one of the largest independent crypto research providers in the world. It offers proprietary methodology for scoring cryptocurrency projects through research and analytics.

Streaming Fast
streamingfast.io

Streaming Fast is a blockchain API company that makes it possible to stream real-time state updates, conduct lightning-fast searches, and provide irreversible transaction guarantees by using a simple API call.

Totle
totle.com

Totle aggregates decentralized exchanges and synthetic asset providers into a suite of tools that makes it easy to access deep liquidity for DeFi assets at the best price.

TradeBlock
tradeblock.com

TradeBlock is one of the longest-standing providers of institutional trading tools, data, and indices for digital currencies. It calculates and publishes industry-leading reference rates for digital assets that are used to price countless OTC transactions, AUM, and derivatives.

TROY
troytrade.com

Troy offers the functions of an aggregated centralized trading platform, data monitoring, and on-chain trading, providing users with a full range of trading services.

zK Capital
zkcapital.substack.com

zk Capital is a research-focused blockchain investment firm.

For an up-to-date list, complete with hyperlinks, visit the
DACFP Yellow Pages
at dacfp.com

Internal Systems

How will your firm manage activities pertaining to digital assets? For example, Excel was not designed to handle these assets. So, if your firm uses Excel for data input and storage, you likely need to consider installing data integration software that allows data to move freely through all the systems in your firm—giving appropriate personnel the information they need at the moment they need it.

Billing and Collection of Advisory Fees

Here's a not-so-trivial item: making sure you're able to get paid!

So, ask yourself, If you recommend that a client move some assets into digital assets, what are the implications for you from a revenue perspective?

You have five choices. The first is not to bill the client for that AUM at all. Obviously, that's not an ideal option—and not merely because it

costs you money. The real problem with this approach is that it raises questions about conflicts of interest and the legitimacy of your advice. "If you tell me that you can't collect your AUM fee on assets placed into bitcoin, and you then tell me not to invest in bitcoin, are you telling me not to invest merely because you don't want to suffer a loss of revenue?" Suddenly, the client can't believe anything you say.

Your second choice is to send a bill to your client based on the amount held in digital assets. But if collecting that fee requires you to invoice the client, you're introducing a new and cumbersome aspect to your practice management. You'll incur a new expense from the effort. And what will you do if the client doesn't pay?

The third option is to split the portfolio into two parts—one holding the usual investments and the other holding digital assets—and then billing only the first part. Here's how that works: Say the client has invested $100,000 with you. Instead of placing all the money into Portfolio A, you put 99% of assets into Portfolio A (which buys the usual investments) and 1% of assets into Portfolio B, where you buy bitcoin. Portfolio A now holds $99,000 and Portfolio B holds $1,000. Next, instead of collecting your fee pro rata from both Portfolio A and B, you collect the entire fee from Portfolio A as shown in Figure 21.1.

The fourth option is to place the digital assets securities in the same account as the rest of the securities. One account, one billing. Simple. Easy. Automatic.

The fifth option is to work with exchanges or custodians that facilitate all your practice management needs—not just billing, but portfolio rebalancing, tax management, and related services.

Billing in Advance

Most advisors debit client accounts quarterly, in advance. That's not in the clients' best interest. By collecting the fee in advance, you're reducing the amount of money they're investing and thus reducing their returns. This problem is even worse when you consider the volatile nature of digital assets.

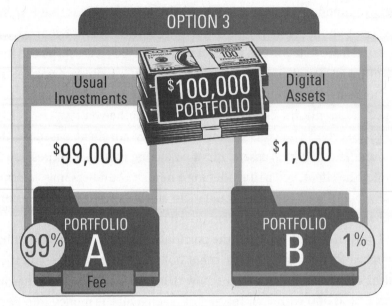

FIGURE 21.1

So, you should collect your fee in arrears—after the quarter has ended. The marketplace has ample technology to let you operate this way, and you'll be demonstrating to your clients that you're engaging in a best practice.

If operations and compliance challenges tempt you to shy away from digital assets, then you should take one of three actions:

1. **Get over it.** This is your job. You have an obligation to serve your clients well, even when you must do work that doesn't describe why you got into this field.

2. **Delegate the chores.** Just because this work is important and must be done doesn't mean you're the one who has to do it. Hire staff or outsource the tasks to consultants.

3. **Quit.** Find another job in a less demanding field, where you don't have to focus on the best interests of other people.

PART FIVE

Getting Started

Chapter 22

The Answers to the Ten Common Concerns

Congratulations! You've learned a lot about blockchain and digital assets. You might still have concerns. I'll answer the most common ones here.

Before we begin, remember that we're talking about investing a tiny portion of your portfolio into this new asset class. So, let's keep the conversation in perspective, okay? As we've learned, a total wipeout of the investment won't impede your ability to enjoy financial security in retirement.

Second, focus on the benefits, not the features. That there's paperwork, for example, or a new custodian, well, those are features. Focus on the benefits, which include improved diversification, lower risk, higher returns, and achievement of your financial goals.

Now, let's consider your concerns.

1. I'm Nervous About Investing in Digital Assets

I know how you feel. When I first encountered bitcoin, it sure seemed strange—like nothing else I'd ever seen. I felt then as you may feel now—that the idea of investing in something so new, so unusual, so "unreal," is uncomfortable.

But the more I learned, the more I understood. And the more I understood, the more comfortable I became. And that comfort allowed me to proceed . . . slowly at first.

You should consider the same approach. Say your portfolio is worth

$100,000. A 1% allocation is $1,000. If you invest that money over 12 monthly installments (using dollar cost averaging, as explained in chapter 17), you'll be investing a mere $83 per month. That's $20 per week, or less than three bucks a day. You spend more than $3 a day on soft drinks and snacks—with no hope of seeing that money again. At least with digital assets, you might get some money back! When you think about it this way, you make it easier to get started.

And if you're still wrestling with your desire to invest versus your fear of losing money, and you don't know how to resolve the debate, use the tactic Benjamin Franklin used whenever he was faced with a choice. Ben described his strategy in his autobiography, published in 1771. He explained that he would take a blank sheet of paper and draw a line down the middle of the page. On the left side, he would list all the reasons to proceed; on the right, he'd list the reasons to decline. Then he'd compare lists.

Nothing is ever perfect, Ben realized; every decision involves pros and cons. By creating both lists, he could easily see which list was longer. If there are more pros than cons, he concluded that the benefits of proceeding outweighed the cautions.

So, let's try Ben's approach. Let's begin by listing the benefits of investing in digital assets. They include:

1. Diversification

2. Noncorrelation with other asset classes

3. Reducing portfolio risk

4. Potentially increasing portfolio returns

5. Increasing portfolio tax efficiency

6. Low investment minimum

7. Inflation protection

8. 24-7 access

Your turn. Add some more benefits:

9. _____

10. _____

11. _____

Now, list your reasons for avoiding digital assets.

1. It's a new asset class, so still somewhat uncertain

2. Potential loss of coins from hacking

Which list is longer? Proceed accordingly, and with confidence that, all things considered, you're making the best choice.

2. It's a Fad

When investing, it's important to differentiate between fads and trends. The former is temporary; the latter is sustained. Clothing, for example, is a trend. Bell-bottom blue jeans were a fad.

Beanie Babies were a fad, not a trend. For a while, the plush dolls were selling for hundreds, even thousands, of dollars. Inevitably, the novelty wore off. Everyone lost interest. The fad was over. And prices crashed.

History is filled with similar stories, dating back to the tulip mania of 1636. All fads experience the same life cycle: they emerge and quickly gain popularity, causing prices to skyrocket. Interest suddenly fades, and prices crash. Pet rocks, yo-yos, Pokémon. All were fads.

So, yeah, I get it. You're wondering if bitcoin is just the latest fad, today's version of Beanie Babies.

It's not. Digital assets are a trend, not a fad. Trends differ from fads in one important way: utility. Beanie Babies are fun to hold and pretty to look at, but that's it. You can't *do* anything with them; they have no practical use.

By contrast, digital assets and blockchain have thousands of commercial uses, as we saw in chapter 2. These benefits, which enable companies to operate faster, cheaper, with greater security and transparency, are the reasons why this technology is here to stay.

"I lost everything in the Beanie Baby crash of '99."

3. It's a Fraud

You've certainly heard lots of stories about fraud involving bitcoin and other digital assets. I've sure heard them, and those stories worried me, too. What I've discovered is that bitcoin itself is not fraudulent; it merely has sometimes found itself involved in fraudulent activities. By the same notion, there's nothing wrong with dollars even though they've been involved in many bank robberies.

Indeed, every asset class has been involved in frauds, scams, and outright theft. The very first security ever sold in the United States—bonds issued by the US Treasury in 1792—got caught up in an insider trading scandal. Despite all the Ponzi schemes, pump-and-dump scams, affinity frauds, and telemarketing schemes involving the stock market, real estate market, and gold market, investors remain confident about investing in those asset classes. We must always be careful when investing. It's no different with digital assets.

4. There's No Legitimate Way to Ascertain the Value

I agree with you. Fortunately, it doesn't matter. When investing, price is what matters—and bitcoin and all other digital assets trade for a price. That price is set the same way all asset prices are set: based on supply and demand. The supply of bitcoin is limited, so all you have to decide is whether demand will increase. That's one of the best aspects of digital assets. Unlike a hotel that sets the price for its rooms, digital assets are decentralized; no single company or person sets the price. Instead, the global network does that. It's a reassuring feature of the asset class.

5. It's Too Volatile

As of this writing, bitcoin has crashed five times since 2014. Most observers believe future crashes are likely.

News flash: the stock market has crashed five times, too, since 1929. Real estate has crashed several times during that same period, as have the gold and oil markets.

Crashes are just part of investing. You don't have to like volatility, but it's costly to refrain from investing in an asset class because of worries that a crash might occur. The reason: every crash in history has been followed by new, all-time highs. There's no assurance that the market cycle will always perform this way, but there's no reason to believe otherwise, either.

So instead of fearing volatility, smile at it. Consider the next crash to be an opportunity to buy while prices are lower. While you wait for that crash, invest regularly via dollar cost averaging and engage in portfolio rebalancing. We learned about all this in chapter 17.

Let's also remember that volatility works both ways: prices go up *and* down, not just down. Guess what? No one ever complains about *upside* volatility. But if you want to enjoy rising prices, you must tolerate occasional periods of declining prices, too.

One final point. Are you sure that digital assets are as volatile as you think? Of the 500 stocks in the S&P 500 Stock Index, in 2020, 112 of them were more volatile than bitcoin. So, if you're willing to invest 40% to 80% of your money in the stock market, you ought to be willing to invest 1% in digital assets.

6. It's Too Risky

All new asset classes are risky. That's why I recommend you limit your exposure to just 1% of your portfolio. Even a total loss of that investment wouldn't cause you significant financial harm.

7. I Don't Think I Need This in My Portfolio

This asset class is needed in your portfolio for the same reason you need everything else in your portfolio: to provide yourself with better diversification.

The more types of assets in the portfolio, the less risk you're taking. That's a key feature of digital assets investments. They're noncorrelated, meaning their price movements are unrelated to those of all the other asset classes you already own.

8. It's Too Late to Buy Because the Price Is Too High

The best time to buy is always in the past. Don't you wish you bought real estate 30 years ago or shares of Apple 20 years ago?

It's human nature to compare today's prices to past prices. But time moves forward, not backward—and all indications suggest that the future price of this asset class will be higher than the current price. Only 300 million people worldwide own bitcoin. That's about 3% of the world's population. What might happen to bitcoin's price if 6% of the population decides to buy? If 12% buy? If 24% buy? The growing adoption rate is a key reason many believe the future price of bitcoin will be higher than the current price.

A rising price also makes the price of bitcoin safer, some say. This theory says that the higher price reflects greater adoption, and the more people who own and use bitcoin, the less likely the price will fall. This is exactly the opposite of how the stock market works, by the way: the more a stock price rises, the more likely investors will sell—because they're relating the price to the profits of the underlying company. But there is no "corporate profit" with bitcoin, and thus that classic "stock market sell signal" does not apply. By this thinking, if bitcoin's price is high, you should be more willing to buy it, not less.

I remember reading about the Wright brothers' early flights. Their first crash occurred on September 17, 1908. The plane was traveling about 150 feet up in the air before it plunged to the ground. Orville was the pilot; he survived, but passenger Lt. Thomas Selfridge died. In reviewing events, Orville said things would have gone much better if he had been flying much *higher*. Doesn't that seem counterintuitive? After all, if Orville had been closer to the ground when problems occurred, Lieutenant Selfridge might not have died. But, no, Orville said. By flying only at 150 feet, he didn't have much time to react to events. At an altitude of 1,000 feet, he'd have had far more time to correct the problem. In the same way, bitcoin at $50,000 in 2021 is much safer than it was at $479 in 2012.

Don't fear bitcoin's high price.

9. Bitcoin Prices Are Volatile, So I'll Wait for the Next Decline Before I Buy

Everyone wants to buy everything for prices that are lower than they are. Few succeed in that effort.

There's a problem with the idea: the price might rise further before it falls. It might rise so much that by the time it crashes, the post-crash price could still be higher than today's price.

So instead of sitting and waiting, hoping you'll catch the best price, engage in dollar-cost averaging. This way, you'll get the average low cost for the duration of your investments.

10. I Don't Know How, or Even Where, to Begin

I have great news for you: you've already begun! You've already completed the first three steps: you discovered digital assets, you had sufficient curiosity to learn more, and you've nearly finished reading this book. You already know enough to decide if you'd like to invest a tiny amount of your portfolio in this asset class and, if so, how you'll likely go about it. At this stage, I'd recommend that you talk with a financial advisor who's knowledgeable about this asset class for additional guidance.

And how do you find that advisor? Go to DACFP.com. The Digital Assets Council of Financial Professionals is the educational organization I created to teach financial advisors about this new asset class. DACFP offers the Certificate in Blockchain and Digital Assets and maintains a directory of advisors from around the world who have attained their certificate. These advisors are far more knowledgeable about digital assets than most, and they'll be able to give you the advice you need. The directory is free to use, so please take advantage of it.

As with all aspects of your personal finances, there's no reason to be alone. Get peace of mind by obtaining the help of a skilled and knowledgeable advisor. The DACFP directory of advisors can help you.

You're well on your way in this exciting journey, and it's been so easy you haven't even noticed!

Acknowledgments

I promised myself I wouldn't write another book. Worse, I promised my wife, Jean, that I wouldn't write another book! It's a long, challenging exercise. The content must be complete and correct—and that means spending more time researching than actually writing. Then there's the matter of sorting the information that's been compiled into a coherent structure. The whole thing is like a chess match where it's always your move. Make a mistake, and the results are disastrous.

Having written 10 books, I promised I wouldn't write another. But this topic is so new, so different, so laden with acute potential to profoundly improve the lives of every American, that I found the need and opportunity too compelling to ignore.

Luckily, I have enjoyed the help and support of several people, and they deserve a lot of credit. We'll start with my longtime agent, Gail Ross, who shepherded the project with my publisher. And many thanks to the Simon & Schuster team, especially executive editor Stephanie Frerich and associate editor Emily Simonson. Other members of the S&S team include production editor Morgan Hart, who masterfully proofread the manuscript and caught literally thousands of typos and other errors; design director Paul Dippolito, who created the page layout; and Beth Maglione, who organized the printing of this book.

Assembling the many lists of products, services, and companies that appear throughout the book are due to the tireless work of members of the DACFP team: Rene Chaze, Don Friedman, Janice Murphy, and Max Torres. In addition to that huge accomplishment, they joined colleagues Maribeth Bluyus, Anna Dawson, Liz Dougherty, Rick

Fowler, Hank Hanna, and Monay James in providing me valuable comments on the manuscript.

Speaking of, I especially want to thank financial planners Scott Butera, Loran Coffman, Pat Day, Alan Facey, Doug Keegan, Felix Kwan, Andrew Massaro, Mark Palmer, and Bob Sargent. They are rare among financial advisors, as they are highly knowledgeable about digital assets—which is why I asked them to read the initial draft of my manuscript. Their comments and suggestions led me to make massive changes in the book, and I thank them for their insightful and invaluable contributions.

Special thanks also to Bitwise Asset Management, for permitting me to include research from their study "The Case for Crypto in an Institutional Portfolio." My readers and I are indebted to the study's authors, Bitwise's David Lawant and Matt Hougan.

A special shout-out to Paul Blumstein, who for decades has diligently sent me cartoon suggestions for my books. Paul turns reading into a participant sport, and I thank him for helping me liven up the otherwise dull subject of money.

And I particularly want to thank DACFP's creative director, Michaele Kayes. In addition to providing a great many comments on the manuscript, she designed and created all the charts and graphics you see throughout the book. Michaele worked long hours until tight deadlines, and her work is masterful. Thank you, Michaele.

Most importantly, I want to express my deepest thanks to my darling wife. Writing is a mentally intensive activity that requires isolation for long, sustained periods. Jean readily encouraged me to embark on this project, because she knows how important it is, and she willingly allowed me the solitude all writers require, breaking it only a few times a day to put food on top of my keyboard. Jean can teach saints about patience, and the rest of us so much more. Thank you, Jean, for your love and support, as strong today as, and more important to me than, *ever*.

And, Jean, I promise, I won't write any more books.

Glossary

51% attack
attempt by hackers to steal a blockchain's data and assets by controlling the majority of the network's nodes

accredited investor
investor deemed to be wealthy or experienced

ADV
federal disclosure document all financial institutions must provide their clients

airdrop
distribution of digital assets by an entity, used for marketing purposes; also called *helicopter money*

Anti–Money Laundering
rule requiring financial institutions to help prevent tax evasion

asset allocation
how a portfolio is invested among a variety of asset classes

assets under advisement
money held by a financial advisor or firm, but not independently managed by them

assets under management
money managed by a financial advisor or firm

authentication economy
an economic system that does not require buyers or sellers to trust each other; instead, their actions are proven valid cryptographically

barter system
economic system where people and entities trade goods and services

base layer protocol
a root blockchain network that allows for the creation, transfer, and storage of digital assets. Also called a *native layer*

Bitcoin
a computer network using blockchain technology

bitcoin
a medium of exchange and store of value that operates on the Bitcoin blockchain

Bitcoin Pizza Day
May 22, 2010. The first commercial transaction using bitcoin

BitLicense
issued by New York to companies doing business in digital assets

block reward
compensation you receive for verifying data placed on a blockchain

blockchain
a ledger that resides on the internet. Also called *distributed ledger technology*

buy and hold
strategy of keeping an investment for years after purchase

central bank
a bank empowered by a government to price money and set interest rates

central bank digital currency
a fiat currency issued in digital form

client relationship summary
short document summarizing a financial institution's services, fees, conflicts, and other facts

code of ethics
policy set by a financial institution governing behavior of its employees

cold wallet
an account holding digital assets that is not connected to the internet and therefore is safe from online hackers

collectible
works of art, rugs, antiques, precious metals or gems, rare stamps and coins

computer farm
an assembly of computers engaged in mining bitcoin

consensus mechanisms
the methodology for generating agreement among those verifying data on a blockchain

convertible virtual currency
virtual currency with an equivalent value in fiat currency

cross-border transmittal
the movement of money from one country to another

crypto asset
any digital asset that uses cryptography to secure transaction records on a ledger

cryptocurrency
virtual currency that uses cryptography to secure transactions digitally recorded on a blockchain

currency
a physical object that represents money

custodian
a person or entity that receives and safeguards your assets for you

deal flow
the discovery of private companies that one might invest in or buy

decentralized autonomous organization
an entity operating independently on the internet, with no one in charge

decentralized finance
online systems that operate on the internet

derivative
investment contract based on an asset

digital asset
the binary representation of anything having an economic value that can be owned

discount
price of a security trading below net asset value

distributed record
data that is posted on the internet for all to see

Dogecoin
a digital pet rock

dollar cost averaging
strategy of investing money in set increments at consistent intervals

donor advised fund
charities that invest donations until donors dictate their distribution to other charities

dual registrant
financial advisor licensed with both the SEC and FINRA

fat-finger risk
accidentally mistyping orders, thus sending the wrong digital asset or amount, or to the wrong party

fiat currency
money issued by a government

fidelity bond
insurance bought by a financial institution to protect itself and its
clients from financial loss due to theft or crime

fiduciary
one who serves your best interests

FIFO
"first in, first out." Your oldest shares will be sold first

FinTech sandbox
government policy that allows companies to innovate without fear of
fines or sanctions

gas fee
fee paid to miners to validate your transaction

Genesis Block
the first block written to the Bitcoin blockchain. Also called Block 0

GTC
a limit order that remains open until executed, no matter how long it
takes for you to get the price you've set. The trade is "good til canceled"

halvening
an event that reduces a block reward by 50%. Also called *halving*

hard fork
the split of a blockchain into two blockchains, the result of
disagreements by developers over how the blockchain should operate

hash
a string of computer code representing data

hedge fund
an investment that strives to reduce risk

HIFO

"highest in, first out." Your shares with the biggest gain will be sold first

hot wallet

an account holding digital assets that is connected to the internet

Howey Test

method used by the SEC to determine if an investment is a security

in-kind transfer

movement of coins or tokens as-is to a different custodian. Also called *trustee-to-trustee transfer*

initial coin offering

a coin released to the market for the first time

intermediary

a person or entity facilitating transactions between two parties

Jamie Dimon

a person who doesn't know anything about bitcoin, and who demonstrates that fact by making ridiculous comments about it. See Warren Buffett

know your customer

rule prohibiting financial institutions from doing business with anonymous parties

ledger

a document that records deposits and withdrawals, or other data

leverage

borrowed money that is invested, to magnify returns

LIFO

"last in, first out." Your newest shares will be sold first

like-kind exchange

selling one investment and purchasing another without paying capital gains. Also called a Starker exchange

limit order
transaction that lets you set the worst price you're willing to accept;
trade will be executed at that price or better. Limit orders are canceled
at the end of the year if not executed.

long-term capital gain or loss
holding period of more than one year

margin call
a demand that you post additional collateral; failure results in the sale
of your asset

market order
transaction to be made immediately or at first opportunity

max drawdown
a portfolio's maximum loss

metaverse
broad term referring to an internet economy supported by virtual
reality gamers

Metcalfe's Law
the notion that a network's value grows exponentially as the network
adds users

micropayment
payment of a small amount of money, often fractions of a penny

mining
the process of validating data on a blockchain

Modern Portfolio Theory
the notion that investing in two risky assets is safer than investing in
just one of them

multiple
valuing a company by dividing its price by its profits

negative correlation
two assets whose prices move in opposite ways at any given time

net asset value
price of a security

node
a computer on the blockchain network

non-correlation
two assets whose price movements are not related to each other

non-fungible token
a token that is unique

oracle
software code that connects the digital world with the physical world

outbound oracle
algorithm that tells a real entity about an event that occurred on a blockchain

over the counter
securities that do not trade on an exchange

permissioned system
an electronic system that is controlled by a person or entity; you cannot access or use it without their approval. Also called a *centralized ledger*

permissionless system
an electronic system that anyone can access

permissive country
a government that does not interfere with the trading of digital assets

play-to-earn game
an online game where participants earn digital assets based on their performance

positive correlation
two or more assets that rise and fall in sync

power of attorney
document giving another person or entity legal control of your assets

premium
price of a security trading above net asset value

private key
secret code giving you access to digital assets you own

private placement
investment fund available only to an accredited investor

proof of stake
protocol that validates data on a blockchain. The more of a digital asset you stake, the greater your chance of receiving a block reward

proof of work
protocol that validates data on a blockchain. Involves solving complex calculations. Success results in receipt of a block reward.

public key
a code you share with others so they can send you digital assets

qualified custodian
a bank, broker-dealer, futures commission merchant, or some foreign entities designated by the SEC or a state agency to serve as a custodian

rebalancing
restoring a portfolio's asset allocation by selling some assets and purchasing others

red flags identity theft program
procedures set by a financial institution to protect its clients and their assets

registered representative
a stockbroker

restricted period
6- or 12-month period during which you cannot sell your investment

Ric Edelman's 1% Digital Assets Allocation Strategy
a brilliant investment strategy, especially for those new to digital assets

second layer protocol
built on a base layer protocol; provides additional features and capabilities

separately managed account
hybrid between owning investments directly and via a fund

Sharpe ratio
a formula that measures an asset's or portfolio's return per unit of volatility

short selling
bet that the value of a company will fall

short-term capital gain or loss
holding period of one year or less

SIM card hijacking
hackers stealing data by accessing the removable memory chip in your smartphone

simple agreement for future equity
a contract whereby a company promises to give equity

simple agreement for future tokens
a contract whereby a company promises to give tokens if they are issued

smart contract
automated movements of money that occur only upon completion of pre-arranged events

soft fork
creation of a new coin that uses the original blockchain

Sortino ratio
a formula that measures the downside volatility of an asset or portfolio

stablecoin
a digital asset whose price is pegged to a fiat currency

staking
posting your digital assets on the internet, to win a block reward or earn interest

standard deviation
the dispersion of an asset's actual return from its average return

strict countries
governments that have banned digital assets transactions

supply chain
the movement of goods from factory to consumer

supply vs. demand
an economic theory that holds that an asset's price rises as demand outpaces supply

taxable event
any event that results in a tax liability

token
small, physical representation of an intangible item

trade lot
a set of assets purchased in a single transaction

trust economy
an economic system that requires buyers and sellers to trust each other's actions

turnkey asset management program
back-office systems deployed by financial advisors

unbanked
a person who lacks sufficient funds to open a bank account, or who doesn't live near a bank

unicorn
company less than 10 years old that is worth more than $1 billion

velocity of money
the speed that money moves through an economic system

venture capital
money invested into an early-stage company

virtual currency
digital representation of a medium of exchange, unit of account, or store of value other than fiat currency

warm wallet
a hot wallet that can only send digital assets to wallets you designate. Reduces hacker and fat-finger risk

Warren Buffett
a person who doesn't know anything about bitcoin, and who demonstrates that fact by making ridiculous comments about it. See Jamie Dimon

wash-sale rule
purchases of a security sold within 30 days are not immediately eligible for capital loss deduction

yield farming
the practice of lending or staking your digital assets to earn interest

Index

When you put clients above all, you end up at the top.

Here at Edelman Financial Engines, we put your interests first and foremost. That's why our planners don't sell products or earn commissions. Our only goal is to help you build, grow, protect and preserve your wealth, so you can accomplish your own goals. That's perhaps why we rank #1 year after year.

Learn more at EdelmanFinancialEngines.com.

Edelman Financial Engines®

GLOBAL X

by **Mirae Asset**

Beyond Ordinary ETFs®

GLOBALXETFS.COM

@GLOBALXETFS

Crypto is the future.
Our mission is to guide you there.

As the world's first crypto index fund manager, we at Bitwise think there are two critical questions investors should ask themselves about crypto.

THE FIRST IS, *DO YOU THINK CRYPTO IS HERE TO STAY?*

Blockchain-based technology has already reimagined the way people transact, organize, and communicate — yet in many ways we've barely scratched the surface. Just think: Bitcoin, DeFi, NFTs, and Web 3.0 weren't a part of most people's vocabulary just a few years ago; now they're redefining entire industries. As an investor, it's important to look ahead and imagine the role crypto will play in daily life down the road.

THE SECOND QUESTION: *IF CRYPTO IS HERE TO STAY, HOW DO YOU PLAN TO PARTICIPATE IN THAT GROWTH?*

For some people, the answer is to try picking the winners, to find the next big thing — the next bitcoin or ether — from a vast array of crypto assets. For others, the market is too mysterious and complex to warrant an investment.

At Bitwise, we think there's also a smart middle road: getting exposure to the market broadly with the help of a trusted guide — in a way that's familiar, simple, and clear. It's why we launched the world's first crypto index fund in 2017, with an emphasis on making crypto widely accessible. It's why we avoid jargon and put a premium on education, helping investors ranging from individuals to financial advisors understand this fast-moving space. And it's why we've made crypto our sole focus from the beginning.

We think crypto is here to stay — and that everyone should be able to benefit from it. What about you?

**LEARN MORE AT
WWW.BITWISEINVESTMENTS.COM**

Bitwise®

Gain digital assets exposure with ETF Simplicity

About the Author

Investment Advisor, *RIABiz*, and *InvestmentNews* have all named Ric Edelman one of the most influential people in the financial profession, and *Barron's* ranked Ric three times as the nation's #1 Independent Financial Advisor. He's in both *Research* magazine's Financial Advisor Hall of Fame and *Barron's* Advisor Hall of Fame. Ric received an Honorary Doctorate from Rowan University in 1999 and IARFC's Lifetime Achievement Award in 2017.

Ric is a leading financial educator and champion of financial literacy. He taught personal finance at Georgetown University for nine years, has lectured at Stanford University, George Washington University, Pepperdine University, and Roger Williams University, and is now Distinguished Lecturer, William G. Rohrer College of Business at Rowan University. *TALKERS* placed him on the Heavy Hundred, its ranking of the 100 Most Important Radio Talk Show Hosts in the country. Ric has also produced award-winning specials for Public Television, and he's a #1 *New York Times* bestselling author of 11 books on personal finance, including a best-selling children's book on money, written with his wife, Jean.

Ric founded the Funding Our Future Coalition, whose 50+ academic, non-profit, corporate, and think-tank members are focused on helping all Americans achieve financial security. He also founded DACFP, the Digital Assets Council of Financial Professionals, which awards the Certificate in Blockchain and Digital Assets.

Along with Jean, Ric also founded Edelman Financial Engines, the nation's largest independent advisory firm, managing $300 billion for 1.4 million individuals and households nationwide. With Ric and Jean's leadership, EFE was ranked #1 for quality by both *Barron's* and *Consumer Reports*.

Ric and Jean serve on a variety of nonprofit boards and are benefactors of the Edelman Center for Nursing at Inova Hospital Foundation, the Edelman Indoor Arena at Northern Virginia Therapeutic Riding Program, and Rowan University's Edelman Planetarium and Edelman Fossil Park. In 2020, Rowan named its communications school the Ric Edelman College of Communication & Creative Arts.

They live in Northern Virginia with their Weimaraner, Satoshi.